Captured at Sea

Captured at Sea

PIRACY AND PROTECTION IN
THE INDIAN OCEAN

Jatin Dua

UNIVERSITY OF CALIFORNIA PRESS

University of California Press, one of the most distinguished university presses in the United States, enriches lives around the world by advancing scholarship in the humanities, social sciences, and natural sciences. Its activities are supported by the UC Press Foundation and by philanthropic contributions from individuals and institutions. For more information, visit www.ucpress.edu.

University of California Press
Oakland, California

Cataloging-in-Publication Data is on file at the Library of Congress.

Names: Dua, Jatin, 1981- author.
Title: Captured at sea : piracy and protection in the Indian
    Ocean / Jatin Dua.
Description: Oakland, California : University of California Press, [2019]
    | Series: Atelier: Ethnographic Inquiry in the Twenty First century ; 3 |
    Includes bibliographical references and index. |
Identifiers: LCCN 2019010308 (print) | LCCN 2019016512 (ebook) |
    ISBN 9780520973299 (Epub) | ISBN 9780520305199 (cloth : alk. paper) |
    ISBN 9780520305205 (pbk : alk. paper)
Subjects: LCSH: Hijacking of ships—Somalia—21st century.
Classification: LCC HV6433.786.S58 (ebook) | LCC HV6433.786.S58 D83 2019
    (print) | DDC 364.16/4—dc23
LC record available at https://lccn.loc.gov/2019010308

28   27   26   25   24   23   22   21   20   19
10   9   8   7   6   5   4   3   2   1

CONTENTS

ILLUSTRATIONS

MAPS

FIGURES

ACKNOWLEDGMENTS

"This wasn't the first time I was captured." With those words, we were all hushed into silence. I was sitting at our usual *maskan* (hangout) on the Lamu waterfront, close to the Somali border. It was 8 PM and the town was enveloped in darkness. In the summer of 2008, power cuts were a daily occurrence. I was in this cosmopolitan corner of the East African coast, with a vague idea of studying contemporary Indian Ocean connections, when I heard Abdul's story. Abdul, a merchant mariner, had returned from a job at sea with a tale of pirates. "The last time was three years ago in Nigeria. There, people came on board and tied us up to steal things from the ship—this was different." We continued to listen quietly as he set the stage for us. "We were returning from a routine food drop in Kismayu. I was down in my cabin getting ready for bed. All of a sudden the alarm went off and captain told us on the announcement system that we had men on board." Someone interrupted to ask how many pirates came aboard, but he was quickly hushed as Abdul continued. "We ran to hide in the reinforced citadel where they have food and supplies, but it was too late. I walked out of the door and there was a man with an AK-47, yelling. He was speaking Somali, but when a man has a gun you don't need a translator."

At this point, Abdul stood up; a diminutive, unassuming man, it was hard to picture him at the center of a tale of piracy on the high seas. Other people had joined our circle and were being brought up to speed by those sitting next to them. Annoyed by the chatter, Abdul silenced the swelling crowd so he could tell more of his ordeal. "We slept on the main deck in the open that night. In the morning at sunrise, I saw that there were six—maybe seven—people, all armed, guarding us. When the sun got too hot, they took us to the upper deck and locked us in the ship's office. As we were walking inside, I saw two small fishing boats tied to the side of our ship. It's unbelievable to think that two small boats with six armed men could capture a big cargo ship, but it happened."

This is a book about capture at sea, about how small boats hijack big ships. Abdul's astonishment over the hijacking of his cargo ship by fishing skiffs immediately struck me, and gave shape to the research and writing that followed ever since that evening in Lamu.

Answering how small boats hijack big ships required inhabiting and researching within a transregional geography. Not only did piracy emerge as part of everyday life, involving all kinds of individuals, organizations, and businesses, but it turned out to be both a local and international/global affair, involving Somali family ties, shipping companies, Lloyd's of London, the U.S. Navy, private security companies, contractors, pilots, negotiators, diviners, and more. This work would not have been possible without the willingness of all these disparate people to allow me in their midst. From coastal Somalia to Washington, DC, to London, South Asia, and Sharjah, as well as onboard a number of ships, this book is built through the hospitality of many who gave time and energy to make this project possible, patiently encouraging me and generously forgiving my missteps and blunders.

Those interviewed remain anonymous or are cited by pseudonym. In some cases, certain details (insignificant to the analysis) have been changed to protect the identities of certain people. That includes the use of composite scenes that contain elements from more than one situation. They accurately reflect actual events, but have been rearranged to preserve anonymity.

In Kenya, Reuben Jemase, Athman Lali, Mohamed Jama, and Ali Hadrami immediately took me in and supported my work throughout. Shafiq Makrani's friendship made Mombasa feel like home. Omar Hassan did the same for me in Lamu, including insisting that I follow up with Abdul, testament to the ways in which he made my research his own. Kadara Swaleh, Charles Appleton, Allan Duncan, Alan Cole, and others at UNODC-Nairobi, the Mombasa Magistrate's Court, Kenya Port Authority, the tireless staff at Mission to Seafarers, faculty at USIU, especially Francis Wambalaba and the staff at the British Institute, were generous with their time and support in Nairobi and Mombasa. Hassan Ibrahim's incisive questions and incredible resourcefulness were essential in navigating metaphorical and literal roadblocks in both Eastleigh and later Somaliland.

In Somaliland, the staff at APD, especially Mohamed Farah, constantly reminded me of the larger stakes of my project. In Berbera, members of the

Somaliland Coastguard, the High Court, and fishing communities generously indulged my questions, all the while noting that I was in the wrong place looking for pirates. Research in Puntland and central Somalia was logistically complicated and made possible by many who, for a variety of reasons, remain anonymous. In particular, to the people I call Sheikh Usman and Aisha, *aad baad u mahadsan tahay*. Your insights into this complex landscape, your patience at every *ma fahmin* made all of this possible. Without Abdirazak Jama's assistance, I would not have been able to land in Puntland. Additionally, Phaisal was tireless in making my project his own and helping me navigate Bosaso. The Ministry of Ports and Fisheries in both Berbera and Bosaso gave me incredible access to the port. Similarly, in central Somalia and the coast, Abubakr was invaluable in making research possible.

In England, I express special gratitude to Andrew Barnes, Mary-Ann Gould, Kristina Koceivich, Keith Miller, Namrata Nadkarni, Ali Shirmake, Dalbir Singh, Mohamed Qazi, and Sridhar Venkatapuram. Finally, thank you to all the ship captains, coastguards, stevedores, merchants, and others who indulged—for the most part—my questions about life at sea: from Captain Simba and the crew of the *Thamani,* who were the best teachers when it came to learning about dhows, to the second mates on bridge watch on container ships who taught me how to read all the dots that light up radar screens.

Many years ago, Montserrat Fontes sparked a curiosity about the world around me, one that somewhat circuitously landed me in Durham, North Carolina, to pursue a PhD in cultural anthropology, where this book began as a dissertation. At Duke University, I was fortunate to encounter a set of teachers, colleagues, and friends who were indefatigable in their intellectual engagements and equally tireless in creating a social world that sustained and enriched my life. I was incredibly lucky to have in Charles Piot and Engseng Ho two deeply supportive and generous advisers whose pedagogical and intellectual commitments continue to inspire. Additionally, I benefited from engagements with a number of faculty members at Duke, especially Anne Allison, Edward Balleisen, Ranjana Khanna, William O'Barr, Anne-Maria Makhulu, Tomas Matza, Diane Nelson, Stephen Smith, and Rebecca Stein. Special thanks also to Attiya Ahmad, Joella Bitter, Fahad Bishara, Leigh Campoamor, Jason Cross, Can Evren, Brian Goldstone, Jay Hammond, Azeen Khan, Louisa Lombard, Ameem Lutfi, Lorien Olive, Erin Parish, Tamar Shirinian, Brian Smithson, Kevin Sobel-Read, and Serkan Yolacan from whom I learned so much.

I could have not asked for a better institution at which to transform the dissertation into a book, than the intellectually stimulating and collegial environment of the University of Michigan-Ann Arbor. I thank my former chair, Tom Fricke, and current chair, Andrew Shryock, for their support of this book project. My colleagues in the Anthropology Department have been a source of great encouragement and intellectual energy. I would like to especially thank Webb Keane, Stuart Kirsch, Mike McGovern, Kelly Askew, Kriszti Fehervary, Matt Hull, Michael Lempert, Damani Partridge, Liz Roberts, Alaina Lemon, Barbra Meek, Erik Mueggler, Brian Stewart, Scott Stonington, Abigail Bigham, Melissa Burch, and Yasmin Moll. I also want to thank Julie Winningham and Amy Rundquist for all their administrative support. My fieldwork does not make their work any easier. Beyond Anthropology, the African History and Anthropology Workshop, Science and Technology Studies, Anthrohistory, the Center for South Asia Studies, and the African Studies Center have provided collegial and dynamic places to present portions from this book. I am especially grateful to Farina Mir, Will Glover, Gaurav Desai, Hussein Fancy, Deidre de la Cruz, Manan Desai, Madhumita Lahiri, S. E. Kile, Amal Fadlallah, and Howard Stein. Students in Cultures of Piracy, Law and Culture, Introduction to Historical Anthropology, and my graduate seminar in Law and Regulation have never shied from asking tough questions and challenging me. In addition, working with Sonia Rupcic, Kevin Donovan, Sam Shuman, Nishita Trisal, Emma Park, Simeneh Gebremariamm, Drew Haxby, and Tara Weinberg has been a constant source of inspiration.

The financial support of the Social Science Research Council's International Dissertation Research Fellowship; the Wenner-Gren Foundation's Doctoral Dissertation Fieldwork Grant; Duke University's Anne T. and Robert M. Bass Fellowship; the ACLS/Mellon Foundation's Dissertation Completion Grant; the National Science Foundation's Collaborative Research Grant (Award number: 1559658); and the Social Science Research Council's Transregional Fellowship Program made possible the often complicated and deeply multi-sited research. The bulk of this book was written while I was a fellow at the International Institute for Asian Studies in Leiden. The institution and Leiden University provided a *gezellige* place to write and think. A special thank-you to Philippe Peycam, Paul van der Velde, Sandra van der Horst, Willem Vogelsang, my fellow Fellows Greg Goulding, Debjani Bhattacharya, Mahmood Kooria, Emilia Sulek, Carola Lorea, as well as Tom Hoogervorst, Nira Wickramasinghe, Alicia Schrikker, and Carolien Stolte. When Leiden with its bucolic canals felt too small, Ajay Gandhi was the perfect host in Amsterdam.

Over the course of this project, I have been fortunate to have the opportunity to present my work at a number of institutions and to think, read, and write together with fellow travelers. In particular, I want to thank Samar Al-Bulushi, Yousuf Al-Bulushi, Hannah Appel, Mark Bradbury, Filipe Calvao, Ashley Carse, Lee Cassanelli, Brenda Chalfin, Sharad Chari, Jason Cons, Jamie Cross, Shannon Dawdy, Elizabeth Dunn, Claudia Gastrow, Aisha Ghani, Pamila Gupta, Jane Guyer, Tobias Haggman, Stefan Helmreich, Karen Ho, Markus Hoehne, Isabel Hofmeyr, Jeffrey Kahn, Laleh Khalili, Julie Kleinman, Darryl Li, Vivian Lu, Pedro Machado, Nidhi Mahajan, Johanna Markkula, Achille Mbembe, Ken Menkhaus, Dilip Menon, Sally Engle Merry, Townsend Middleton, Kris Peterson, Michael Ralph, Joshua Reno, Meg Samuelson, Judith Scheele, Ed Simpson, Ajantha Subramanian, Noah Tamarkin, Gabriela Valdivia, Francois Verges, and Caitlin Zaloom. For their invaluable feedback and engagements, I am truly grateful. Derek Peterson and Jason De León generously read the entire manuscript, and Naor Ben-Yehoyada has been a constant source of wisdom and thinking and acting kinship. Kevin O'Neill is mentor, collaborator, and editor par excellence. Their insights, as well as Jim Ferguson's and the second reviewer at the University of California Press, have made this a richer work, though all shortcomings and errors remain my own.

It has been a privilege to publish with the University of California Press. Kate Marshall has been a wonderful editor, pushing and prodding the manuscript along, and I am grateful to her editorial vision. Enrique Ochoa-Kaup's email reminders have made the process smooth and painless. I thank Bill Nelson for locating readers in the text with his maps, Ben Alexander for his copyedits, and Victoria Baker for her insightful indexing. Sarula Bao's illustrations accompany the writing, and I am immensely grateful to the ways in which she translated those words into art.

Close friends and family in Los Angeles, India, Netherlands, South Africa, and New York have sustained me through this process. I am grateful to them all, especially Amrita Singh, Arunjit Singh, Ravideep Sethi, Sangeet Sethi, Gurpreet and Ranjit Singh, Satindar Dua (Bhuaji), Kiran and Prithipal Sethi, Carla Hung, Christina Tekie, Matthew Smith, Spencer Orey, Mina Leazer, Jacqueline Stam, Aukje Ravensbergen, and Maarten Meerman. Anjali Singh's literary sensibilities and editorial acumen have inspired me to be a better storyteller. Melinda Barnard has the unique ability to blend being a dear friend and stern editor, even from a hemisphere apart. I thank Cees and Herma for their enthusiasm, cozy dinners, and support, and my parents, Apjeet and Surinder, who have always believed; their unquestioning confidence has given me the strength to keep going.

In the course of writing this, I have been lucky to meet Sanne. I have shared every idea, and every word within this book multiple times with her as we have shuffled between two continents and many time zones. My sharpest critic and my strongest supporter, she truly is my world (even as she pushed me to excise that word from the book!). Finally, I wish to dedicate this book to my grandparents, particularly Beeji and Nani. Whilst neither lived to see the completion of this project, their lives and stories of mobility, exile, and family—from Peshawar to Bangkok—shaped my interests in anthropology and continue to inspire me to write and wonder.

Excerpts from Chapters 2 and 3 have appeared in the journals *Comparative Studies in Society and History* and the *Journal of East African Studies*. Portions of chapter 1 and 3 are revised from book chapters published in edited volumes *Legalism: Property and Ownership* and *Panic, Transnational Cultural Studies, and the Affective Contours of Power*. I wish to acknowledge the editors for their generosity in the peer review process and in allowing me to republish this material.

A NOTE ON LANGUAGE

In this book, I use common English spellings for words in languages other than English. Given the prevalence of regional variations and multiple orthographic systems in Somali for the time periods covered in the book, I have opted for a simplified Somali spelling. For transliterations from Swahili, Hindi/Urdu, Arabic, and Gujarati, I either use the transliteration from the source text in case of direct quotations or follow the *International Journal of Middle East Studies* system for Arabic script.

ABBREVIATIONS

BEIC	British East Indian Company
EU-NAVFOR-ATALANTA	The European Union Naval Force Operation Atlanta
EU	European Union
H&M	Hull and Machine
IMB	International Maritime Bureau
IMO	International Maritime Organization
IRTC	Internationally Recommended Transit Corridor
IUU	Illegal, Unreported, and Unregulated
JWC	Joint War Committee
K&R	Kidnap and Ransom
MSV	Motorized Sailing Vessel
MSY	Maximum Sustainable Yield
MtS	Mission to Seafarers
NATO	North Atlantic Treaty Organization
P&I	Protection and Indemnity
PMC	Private Military Company
PMSC	Private Maritime Security Company
PSC	Private Security Company
PMPF	Puntland Maritime Police Force
SOMAFISH	Somaliland Fishing Association
UNCLOS	United Nations Convention on the Law of the Sea

UNODC	United Nations Office on Drugs and Crime
VLCC	Very Large Crude Carrier
VOC	Vereenigde Oostindische Compagnie (Dutch East India Company)
WFP	World Food Program

Introduction

AN ANTHROPOLOGY OF PROTECTION

TWO SMALL SKIFFS APPROACHED the aft side of the ship. On October 28, 2007, eight nautical miles off the coast of Somalia, the *MV Golden Nori* carried a cargo of highly flammable benzene as well as a crew of twenty-three merchant mariners primarily from the Philippines, South Korea, and Myanmar. A US naval official in Washington, DC, appraised the situation: "It was a perfect day for a hijacking, the waters were calm, the visibility was good, and the ship was moving along at a slow cruising speed of eight knots an hour." Weighing 11,676 deadweight metric tons (DWT) and the approximate length of one soccer field, the *Nori* was a relatively small cargo ship, though it would have towered over the fishing skiffs. Careful not to get caught in the wake of the ship, the pirates hooked a rickety ladder onto the side and climbed onto the ship. Once on board, things became a little tricky for the hijackers. The captain had sent a distress call just before they entered the bridge and the *USS Porter,* a naval destroyer patrolling the Horn of Africa as part of Operation Enduring Freedom—Horn of Africa (the African outpost of the US-led global war on terror), received this call. The *Porter* arrived shortly afterwards and shot warning rounds in the direction of the *Nori,* sinking the skiffs attached to the rear side of the tanker. Soon, a German naval vessel and a French Chinook helicopter also started following the ship. Given its highly flammable cargo, the owners of the *Nori,* a chemical tanker company based in Japan, urged the navies to cease fire, and the ship, which had changed course towards Somalia, continued on its way to Bosaso in the autonomous region of Puntland in northern Somalia. As the *Nori* arrived in Bosaso, the *Porter* and other warships blockaded the port, preventing the ship from entering. For the next two months, hijackers and hostages were trapped on board as negotiations for release ensued.

"Benzene is a highly volatile chemical," explained Samir, a broker for a tanker-chartering firm. "It evaporates quickly at room temperature, so the air in the immediate proximity of containers carrying benzene—and remember, the *Nori* has twenty cargo tanks, so about seventy-thousand-plus barrels of this material—is rich with hydrocarbons and oxygen. All it needed was a spark and the whole thing would have gone boom." Tanker-chartering firms are companies that hire chemical tankers from shipowners, and Samir was explaining to me why the *Nori* owners negotiated a tenuous ceasefire between the navies and the hijackers. "That would be our protocol as well," he said. "You want to avoid the risk of fire at all costs in that situation." We walked over to a model of a chemical tanker displayed prominently at the entrance to his office, a large open room of cubicles humming with activity and boasting an enviable view of the Singapore skyline. "See this whole thing?" He gestured towards the deck of the model tanker. "It's one big floating powder keg." As we both stood admiring the labyrinth of pipes and barrels that make up a chemical tanker, he added, "They got lucky—the pirates got lucky with their cargo."

The pirates did get lucky. The flammability of benzene prevented the navies from doing anything more than blockading the Bosaso port and keeping a watchful eye as negotiations commenced between the shipowners in Japan, maritime insurance companies in London, and the hijackers in Bosaso.

During my time in Bosaso in 2011, a range of people would recall with vivid detail the standoff between the *Nori* and the international navies. One day as I sat with Gurey, a port inspector, at the edge of the fishing jetty, he gestured past the sunken Pakistani dhow[1] that marks the entrance to the Bosaso port. "From here," he said, "we would have seen the *Nori* and the warships." As we watched a dhow glide out to sea in the hazy evening light, he continued, "For weeks we heard helicopters overhead and warnings from the navy to convince the pirates to give up. But they never attacked the ship because of the chemicals and hostages on board. You could see small boats going to and from the ship every day. Negotiators would travel to the ship and supply boats with food, water, and khat[2] . . . [They] would leave from this jetty at night to keep the hostages and the crew members fed."

This almost-daily movement of supplies and negotiators was crucial for ransom negotiations. But as time wore on and they accrued more debt, the pirates grew more nervous. "No pirate acts alone," Gurey told me. "They had procured the money to buy supplies from financiers belonging to their *diya* [group responsible for payment of restitution], and each passing day meant less reward [ransom] for the pirates."

Meanwhile, in a glass building in the city of London a group of insurance underwriters were also getting nervous. An underwriter whose company insured chemical and gas tankers explained to me the complexity of cases like the *Nori*. Given the high cost of chemical tankers, ranging from $6 million to $10 million, vessels are often leased through large shipping pools. A hijacking, then, meant that shipowners lost money daily during ransom negotiations. Additionally, given the volatility in chemical prices, delays meant potentially large losses to the cargo owners. "The adage 'time is money' was certainly relevant in the case of *Nori*," he remarked, noting that long negotiations make everyone nervous, not only the families of seafarers. "The insurance company has the responsibility to protect the crew and cargo. In these cases, we always recommend hiring a negotiator, otherwise things can get derailed very easily. Luckily with the *Nori*, the hijacking was resolved in two months. I've heard of ships stuck for over two years."

Back in Bosaso, Gurey remembered when the *Nori* was released. "There were rumors the night before that an airplane had dropped a package [containing a million-dollar ransom] onto the ship. I didn't see anything, but the next day from the jetty I watched the *Nori* sail away." Pointing to a small settlement next to the port with fishing skiffs anchored in the little bay, Gurey recalled that a fisherman had reported watching the pirates slip away from the ship back onto land. "The pirates won that day: all these big navies were watching and they could do nothing." Gurey had almost a hint of awe in his voice and a grin was faintly visible in the post-dusk hour. "It was the *Nori* that made piracy into a big business. After that people went from catching fish to capturing ships."

The successful hijacking of the *Nori* was followed by an unprecedented upsurge in incidents of maritime piracy off the coast of Somalia. From 2007 to 2012, over one hundred fifty ships and over three thousand crew members of one hundred twenty-five different nationalities were held hostage in the western Indian Ocean (UNODC-WB 2013, 2). In contrast to maritime piracy in other parts of the world, piracy in the western Indian Ocean operates almost exclusively on a hijack-and-ransom basis, with crew, cargo, and ship held hostage until negotiators secure a ransom—a process that can take from as little as a few weeks to as long as three years. A ransom requires willing parties and a structure of exchange. Piracy could not exist without some kind of agreement, however forced, between the various actors involved in this world, or the infrastructures of communication and mobility that make negotiations and ransom payments possible. The *Nori* incident and subsequent hijackings foreground this complex network of insurance companies, shipping conglomerates, and coastal Somali piracy syndicates.

A chemical tanker hijacked by a few men on small skiffs who outsmarted international navies seems like an improbable story. In an era of US naval hegemony, drones, and near-constant surveillance, pirates and piracy should be anachronisms, relics of a different time. And yet, not only was the *Nori* hijacked—under the watchful eyes of naval destroyers—but a million dollars landed on the ship securing its release. Why did shipping companies pay this ransom (and even larger sums after the *Nori* hijacking)? Why were so many actors involved in negotiating the release of the ship? Why *did* pirates win that day?

This book examines the making of a hijack-and-ransom economy in the western Indian Ocean to show how the capture of a ship makes visible systems of protection that exist not only in coastal Somalia, but also in the offices of maritime insurance companies in London and on board NATO warships. In contrast to the common notion of piracy as *hostis humani generis* (enemy of all mankind) (Greene 2008; Heller-Roazen 2009), or "mere theft at sea" (Rubin 1986, 1), or even the romanticized figures of popular culture, the concept of protection emphasizes parallel and competing systems, where piracy represents not only an interruption but also an attempt—framed through the threat of violence—to insert oneself within a global sea of trade. The hijacking of a ship forced these varied systems of protection to come into contact with each other and reveals the often-surprising ways in which these seemingly distinct systems become legible, however briefly, to each other.

From insurance contracts to the protection of kinship groups, and from armed guards to the presence of naval destroyers, long-distance trade has been shaped by practices of protection. As this book will show, protection emerges clearly at sea because maritime journeys are always vulnerable. Waves engulf, boats sink, people drown, cargo transforms into flotsam and jetsam, and pirates (and navies) arrive at the threshold, armed. Before, during, and (importantly) in the aftermath of a hijacking, each of these actors *protects* their investments, interests, reputations, human lives, or all of them at the same time. These multiple forms of protection undercut the empirical and analytical divides between piracy and counter-piracy. In the popular imagination, the worlds of piracy and counter-piracy are generally seen as distinct and diametrically opposed, with a ragtag set of "desperados from a dysfunctional land" (Lane 2013, para. 5) pitted against the global leviathan of the shipping industry and naval forces from several powerful nation-states. "Bad"

FIGURE 1. Shipping containers in a Red Sea port, 2018. Photo by author.

pirates and the "good" coalition of counter-piracy are divided both spatially and analytically. In opposition, the presence of protection across this global field of claim-making over ships and mobile objects at sea, from northern Somalia to the offices of Lloyd's of London, reveals an alternative system of connectivity, forged through protection.

SOMALIA AND THE WESTERN INDIAN OCEAN: CONNECTIONS AND INTERRUPTIONS

Millions of ships are at sea. From small fishing boats stitched together with balsa wood and rope to lumbering supertankers—leviathans of metal and machine—millions of vessels and millions of seafarers are currently afloat in the ocean. Almost everything we eat, wear, or otherwise consume on a daily basis has some connection to these vessels and to global shipping. Some 90 percent of global trade—approximately six billion tons of cargo—travels on over one hundred thousand cargo ships that are operated by 1.25 million seafarers (UNCTAD 2018).

The western Indian Ocean is central to this world of trade, with anywhere between twenty-two thousand and twenty-five thousand vessels transiting through the Suez Canal each year. Every day, in fact, 4.8 million barrels of oil move through the Bab-el-Mandeb Strait, representing over 30 percent of the world's oil supply (USEIA 2017). These numbers do not include the many millions who traverse these restive waters on a daily basis—the fishermen, the migrants, the smugglers, the pirates—whose journeys (both failed and successful) are equally central in shaping the contemporary world.

Despite its importance, life at sea, as well as the labor of those who toil in these waters, often remains murky to those on land. We suffer from a form of "sea-blindness"[3] that keeps us oblivious to the deep maritime connections essential to everyday life. Accidents and disasters such as oil spills, migrants drowning at sea, the search for the wreckage of commercial airlines downed at sea, and shipwrecks offer the fleeting moments when global attention turns to the ocean before returning again to land.

Coastal Somalia has a vexed relationship and a long history with the highways of maritime commerce. Adjacent to some of the busiest shipping lanes in the contemporary world, with the longest coastline in mainland Africa, Somalia abuts against the sinews and circuits that connect Europe to Asia by way of the Red Sea and the Indian Ocean. Yet one of the first and most enduring impressions of the Somali coast is its geographic inhospitality. North of Mogadishu, the East African coast transforms from the verdant forest-and-sea region that begins in Mozambique in southern Africa into a desolate desert-and-sea region that extends from Mogadishu across the Horn of Africa, South West Asia and the Indus Basin. Occasionally interrupted by small coastal settlements, this desert region is flanked by the jagged peaks of the Ogo Mountains as the coastline veers away from the Indian Ocean towards the narrow Red Sea.

Offshore, a series of wind patterns and oceanic currents circulates between Asia and Africa, between the Red Sea and the western Indian Ocean, creating both a rhythm to life on land and sea and, prior to the coming of steam, an infrastructure to transoceanic movement. This dynamism of hinterland and coast, of wind and currents, is central to the varied interactions that have shaped coastal Somalia from Zeila in the North on the Red Sea coast to the Bajuni Islands and the Lamu archipelago in the South.[4] As early as the first century AD, tales from Somali ports appeared on papyrus in ancient Greece. Compiled and copied to parchment by a Byzantine scribe in the early tenth century, the *Periplus Maris Erythraei* is one of the few extant chronicles of an Indian Ocean world prior to the coming of Islam. This practical handbook lists in great detail the prevailing wind patterns and offers tips on sailing the monsoonal seas, advice on goods to buy and sell, and brief references to the nature of political authority along the coast from Egypt to the Malay

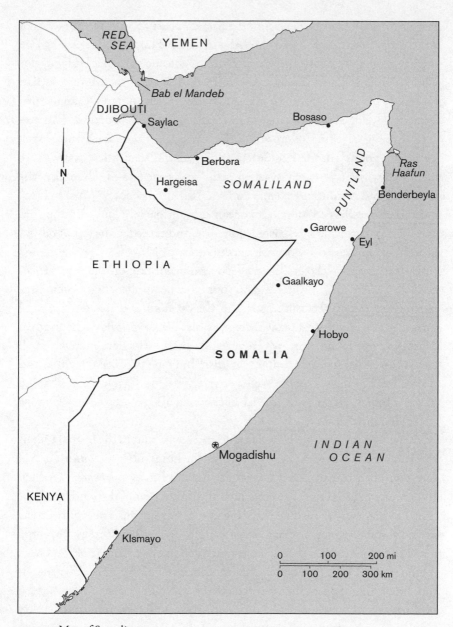

MAP 1: Map of Somalia.

Peninsula. Following the *Periplus,* the Somali coast appears in the works of Arab geographers such Yāqūt ibn 'Abd Allāh al-Ḥamawī (d. 1229), whose literary geography, *Kitab Mu'jam al-Buldan,* chronicles a lively and polyglot world of exchange in the port cities of the Red Sea and the western Indian Ocean. What emerges in these texts, as well as a rich Indian Ocean historiography developed over the past three decades, is a zone of connections created through centuries of cross-cultural trade and the mobility of people, ideas, and goods.[5] In the Red Sea and the Indian Ocean these routes were identified with an ecumenical Islam, specifically the Shafi'I school of jurisprudence and Muslim merchants and states. This was not a "Muslim lake" but rather a restless cosmopolitan ocean of multiple religious communities and social movements that existed alongside, and exceeded the temporalities of, various empires in this oceanic space (Ho 2004).

In recent years, scholars, particularly those working on the nineteenth-century western Indian Ocean, have sought to detail not only specific connections across oceanic space but also the economic, political, legal, and infrastructural forces that made them possible (Bishara 2017; Machado 2014; Mathew 2016; Huber 2013; McDow 2018). These works productively push beyond an earlier focus on cosmopolitanism by emphasizing inequalities and unfreedom (Hopper 2015) as well as the centrality of violence in shaping western Indian Ocean connectivity in the long nineteenth century (Prange 2018; Subramanian 2016).

Drawing from these archives of trade and navigation in the Indian Ocean as well as the more recent oceanic turn in the humanities,[6] *Captured at Sea* foregrounds a transregional geography and the dynamic ways in which Indian Ocean histories shape contemporary forms of mobility and interruption in this oceanic realm, including the interruptions and connections forged through piracy. In the western Indian Ocean, ships, crew, and cargo move and moor through ports and traverse geographies that are old and new. As the Indian Ocean emerges as a renewed locus for global trade and geopolitics, including South-South interactions (Kaplan 2010; Verges 2003; Hofmeyr 2010; Prestholdt 2015), new infrastructural visions of connectivity such as port projects, rail networks, and shipping lines find themselves traveling much older paths. Take for example recent megaport-development projects funded by new investments, particularly from China and its One Belt One Road Initiative, across the western Indian Ocean littoral from Lamu to Gwadar. In the everyday working and contestations over such projects, old networks of trade and exchange are both made visible and also reenergized (Dua 2017b; Jamali 2013). The contemporary mobility of ships, goods, and capital thus emphasizes the salience of long histories not as static contexts, but as both "project and process" (Ben-Yehoyada 2016, 24) in shaping the western Indian Ocean.

Thinking through the ocean has important consequences for how we understand Somalia as well. The collapse of the central government in 1991, warlords, haunting images of large-scale famine, and an American soldier being dragged through the streets of Mogadishu are often the only visual register through which the rest of the world understands this corner of East Africa. Somalis and others have sought to write against these images, noting the ways in which life continues and indeed thrives amidst this suffering. They have also emphasized western complicity in producing and perpetuating conflict in this region.[7] The absence and presence of the Somali state has been a central feature in thinking and writing about the region, often for good reason given the hardships endured by Somalis due to over twenty years of statelessness.[8]

Academic and nonacademic responses to maritime piracy similarly foreground this emphasis on state failure. The first camp of scholarship locates piracy primarily as a maritime offshoot of larger issues with governance and the consequences of state failure in Somalia (Daniel 2012; Ibrahim 2010; Stevenson 2010). In this narrative, pirates exist in Somalia because the state does not. Piracy, for these analysts, is often conflated with Al-Shabaab and other militant groups operating in the region.[9]

A second set of literatures has sought, with varying emphases, to critique and contextualize the narrative of failed states and the ways it obscures forms of governance and order without government. The rise and success of piracy in Somalia, as these works note, while tied to failures of governance, also requires a degree of stability in order to make possible the recruitment and redistribution that is central to the kidnap-and-ransom economy of Somali piracy. Empirically, if ungoverned space were a critical factor, piracy in Somalia would be concentrated in south-central coastal areas, which have been the most lawless, violent, and crime-ridden areas since 1991. But pirates have not been very active on the southern coast. Instead, they have clustered on the northeast coast in Puntland and in several fishing villages in central Somalia, where a weak, but functional, local administration holds power.[10]

While inspired by a number of these works, particularly scholarship that has nuanced understandings of state failure, the transregional oceanic geography that frames this book offers the possibility of a different kind of story.

Here, I emphasize worlds of obligations and long histories to show how spaces like Somalia and the Indian Ocean and practices like piracy are constituted through transregional connections and interruptions. Far from being an anachronistic practice or aberration, maritime piracy calls attention to the logics of contemporary capitalism and new forms of regulation while emphasizing longer histories and the oceanic contexts of these systems.

WHO IS THE PIRATE? A TALE OF TWO THALASSOCRACIES

Where the Indian Ocean and the Red Sea meet is a mist-covered promontory, Ras Asir (Cape Guardafui) in contemporary Somalia. In the early nineteenth century, this area had become infamous as a graveyard for ships making their way from the relative calm of Aden or Berbera in the Red Sea to the Indian Ocean. During the southwest monsoon, lasting roughly from May to November, when strong currents and gusty winds blow from the south, ships would often get caught in a whirlpool that developed northeast of Ras Asir. An unfortunate ship caught in this whirlpool would find itself thrown westward towards the treacherous rocky coast. By the beginning of the nineteenth century, this coastline and the Majeerteen inhabitants of the area had developed a ferocious reputation for plundering vessels that had the misfortune of being stranded along this desolate coast.

To curb this annual share of shipwrecks, the construction of a lighthouse was proposed to protect ships and provide comfort to sailors in these treacherous waters. From the beginning this project was staunchly opposed, and acts of sabotage occurred regularly. Writing in a briefing, a representative of the Italian Protectorate noted:

> A little beyond Obok rises the majestic promontory of Guardafui, where these many years past a lighthouse has been projected, though up till now the only ascertainable result of these projects has consisted in words and promises. The inhabitants are violently opposed to the idea, seeing themselves about to be deprived of a very profitable source of income, and Sultan Osman, himself being the person principally interested, is the head and front of the opposition. (Baldacci 1909, 71)

Shipwrecks, as the report highlights, provided the Majeerteen with a steady source of profit, and, importantly, the flotsam and jetsam of these wrecks was their ticket into the world of Indian Ocean trade and a source of political power on land. In particular, the Majeerteen created a redistributive economy through the sale of these goods in Arabia and the distribution of profits to kinsmen-turned-clients, creating obligations that could be exchanged later for rights in labor, water, and the use of pastures. Prior to the creation of this shipwreck economy, Majeerteen political organization consisted of small groups of inland herders and fishing communities along the coast interlinked through claims of common descent. By the mid-nineteenth century this world had significantly transformed. The Isman Mahmoud, one of the three major lineages of the Majeerteen, had consolidated power and created a new regional political economy built around shipwrecks (Durril 1986). All that came from the sea belonged to *Boqor* (Sultan), proclaimed the Isman Mahmoud as they jealously guarded the bounty of the sea with the Sultan's house exercising ownership over the profits of plunder. Within the Majeerteen Sultanate, plunder and trade were inextricably linked.

In the nineteenth century, as ships transformed into flotsam and jetsam and crew members found themselves marooned on the northern Somali coast, they were claimed within multiple regimes of protection. What the Majeerteen understood as redistribution, the Italians and the British called piracy. Efforts to curtail this shipwreck economy entailed port blockades and aerial bombardments (Portenger 1819) as well as the signing of protectorate treaties with various rulers of Puntland. The first treaty a Somali *Boqor* ever signed with a Western power was an agreement with the British in 1838.[11] It engaged him to protect British ships and nationals when passing by or shipwrecked on the shores of his chiefdom. Plunderers of shipwrecks had been transformed into protectors, and rulers into clients.

These contests over shipwrecks are part of a longer history of claim-making at sea. One of the first instances of the terms *pirate* and *piracy* appears in classical Greek. *Peirates* was used not to describe individual acts of banditry or takings on sea, but rather to describe the political structure of bands along the Aegean "where forcible seizure was one way to acquire metal or other goods from outside sources" (Rubin 2006, 5). For the Greeks, piracy had little to do with legality, but was an economic system practiced by diasporic[12] seafaring communities in the Aegean where raiding was a secondary system of transfer and redistribution. Opposed to this understanding of piracy as a form of commercial transaction, Roman law focused on pirates as rebels or enemies who refused to recognize the supremacy of Roman law. Daniel Heller-Roazen (2010) notes that Roman commentators, such as Livy, framed actions against pirates through a language of war (*belloque*). For the Romans, pirates were treated, not as criminals, but as enemies to be met in war and defeated—enemies that as Cicero notes were *communis hostis omnium* (common enemy of all).[13]

From piracy's earliest beginnings, then, we see a vision of two different thalassocracies (maritime empires)—one diasporic, the other imperial. From the vantage point of a diasporic empire, like that of the Greeks, piracy was part of an economic world that constantly blurred between seizure and exchange. For the Romans, piracy represented a political challenge to imperial legitimacy, one that required a moral and legal response—a war against piracy. This second vision of piracy, as a threat to imperial order at sea, emerged again in the context of the changing Mediterranean and Atlantic world of the fifteenth century, an era of imperial competition and transatlantic slavery. In a world dominated and divided through papal decree between Spain and Portugal, newcomers (such as the English, French, and Dutch) relied on a form of privateering initially financed by monarchs, and later funded by private enterprises and legally supported by natural-law and positive-law claims to legitimacy (Starkey, van Heslinga, and Moor 2001; Greene 2010). These new states desired empire but had neither the resources nor the military might to achieve these goals. Thus, a form of outsourcing emerged where "violent entrepreneurs"[14] carried out state policy by private means.

Through the issuance of letters of marque, European monarchs and republics "legalized" piracy and ensured that a percentage of the profits would finance state expansion and consolidation. Yet legalized privateering was always a precarious identity, and wartime privateers often turned pirate in peacetime. These pirates then threatened the very empires they had helped create, defend, and finance. Such fear of privateers gone rogue turned into a full-scale "war on pirates" in the late seventeenth and early eighteenth centuries, but, unlike the campaigns of Pompey and the Roman Empire, the end of the golden age of piracy was ushered in not through a declaration of war but through naval police actions and trials by admiralty courts and other municipal jurisdictions. Piracy, as jurors were regularly reminded in the seventeenth century, was *merely* robbery committed at sea. It was during this time that figures such as Captain Kidd and Samuel Bellamy, whose operations extended from the Atlantic to the Indian Ocean, were brought before admiralty courts in England and publicly executed in order to serve as a warning to other sailors who harbored dreams of "turning pirate" (Rediker 2004; Ritchie, 1989; Benton 2005).

In the Atlantic (and later the Indian) Ocean, this battle against piracy was central to promoting what the historian David Armitage (2000, 101) has called the "myth of an empire of the seas [as] critical to defining the British Empire as both free and benign." Campaigns against piracy (and slavery) became tools through which to transform oceanic space and to project a monopoly on violence at sea, especially in the Indian Ocean. The eradication of shipwreck economies on the coast of northern Somalia was part of this attempt to legitimize empire on land and sea.[15]

Contestations over piracy and protection in the Indian Ocean thus became a mode of delegitimizing local power and expanding European influence in the region. Importantly, they also became part of the vocabulary of resistance to European expansion. Rulers across the Indian Ocean claimed they were not pirates but legitimate protectors, thus turning the claims of piracy back onto their accusers.[16]

I was reminded of these longer histories and contests over the meanings of piracy when I started doing research in Puntland in 2010, specifically in my encounters with Asad. A former politician and an avid reader of *The Guardian,* Asad and I used to meet for weekly coffee to discuss the news, a meeting that would end—much to my delight—with Asad giving me his weekly pile of newspapers. We met when I first arrived in Somalia, and upon learning about my research he suggested a follow-up meeting so he could give me what he termed "the truth about piracy." The next day, he handed me a newspaper article written by a British journalist that proclaimed we had all been lied to about Somali piracy. "See, it says right here, piracy in Somalia is a revolt against illegal fishing. These people are just fishermen who had no other choice but to fight against the looting of our resources!" As he encouraged me to write about piracy, he noted that I should not fail to mention that "Who the West calls pirates, we call *geesiyaal* [heroes] in Somalia."

But a few months later, Asad's story had changed. Over coffee, I was asking him about fishing cooperatives as a potential solution for piracy, when he dismissed the question with a wave of his hand. "You won't understand piracy by studying fishing—it's a business. Even Harvard Business School teaches about piracy as a business. They're businessmen, that's it." I was somewhat taken aback by this change of tune, though not surprised. I was increasingly encountering a number of self-proclaimed pirates who were re-narrating piracy as a business enterprise, with one group in central Somalia changing its name from "coastguard" to "private investment group." Asad was fascinated by that group's business model, emphasizing, "That's what you should be writing about. It's very Somali, really: we are the most entrepreneurial people."[17]

When I returned to Puntland in 2013 for a follow-up research visit, I called Asad. When he found out I was still working on piracy, he somewhat abruptly replied, "Those people are bad, they are *tuugag* [criminals]. Why waste your time writing on them?"

For Asad, as for many in Somalia, the transformation of pirates from *geesiyaal* to *tuugag,* from heroes to criminals, reflects debates over piracy in Somalia during its rise and fall (and possible renewal) from 2007 to 2013. This transformation also points to a wider slippage in the meaning of piracy and pirates. Across space and time—from nineteenth-century shipwreck economies in coastal Somalia to Greek and Roman visions of maritime piracy, and from Atlantic and Indian Ocean debates on piracy to shifting meanings of piracy within Somalia—these terms are notoriously difficult to define. Yet, this is precisely why they remain central in shaping ideas about legality and economy.[18]

THE RETURN OF THE PIRATE

Late-nineteenth-century transformations in steamship technology that made vessels bigger and faster at sea, in addition to consolidating British and later American global control over the world's oceans (Mahan 1890), are broadly understood as sounding the death knell for large-scale organized maritime piracy. By the early twentieth century, the pirate and maritime piracy was seen as a relic of the past and by 1924, legal scholar Edwin Dickinson asked in the pages of the *Harvard Law Review,* "Is the Crime of Piracy Obsolete?"[19]

The codification of a definition of maritime piracy in the early twentieth century emerged, therefore, not in response to an immediate need for clarifying the definition of piracy, but instead as part of a larger project of legal codification of international law. Maritime piracy in these debates was hardly understood as an immediate problem. Instead, this codification reflected the institutionalization of a liberal international order and its desire for legal rationalization, as well as for the solidification of the role of the state in the governance of territorial waters; the codification of maritime piracy was thus part of a larger process of territorializing the ocean (Ranganathan 2015).

The end of the Cold War saw the surprising return of maritime piracy, a seeming vestige of a bygone era, to the world's oceans. Shifting regulatory regimes, a proliferation of small weapons, the growing demand for fish, and the de-peopling of global shipping made the busy shipping lanes of Southeast Asia and Africa once again sites of predation, profit, and plunder (Dua 2019; M. Murphy 2009). According to the International Maritime Bureau (IMB), beginning in 1991, a number of regions including the Straits of Malacca in Southeast Asia, the Gulf of Guinea in West Africa, and the Red Sea off the coast of Somalia saw a sharp increase in maritime predation.[20] From 1991 to 2006, the Straits of Malacca were the most heavily pirated waters traversed by global shipping. The attacks in Southeast Asia primarily involved the theft of cargo and (sometimes) entire vessels as ships passed through the dense archipelago of these straits. Operating from small islands in the shadow of bustling ports like Singapore, piracy in Southeast Asia in the 1990s was, in the words of one author, a sophisticated form of "maritime mugging" (Lehr 2006, 3).

Somali piracy had a very different character, because ransom making was its main objective. Prior to the 2007 hijacking of the *Nori,* the story at the beginning of this book, piracy off the coast of Somalia had been a sporadic and localized affair, with fishing vessels and dhows the primary target of the hijackers. Ransom payments were smaller, ranging from $50,000 to $100,000, and piracy seldom left the coastal region.[21] The hijacking of the *Nori* marked a significant scaling up of ransom payments. The *Nori* was released for an estimated $1 million and, importantly, set the stage for the ransom economy of maritime piracy. By 2008 Somali piracy had overtaken piracy in the Straits of Malacca such that, according to the IMB, 23 percent of all global piracy attacks were taking place off the Somali coast (IMB 2008). By 2011, the majority of all reported piracy attacks occurred in the western Indian Ocean. A listing of the number of attacks and crew members hijacked makes for sobering reading. A World Bank report published in 2013 noted that, since 2005, "pirates from Somalia ha[d] carried out 1,068 attacks. Of these, 218 resulted in successful hijackings with [the] abduction of at least 3,741 crew members of 125 different nationalities, and payment of US$315 million–US$385 million in ransoms. Between eighty-two and ninety-seven non-Somali seafarers are believed to have died in attacks, detention, or rescue operations" (World Bank 2013, 1).

This upsurge in incidents of maritime piracy led to a coordinated global naval and legal response. Acting under the legally binding Chapter VII

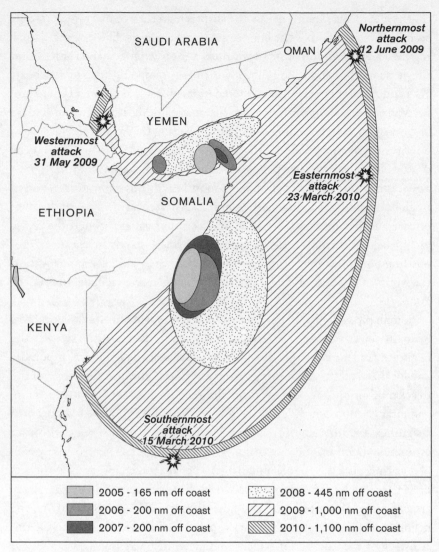

MAP 2: Map of range of piracy attacks.

powers of the United Nations, the Security Council called on "flag, coastal and port states ... with relevant jurisdiction under international law and national legislation, to cooperate in determining jurisdiction, and in the investigation and prosecution of persons responsible for acts of piracy and armed robbery off the coast of Somalia" (Resolution 1816). This resolution authorized a naval presence in the Red Sea that ended up pushing pirates farther out into the Indian Ocean. As pirates shifted to the Indian Ocean, this required the hijacking of dhows first to navigate the open ocean, transforming the geography and actors involved in piracy. In addition, this resolution sought to legally prosecute pirates in domestic courts across the Indian Ocean littoral. In 2009, as part of a deal brokered between the European Union, Britain, the United States, and Kenya, the coastal city of Mombasa in Kenya was selected as the location for the largest, most systematic attempt at prosecuting maritime piracy in over a century. Over a hundred suspects were to be tried in the Magistrate's Court in return for technical and capacity-building assistance for the Kenyan judiciary (Dua 2010).

The selection of Mombasa was not without controversy. Critics pointed to a lack of infrastructure and technical expertise for handling the increasing caseload as the naval patrols began to intercept more and more pirate ships. The agreement was finalized at a time when the capacity of the Kenyan judicial system was being questioned in various quarters. The judiciary was criticized for being unable or unwilling to prosecute suspected perpetrators of the 2007 post-election violence, in which over one thousand people died and over one hundred fifty thousand were displaced (Taussig-Rubbo 2011). Others were skeptical of Kenya's jurisdiction in the matter. A Mombasa-based defense attorney accused the United States and the European Union of "dumping" pirates in Kenya. It was within this context that I began my research in the courtrooms of coastal Kenya.

In June 2009, I was in the audience at the Mombasa High Court to observe the beginning of a piracy trial. It was a muggy afternoon. "*Maharamia wamekuja*" (the pirates have come), whispered the person sitting next to me in hushed anticipation. As murmurs about their impending arrival circulated through the courtroom, conversations gradually faded and a thick stillness enveloped the room against the best attempts of an unusually loud fan.

The suspected pirates paraded in one at a time, eventually taking their seats in courtroom number seven at the High Court. Dressed in ragged blue jumpsuits, the group of eight silently walked to the stand without acknowledging the crowd or their court-appointed lawyer. Once the suspected pirates sat, the courtroom began to hum with renewed conversation as the packed visitors' gallery traded stories about pirates and their exploits in the Indian Ocean. Some surreptitiously snapped pictures with their camera phones, prompting angry glares from the policeman standing near the empty magistrate's chair. A few minutes of restless rumbling later, the policeman shouted to us to stand up as the magistrate made her way into the courtroom. Shuffling to its feet, the crowd bowed respectfully, enacting a centuries-old common law ritual—one of the many legacies of Kenya's British colonial past.

The magistrate first summoned the state attorney and the defense lawyer to her bench to discuss procedural matters. After a few minutes of animated discussion, the magistrate gestured to the defense and prosecution to return to their tables and turned her attention to the suspected pirates. In a mix of Swahili and English, she explained that the defense appeal for dismissal, based on lack of jurisdiction, was rejected and the trial would proceed. A sprightly young Somali man dashed up to the stand and translated the magistrate's declaration into Somali to the eight unexpressive men. Over the course of the next several hours, numerous EU naval officers, Kenyan police, and customs officials testified that these silent men were not the coastguards their lawyer claimed they were, but in fact pirates.

After the first hour, the crowd started to slowly trickle out, and by the end of the hearing I was one of the few spectators left in the courtroom, along with a scattering of committed journalists. Even a piracy trial is a tedious affair. In this hearing, the multiple languages and translations employed (including French, German, Spanish, Somali, Swahili, and English) over the course of testimony and counter-testimony made an already ponderous process even slower. At one point, the proceedings were punctuated by an irritated, off-script outburst. In response to the defense lawyer's constant questioning of the legality of the arrest of the suspected pirates by the EU naval force, the German captain who had conducted the arrest remarked agitatedly, "There is no jurisdictional issue here. Pirates are enemies of all mankind." At this point, the defense attorney jumped up and urged the magistrate to strike down this claim for jurisdiction. "We are in a Kenyan court. As you know, the case is being tried under the Merchant Shipping Act." The defense was referring to a 2009 law passed with EU assistance that sought to streamline the ability of Kenyan courts to prosecute piracy. The defense attorney then continued, "Kenya has no interest in this matter—the pirates were arrested far away from Kenya. Why don't they [the EU] take them to Europe for prosecution?" Turning to the audience in a manner befitting a trial attorney, he answered his own question: "They don't want the possibility of pirates seeking asylum." After a brief pause, he theatrically delivered the closing line of his argument. "They are dumping pirates in Kenya, just like the ships dumped toxic chemicals in Somalia, which is why we have coastguards in the first place." These exchanges reflected wider controversies about piracy trials in Kenya and elsewhere.

The German captain who referred to pirates as enemies of all mankind and the defense attorney who sought to transform them into coastguards located the prosecution of Somali pirates within a long legal history where piracy has moved between the *hostis humani generis,* the privateer and the petty thief, between war and criminality. But there is another side to this history: this is the story of protection. In that same testimony, the German captain explained the role of the navies as *protecting* global trade. In another particularly heated moment, as the defense attorney kept pushing the captain on how he could tell a pirate skiff from a fishing vessel, the captain snapped, "The sea is not an empty place, it is full of many kinds of vessels! There are merchant ships, pleasure boats, and fishing vessels. A skiff used for piracy today can be used for fishing tomorrow. Someone who is a pirate can show up as a dhow captain or on a smuggling boat." The work of counter-piracy, the captain claimed, was to try and distinguish between fishing vessels and pirate boats. This is how navies, he claimed, protected this sea of trade—a form of protection that distinguished between pirates and fishermen.

As legal trials in Kenya got enmeshed in questions of jurisdiction (Scharf, Newton, and Sterio 2015) and were temporarily halted in 2010, I found myself encountering these claims over protection in many, often unexpected, places. From boat captains to seafarers, protection was a key framing through which disparately placed actors were talking about piracy and maritime trade. This led me to a move away from courtrooms towards a broader field and longer histories of protection.

PIRACY AND PROTECTION

Central to making things move within the economy of long-distance shipping are what can be understood as practices of protection.[22] These forms of protection occur across multiple scales from those protecting their lives and goods as they travel through liquid domains, to those making claims over trade routes, and finally, to those claiming to protect free trade. In addition to being enacted at multiple scales, protection also ranges from promise to contract and from a willing form of engagement to a coercive force. In the Indian Ocean, the question of protection is tied to long-standing debates over the role of violence in shaping maritime trade. An earlier historiography sought to distinguish the Indian Ocean from other oceanic realms by noting the absence of a centralized state authority and emphasized the "free" nature of trade (Pannikar 1959). According to this historiography, European incursion—specifically the arrival of Vasco da Gama in 1498—disrupted a peaceful trading world through the introduction of the *cartaz* system: an attempt to monopolize trade through the use of sea passes. Other European powers (notably the Dutch and the British) similarly followed suit, melding commerce and cannon, and thus increasing protection costs for Indian Ocean merchants, requiring them to pay tributes or risk seizure.

The historical record belies this story of transition from a premodern *mare nullum* to a post-Portuguese *mare clausum*. As scholars like Prange (2011) and Margariti (2008) have emphasized, forms of predation and violence accompanied the peaceful cosmopolitan flow of people and goods before the arrival of European imperialism. In his tenth-century treatise *Aḥsan al-taqāsīm fī ma'rifat al-aqālīm,* the geographer al-Muqaddasī notes the presence of *asakir al-marakib* (ship guards) on board vessels sailing in the Red Sea. He goes on to describe the armory of these guards, including heavy weapons and flammable liquids that were frequently used in their encounters with pirates in the Red Sea. The presence of ship guards on vessels transiting through the Red Sea and the Indian Ocean can be traced back to the first extant chronicles of trade in the region. For Margariti (2008, 164), "Protection against pirates was vital, for piracy shadowed trade in the Indian Ocean at least from the time of the *Periplus* and probably earlier." The use of *asakir al-marakib* and traveling in armed convoys at sea, in addition to the presence of *ushur al-shawani* (protection taxes) levied by rulers across the Red Sea and the Indian Ocean to protect merchants from pirates, highlights an Indian Ocean political economy of violence (Subramanian 2016; Clulow 2012).

In fact, as the historian Frederic Lane shows for the medieval and premodern Mediterranean, protection (what he terms "protection rent") makes possible long-distance trade more generally. As Lane (1979, 251) notes, in the medieval and premodern world, "a very large part of the costs of the long-distance merchant was payment for protection or insurance against losses by bandits or pirates." At the same time, the distribution of protection across the spectrum of premodern trade was hardly uniform: some merchants could buy protection of a better quality than others or buy the same quality at lower costs. This difference between the cost of protection and the payment made by merchants for protection was for Lane a "more important source of income than profits due to superiority in industrial techniques and industrial organization" (251). This framework of protection costs has been useful in explaining the rise and fall of various imperial projects in the Indian Ocean. Where the Portuguese failed to control the western Indian Ocean world with warships and the *cartaz* systems, the Dutch—and later British—expansion in the Indian Ocean "internalized" the costs of protection by giving large joint-stock companies the right to monopolize trade and to conduct warfare east of the Cape of Good Hope. For Niels Steensgaard (1974), these shifting practices of protection partly explain Western European success and Portuguese decline in the Indian Ocean.

If protection (and specifically protection costs) are frameworks through which to understand imperial expansion and failure in oceanic space, Charles Tilly territorializes Lane's concept of protection as a way to reread the rise of the nation-state. Through protection, Tilly recasts this history as part of a long continuum that takes in "banditry, piracy, gangland rivalry, policing, and war making" (Tilly 1985, 170). Highlighting the double-edged nature of protection, Tilly notes that "in contemporary American parlance, the word 'protection' sounds two contrasting tones. One is comforting, the other ominous. With one tone, protection calls up images of shelter against danger. . . . With the other it evokes the racket in which a local strong man forces merchants to pay tribute in order to deliver" (170). Critiquing Lane for "containing his analysis within the neoclassical theory of industrial organization" (181), Tilly gestures at a way to think more broadly about protection, and specifically its imbrication with practices of war-making and state-making where protection provides one genealogy for the rise of the modern state (Shah 2006; Gambetta 1996). Protection was also central within the jurisprudential politics of nineteenth-century empire and international law (Anghie 2005; Grovogui 1996). The instability of the meanings of protection in international law framed encounters between Europeans and others, including justifications of conquest and annexation (Benton and Ford 2016). This continues to shape contemporary logics of humanitarian intervention and the international and domestic politics engendered through claims of protection (Babül 2015).

Limited to neither states nor the realm of international law, the anthropology of protection emphasized in this book brings together law and economy to reveal a multiplicity of systems that are engaged in facilitating mobility. There are piracy trials in courts around the globe (international law), navies patrol the high seas (states), and yet ransoms are paid. The existence of this hijack-and-ransom economy in the western Indian Ocean makes visible alternative systems of protection that connect, in ways that are both brief and unstable, disparate places like insurance offices in London and pirate villages in coastal Somalia. Protection, as this book will show, is the logic through which these otherwise quite distinct locations with different participants, histories, demands, and infrastructures become legible to one another. Beyond disruption (Cowen 2014; Mezzadra and Neilson 2013), protection transforms the story of piracy into an alternative form of connectivity and possibility.

This mode of understanding protection as temporary form of connectivity and possibility linked to itineraries and routes emerges from a wider moral geography of protection in the western Indian Ocean, including land-based modes of escort such as *jiwar, aman,* and, in the Somali context, the practice of *abaan,* a guarantee of safety for strangers in return for payment.

A claim of payment in exchange for safe transit, land-based forms of escort known in Arabic as *aman* and in Somali as *abaan* were long-established modes of claiming power and prestige over mobile trade networks that criss-crossed the hostile deserts of Northeast Africa, connecting the African hinterland to the wider trading worlds of the Indian Ocean and the Mediterranean. *Abaan* existed in a noncentralizing system that worked sideways—horizontally extending protection for a limited time to a stranger who traversed temporarily through one's territory. Located within a world of a "shared and layered concept of [Indian Ocean] sovereignty" (Bose 2009, 25) and *suzerainty* (Brennan 2008), *abaan* had a dual orientation. To provide protection required an ability to control and exert jurisdiction over itinerant merchants, traders, and other foreigners without a (necessary) claim of sovereignty or incorporation. At the same time, *abaan* was always oriented within local political structures and was a means of moving within the world of clan, kinship, and genealogy. A successful protector was exalted in idioms of Somali poetry, and the failure to protect was simultaneously memorialized in these oral idioms. This dual orientation of *abaan* was thus both a mode of engaging circulation on land (and, in the nineteenth century, at sea) through jurisdiction without necessary claims of sovereignty and a way of grounding prestige and honor territorially.[23]

As noted earlier, in the nineteenth century, practices such as *abaan* and the larger question of protection were central to the encounter between European and local powers. The arrival of the British into the trading world of Somalia, as for the French and Italians, was initially facilitated through trusty protectors such as Rooble Afdeed, of the GadaBuursi, in trading towns like Zeila.[24] In opposition to a centralized system of governance, *abaan* and these other forms of protection in the Indian Ocean work "sideways"

(Dresch 2012, 154) and are tied to a field of action dedicated to the encounter between strangers. Here, it is space as the reach of a person that determines questions of jurisdiction as opposed to control over territory or a monopoly of violence. Prestige and violence structure this claim of protection, and hospitality can blend quickly into capture. These forms of protection deal with the mobility of objects and persons, and are about keeping spaces open and providing restitution.

These varied forms of protection—from the histories of protection in the Indian Ocean to maritime insurance, and even the protection of the pirate—and their encounters on land and sea are central to the argument of this book. Emphasizing a wider geography and set of actors is a mode of deparochializing piracy from a question of failed states and crisis, while also acknowledging their productivity as a way to claim legitimacy, capital, and jurisdiction. Instead of highlighting the absence of a regulatory authority, protection emphasizes a plurality of regulatory figures encountering each other in the watery expanses of the ocean. A unifying category deployed by differentially situated actors, the anthropology of protection offers a conceptual framework through which to understand modes of encounter in the Indian Ocean and beyond.

Maritime adventures, as journeys beyond the threshold of the *oikos,* are premised on the comingling of risk and opportunity.[25] To leave behind the solidity of *terra firma* and traverse liquid paths is to embrace a universe of peril (and possibility). Beyond the Indian Ocean littoral, protection, as this book will show, offers a unique vantage point from which to reflect on the seemingly intractable questions of safety in an insecure world: What does it mean to be safe? Who gets to be safe? As juridical engagement, as an offer of refuge and sanctuary from the wrath of another, as a form of labor, and as a mode of intimacy, protection helps explain the rise and fall (and renewal) of maritime piracy in the western Indian Ocean and the processes of mooring and moving in a world that constantly blurs hospitality and hostility, capture and freedom, land and sea.

AN ANTHROPOLOGY OF PROTECTION

In this book, claims to protection animate an entire set of actors and create geographies of interaction, from insurance markets in London to fishing communities in northern Somalia. The methodology of the book was therefore to be immersed in these very different spaces and groups of actors. At a practical level, this required devising specific methods for the various sites where research was conducted. This meant learning risk analysis for insurance underwriting whilst in London, apprenticing on a dhow, and learning to chew khat and understand the regulation of the *suqaa* (market) in port cities of northern Somalia. The methodology of fieldwork, then, is the comparison, overlap, and conflicts between these various sites and the conceptual vocabulary that emerges from these differently located spaces. Piracy cannot be understood in one locale or scale, but rather can only be comprehended by lifting geographic and analytic divides between piracy and counter-piracy, history and anthropology, as well as land and sea. As a transregional phenomenon, piracy as protection requires a transregional methodology.

My research began in courtrooms in coastal Kenya. When the piracy trials were halted in 2010 due to debates over jurisdiction, I moved the research to the port and various freight and cargo companies in Mombasa. Here I noted the ways in which the protection of crew and cargo led to drastic shifts in shipping governance and insurance. Piracy was transforming not just what was happening at sea but also practices on land. I quickly realized that important (and often hidden) actors in the world of piracy were not only based in East Africa, but in fact scattered globally.

The methodology for this first phase of research sought to explore these other economies, ranging from insurance companies in London to the dhow trade that brings most of Somalia's imports and exports. Thus, research moved from East Africa to the United Kingdom, western India, and the United Arab Emirates. In London, the de facto headquarters of global maritime commerce, I ended up working as a risk analyst for an insurance underwriting firm. In addition to understanding the governance facilitated through insurance contracts via focused interviews, this work also entailed attending workshops and training, and learning the dynamic and everyday modes of protection enacted in insurance underwriting.

In western India and the United Arab Emirates, I learned from sailing crews and wholesalers the modes of risk pooling and protection entailed in sailing in waters populated by pirates and navy vessels. In addition, these merchants and sailors provided valuable contacts that facilitated my research in Somalia. Armed with these contacts, I arrived in Somalia, specifically Somaliland and Puntland, to again understand how piracy was reshaping other economic practices. But in the course of my research in Somalia the boundaries between piracy and other economies started to blur. Merchants turned out to be piracy financiers or antipiracy advocates; stevedores at ports turned out to be failed pirates. I soon discovered that piracy was not a shadow economy but part of everyday worlds and norms of sociality. This made research feasible, but also made certain aspects of piracy invisible to me. I never inquired about, nor discovered, the political complicities between local governments, Islamist movements, and pirates—those questions fall within the purview of intelligence agencies and other policing organizations. Most of my encounters in Somalia were in public or semipublic locales, and I learned a lot from them about the socialization of piracy within cities and villages in the region. The ways that individual pirates privately negotiated their status as pirates or itineraries beyond piracy, with wives, mothers, or children, only emerged in interviews and not in any observed settings.

As a young, male, South Asian American, I was both familiar and strange within this space. Many in Somalia treated me as a Kenyan-Indian business-man (due to the fact that my Swahili was always better than my Somali), an Egyptian (due to my Egyptian-inflected Arabic), or sometimes a journalist, and on a few occasions a CIA agent. These different identities reveal the modes of intimacy and estrangement within which my research was under-stood. Instead of ever-increasing intimacy, my fieldwork in Somalia was highly contingent on political and other currents onshore and offshore. This also made research somewhat episodic, with the maximum consecutive dura-tion of time I could spend in Somalia, due to security and financial limita-tions, being three months. But through repeated visits, ranging from a week to three months at a time, from 2011 to 2013, I was able to interview and otherwise spend time with a number of people involved in the world of piracy in Somalia. In these encounters, I sought to distinguish myself from journal-ists, partly because I wanted to stay longer and also not have to pay for inter-views. Many pirates refused to speak to me because they wanted money; others would only give the occasional interview. While those interviews fea-ture in the book, most of the material comes from long periods of time spent in government offices, ports, and khat chews in northern Somalia. In each of these places I sought to work with administrative officials, port workers, pastoralists, fishermen, and merchants to understand how they navigated piracy, and these encounters also helped facilitate interviews and travel throughout the region. These places were also important sites where I was introduced to both active and former pirates. While fieldwork in Somaliland was less constrained and I was able to freely move around, research in Puntland and central Somalia required constant mediators, including at times armed guards. Working with a plurality of actors was a way to avoid being "captured" by any one of these groups and ensured my mobility through the region. This also allowed me to cross-reference stories and often to pit competing explanations against each other. Somalia and the western Indian Ocean—due to their histories of mobility—are a multilingual space, and the fieldwork engaged multiple languages, including Arabic, Swahili, Somali, Urdu, and Kutchi, where I have varying degrees of fluency.

Finally, I got to spend some time on board a variety of ships, including container ships, dhows, and naval patrols. These voyages ranged from smaller forays of two to three days on fishing boats, dhows, and naval patrols to three weeks transiting the Red Sea and the western Indian Ocean in a container ship, and were important in getting my sea legs and learning about the gendered and racialized forms of labor and conviviality that shape life on board vessels. Learning from dhow crews how to sail dhows, working with crew members on container ships as they went about pirate patrols in the Red Sea, and sharing conversations with crew members and captains aboard these very different vessels underscored the centrality of protection in shaping understandings of being at sea and the materiality of navigation in the Indian Ocean.

The book thus moves between these spaces and brings into view parallel, and often competing, regimes of protection in order to think beyond methodological and analytical divisions between piracy and counter-piracy.

Chapter 1, "Protectors of the Sea: The Rise of Maritime Piracy off the Coast of Somalia," provides a prehistory to the contemporary upsurge in maritime piracy by emphasizing the interplay between pastoral idioms of property and the development of a maritime fishing economy in coastal Somalia. By emphasizing the centrality of capture—and notions of bounty, payment, and redistribution nested within it—this chapter illuminates shifts in relationships of property and profit across scale and historical time, and suggests that understanding the emergence of piracy requires an explication of the interplay between sea and land (fishing and pastoralism) within regimes of governance in Somalia and the western Indian Ocean.

Based on ethnographic work in northern Somalia, Chapter 2, "Anchoring Pirates: Grounding a Protection Economy," turns to the concrete processes through which the economy of piracy was anchored within forms of obligation on land in Somalia, Puntland, and Somaliland. As piracy expanded, partly as a result of international naval policing, from the coastal waters of the Red Sea to the monsoonal Indian Ocean, it required new forms of risk pooling that anchored piracy to land even further. Given the uncertainties of the ransom economy, modes of financing such as diya kinship groups and economies of khat provided the capital, collateral, and connections that made possible deep-sea voyages to capture container ships. Diya and khat make piracy possible and socialize it within forms of obligation and exchange that both offer protection and govern the economy of piracy.

Chapter 3, "Regulating the Ocean: The Governance of Counter-Piracy," moves to counter-piracy and specifically the naval response to Somali piracy and the maritime insurance contracts that govern global shipping in the western Indian Ocean. Counter-piracy as a global response to Somali piracy is constituted both through practices of policing at sea and through the contractual and bureaucratic logic of insurance agencies and their forms of underwriting risk. An ethnography of counter-piracy, foregrounding both military bases and insurance offices, emphasizes that force and contract are not distinct, but rather blend into each other. This spillover between the boundaries of naval policing and insurance contracts reveals practices of discernment and distinction that make possible a system of governance and an economy of protection over people and objects in mobile spaces, including over those understood as piratical.

Chapter 4, "Markets of Negotiation: The Making of a Ransom," turns to the multi-actor and multi-spatial process of the making of a ransom. In popular and academic discourse, "bad" pirates and the "good" coalition of counter-piracy are divided both spatially and across the boundary between legality and illegality. Lifting the divide between these geographically and legally distinct worlds of piracy and counter-piracy, this chapter reveals a shared, if internally competitive, world that emerges in the aftermath of capture. Moving between coastal Somalia, the offices of negotiators, shipowners, and the families of hostages, I explore the production of the ransom and the possibilities of both profit and loss and failure that are central to this process. This is a world not only of pirates and navies locked in an endless battle at sea but also of contractors, negotiators, pilots, consultants, and diviners. These various figures and their numerical and nonnumerical modes of valuation—including the gendered and racialized forms of value that shape piracy, counter-piracy, and the wider economy of maritime labor—are essential to transforming capture into a ransom.

Finally, Chapter 5, "Captivity at Sea: Pirates on Dhows," turns to a curious form of hijacking at sea characteristic of Somali piracy. Somali pirates sought to capture Indian dhows as they traveled from ports in western India to Somalia. These vessels were not captured for their value as ransom, but rather transformed into motherships—ships hijacked by pirates to go farther into the Indian Ocean and blend into oceanic traffic in order to capture cargo ships. Based on interviews with former hostages and hijackers, I unravel the interplay between hostility and hospitality in these moments, contrasting the narratives of the hijacked dhow crews with the more publicized captivity narratives of Western hostages, and reflect on what these moments of captivity can tell us about freedom and safety in this contemporary moment.

ONE

Protectors of the Sea

THE RISE OF MARITIME PIRACY OFF
THE COAST OF SOMALIA

BERBERA WAS MY FIRST INTRODUCTION to the Somali coast. As I waited for a visa and security guarantee to travel to Puntland, the autonomous region in northern Somalia and home to most pirates, I decided to begin my research in the relatively safe confines of secessionist Somaliland. I arrived in the capital, Hargeisa, in the winter of 2010, armed with contacts obtained from boat captains, Somali wholesalers, and traders in Sharjah and Mombasa. In Hargeisa, people constantly informed me that I was in the wrong place looking for pirates. "We have honest fishermen, and law and order in Somaliland," remarked Admiral Ahmed during our weekly chats in the small Somaliland Coastguard Office. Visibly bored after imparting yet another history lesson on Somaliland and the Somaliland Coastguard's problems of underfunding, the admiral suggested a trip to Berbera: "You won't find pirates—but you'll learn about fishing, and you must meet Musa, the director of the Somaliland Fishing Association (SOMAFISH) who will explain everything." With the admiral's invitation letter in hand, a couple of days later I was in a Land Cruiser racing towards the *Badda cas* (Red Sea) and the port city of Berbera.

Located a hundred or so miles before the Red Sea empties into the western Indian Ocean, Berbera is the main trade port for Somaliland. Unlike the mythical Indian Ocean port cities with their labyrinthine coral buildings that echo long histories of trade and mobility, Berbera is by every measure architecturally unremarkable. Drab concrete buildings, shops, and warehouses line the dusty, rough road connecting Berbera to the capital, with the relentless and harsh sun a constant reminder of why the *Saaxil* (coast) remains relatively peripheral and often inaccessible in northern Somaliland/Somalia. But this initial impression of inaccessibility belies a rich world of trade and exchange.

In the nineteenth century, traders and merchants from far and wide annually transformed this dusty speck on the Red Sea into a hub of activity during Berbera's annual trade fair. In his travelogue, Lieutenant C. J. Cruttenden of the British Indian Navy described arriving in Berbera at the height of the trade fair in 1848 as anchoring into a "perfect Babel, in confusion as in languages" amidst the chaos of "small crafts from the ports of Yemen; the valuably freighted *Bagalas* from Bahrein [Bahrain], Bussorah [Basra, Iraq] . . . and the clumsy *Kotias* of the fat and wealthy Banian traders from Porebunder, Mandavie, and Bombay" (Cruttenden 1849, 54). Gazing from his ship, Cruttenden noted a constant dust cloud on the horizon as rows and rows of livestock marched through the harsh Somali interior in order to be loaded onto waiting boats ready to transport them across the Red Sea.

While few physical reminders exist of this vibrant nineteenth-century trading port, the cycle of commerce continues with dhows, and increasingly container ships, arriving in this heavily import-dependent economy laden with goods from dentist chairs to rice. In addition to this long history of trade, Berbera is also littered with remains of other, more recent and more violent histories. On the road between Hargeisa and Berbera, I occasionally encountered shelled-out and bullet-pocked buildings and abandoned and rusted tanks—reminders of the civil war that pitted the inhabitants of Somaliland against the dictatorial regime of Siyad Barre (1969–91). Adjacent to the port, half-sunken ships from aerial bombing campaigns testify to the twilight years of the Barre regime when all dissent was viciously quelled.

Legacies of the Cold War, when Somalia oscillated between the Soviet Union and the United States, also linger in the shadows of the city. The seemingly endless airport runway constructed by the Soviet Union and used by NASA as an emergency space shuttle landing site is perhaps the most visible reminder of Berbera's former strategic importance. But there are also smaller imprints of the Cold War and Somalia's recent history. Health clinics, fishery cooperatives, and schools, built with Soviet assistance, dot the coastline and are now reduced to rubble due to shelling or simple neglect. New construction, the result of investment by the Somali diaspora, occurs closer to the market area away from the sea. One of these buildings along the coastline, a former Cuban health clinic, now hosted the office of SOMAFISH.

After a week of back-and-forth phone calls and text messages, Musa, the director of SOMAFISH, agreed to meet with me right after the afternoon prayers. To get to his office I passed a veritable graveyard of fiber fishing skiffs, the preferred vessels of local fishermen as well as the pirates who roamed farther out in the Gulf of Aden. Sitting behind a desk littered with papers and a triptych formed by a Somaliland flag, a shark jaw with teeth intact, and a replica of an anchor, Musa recounted his personal biography, which intersected with the story of Somali fisheries—from the heyday of industrialized fishing in the Barre regime to the calamities of war and the tentative reemergence of this industry in Somaliland, in the shadow of piracy and foreign interlopers.

Born in Berbera, Musa, like many of his generation, went to university in Mogadishu. "I studied business administration at university. In those days, the Soviet Union was heavily involved in funding development projects. So, after finishing my degree I got a job in one of these projects, a fish factory in Las Qoray." Pausing, he asked me if I knew where Las Qoray was. I nodded. "In Sanaag, between here and Puntland," I replied, and told him I was planning a trip there to see the fish factory. "Oh, you won't see anything of the old factory anymore. I worked at the factory until the war began [1991] . . . it was all destroyed during the war." Leaning further back into his chair, he started telling me about the end of the Barre regime: "During the war, after the government ended, most people started to return to their clan homelands. So, we moved from Las Qoray and ended up here in Berbera because my father is from Somaliland. Those were hard days. People were leaving, going everywhere they could, but many of us who stayed, we built Somaliland." After a long chat about the successes of Somaliland, Musa returned to the fish factory in Las Qoray. "One morning people came in and took everything at the fish factory: the machines, roofing material, anything that could be taken was taken from the factory and sold. I hear they've rebuilt the factory and it sells fish to China and even Australia." I asked Musa if he ever wanted to go back to work in Las Qoray. "No, no," he responded somewhat angrily, "that factory is controlled by Puntland." I had inadvertently stumbled into the thorny issue of conflict between Somaliland and Puntland.[1]

Trying to change the subject, I asked instead about plans for the Berbera factory. Musa detailed his ambitious vision to create a fishing store and export house in Berbera. "But to do all that we need air-conditioning. Fish need ice." Sitting in his decidedly not air-conditioned office, we were discussing plans to find ice and air conditioning when Musa suddenly remembered another meeting. We walked outside into the humid evening and back through the graveyard of skiffs. Pointing to these vessels, even more eerie in the dim light, he remarked that these were the lifeblood of SOMAFISH. "We need more boats; we need to be able to repair these boats. Without the

FIGURE 2. Author with Somaliland
coastguard in Berbera Port, 2011.
Photo by Hassan Ibrahim.

skiff we cannot profit from the sea." He walked closer to the skiffs and continued, "Without fuel, the fishermen cannot compete with the Yemeni fishermen or the trawlers." Seemingly to underscore his point, Musa jumped into
one of the skiffs: "If they [the fishermen] can't fish, they might become
pirates. You know the pirates in Puntland, many of them were fishermen,
before they started *catching different fish.*" As he stepped out of the skiff, he
remarked, "Now they call themselves *badaadinta badah* [protectors of the
sea]." Nodding in agreement, I offered to take Musa to the seafood restaurant
after his meeting, a place favored by the occasional UN official visiting
Berbera, as a gesture of appreciation. Musa politely declined, explaining that
he was a "true pastoralist" and found the idea of eating fish "repulsive." As he
emphasized, he had no plans on being *afkalluun* (a fish mouth).

Musa's story, his reliance upon and revulsion of fish, and the physical landscape of Berbera bring into view geographies of commerce, conflict, and community that have shaped this region's past and present. From his work at a
fish factory in Las Qoray to his return to Somaliland, Musa's career trajectory
reflects both the fantasies of the developmentalist state and the disruptions
of internecine conflict. Similarly, the terrain of Berbera underlines a port city
whose fortunes depend on both land and sea, ebb and flow, alongside political, social, and economic shifts. These histories of rubble,[2] these visible and
invisible legacies of trade, war, and geostrategic rivalry, all serve to remind us
of Berbera's role in a wider world. These connections, reflections of a simultaneous interplay of marginality and strategic importance, continue to shape
the Somali coast's relationship to a wider oceanic world. As Admiral Ahmed
had rightfully predicted, I did not meet pirates in Berbera on that trip. But
what was made visible in Berbera—the movement between land and sea, the
longer political and economic histories, and the ambiguous status of fish and

fisheries (and pirates)—is key to understanding maritime piracy in the western Indian Ocean.

From 2007, the dramatic upsurge in maritime piracy off the coast of Somalia drew global attention to fishing, specifically to the problem of illegal fishing in the western Indian Ocean. While reports emphasizing the prevalence of illegal, unreported, and unregulated (IUU) fishing vessels in Somali waters date back to the early 1990s, when large-scale foreign trawling first made its appearance in the western Indian Ocean, this renewed emphasis on IUU fishing in popular and academic scholarship can be directly linked to the rise in incidents of maritime piracy and international efforts to curb this practice. Whether writing about the connections to the Sicilian mafia or the exploitation of these waters by foreign trawlers,[3] these works have been crucial in critiquing a simplistic narrative of piracy as criminality. They remind us that in global coverage only certain actions are labeled as piratical: "piracy" and "legality" are loaded and polemical terms that legitimize certain actions while condemning others. But while importantly contextualizing the rise (and fall) of maritime predation in the western Indian Ocean, these works still narrate a story of failure—of governance, of states, and of other international institutions.

A focus on failures of governance has been central in explaining not only the rise of maritime piracy, but also contemporary understandings of global commons regimes more generally. From land appropriations across sub-Saharan Africa to toxic dumping in the world's oceans, we are in an era of renewed global dispossession, one seemingly aided by failures of governance. Drawing on Karl Marx (1867) and Rosa Luxembourg ([1913] 2003), scholars like David Harvey (2005) have emphasized an ongoing primitive accumulation characterized by new and increased forms of enclosure and expropriation. This primitive accumulation produces geographies of toxicity in its wake, a toxicity that is felt unevenly along lines of race, class, and gender. This scholarly focus on dispossession, toxicity, and ruination is a powerful diagnostic of the current moment and has given rise to new, emergent scholarship in anthropology and beyond that chronicles the (im)possibilities of life "at the end of the world" (Tsing 2015).

While remaining attentive to dispossession and exploitation, this chapter tells a different story. Locating Somali piracy within longer histories that emerge from places like Berbera, I highlight commons (such as oceanic spaces) that emerge through the interrelationship and interdependence of land and sea, of capture and redistribution. The transformation to what Musa referred to as catching a different kind of fish requires us to focus simultaneously on the making and unmaking of relationships, including property relations—a process that occurs across scale and time. The rise of piracy, then, is not just a story of failure or absence—even though that absence profoundly shapes what happens off the coast of Somalia—but also of the development of a modality of governance (and extraction), built on the intimacy of capture and redistribution, through which one could claim to be a protector of the sea.

This chapter unfolds along two interrelated lines. At one level, what follows is the story of the emergence of maritime piracy that captivated global attention from 2007 to 2012—a period in which over one hundred fifty ships and three thousand crew members were held hostage off the Somali coast. Through this story of piracy, one shaped by local and global regulatory shifts, I reflect on the broader making and unmaking of the commons and focus on what piracy tells us about possession and dispossession on land and sea.

I begin on the Somali coast and explore the role of fish and fishing within a pastoral world. Moving between ethnography, history, the archive, and theories of property, the first part of the chapter builds what I term a *pastoral commons* that emphasizes mobility, capture, and redistribution. This mode of property-making is central to understanding how claims are made upon objects at sea, claims that shape the encounters between pirate skiffs, oil tankers, and other vessels in the Indian Ocean. The focus then shifts to the heyday of the Somali state and the period of Scientific Socialism (1969–75). The argument here tracks the transition from a "sea of fish" (Dua 2013), a world of artisanal fishing, to a sea of licenses from the 1970s onwards: the sea as a natural resource belonging to the state that could be harnessed and exploited by the Somali government and other private actors through licensing (Dua 2017a). The government's extraction of profits through this form of licensing was crucial to the establishment of fisheries and constituted more generally a central logic of statecraft in Somalia. In this sense, the contemporary upsurge in maritime piracy off the coast of Somalia can be understood not as a moment of rupture resulting from the absence of a centralized government but rather as an extension of the licensing regime, now pursued by nonstate actors in the guise of piracy.

LAND AND SEA

What does it mean to make property at sea? In the classical world, Roman jurists divided the universe into things over which humans had patrimony and things that were seen to lie outside this system (*res extra nostrum patrimonium*). Land could be fenced in and enclosed, and so was fair game for conquest and control. Things outside the threshold of human patrimony and ownership included those which belonged to the gods and those over which no single being, divine or human, could lay claim. This latter realm of law included the air, flowing water, and the sea. This elemental distinction has been at the center of Western legal thought. In his aptly titled *Land and Sea*, Carl Schmitt reframes world history as the "history of the wars waged by maritime powers against land or continental powers and by land powers against sea or maritime powers" (Schmitt 2008, 5). To Schmitt, land and sea, exemplified in the figures of the behemoth and the leviathan, are in eternal opposition—land and sea are fundamentally, radically different.

This sense of distinction was also the basis for a young Dutch jurist's defense of acts of seizure at sea by the Dutch East India Company (VOC) in the early seventeenth century. Writing in the aftermath of the capture of the Portuguese carrack *Santa Catarina* in the Straits of Singapore in 1603, Hugo Grotius sought to justify Captain Jakob van Heemskerck's action through recourse to natural law and divine will. Grotius located van Heemskerck's actions within a wider context of freedom of trade and navigation. Property (or what we now would term a "property right") could only be derived from physical possession and use. Given the fluidity of the ocean and its seeming inexhaustibility, no one could possess, and thus exclude others from, the sea. As he notes in his *Mare Liberum*, "The sea therefore is in the number of things which are not in merchandise and trading, that is to say, cannot remain property" (Grotius [1609] 2004, 30). Thus, the Portuguese attempt to exclude Dutch shipping from the Indian Ocean was an act of aggression justifying van Heemskerck's seizure as a legitimate act of reprisal. As David Armitage has noted in his introduction to Grotius's *Mare Liberum*, "This fundamental contrast between the properties of sea and land would remain central to later conceptions of property within the natural-law tradition up to and beyond John Locke's agriculturalist argument for appropriation, which similarly exempted 'the Ocean, that great and still remaining Common of Mankind' (Locke, *Second Treatise*, § 30) from the possibility of exclusive possession" (Grotius [1609] 2004, xvi).

This elemental bias of Western natural law, this distinction between property on land and commons at sea, has shaped a long history of understanding property and possession. In particular, the natural law vision of commons is central in the justification of colonial and postcolonial appropriations. It is precisely the idea of the commons—as a space with no prior claim of ownership—that allows for the possibility of expropriation. This vision of the commons is what allowed Locke to imagine all the world as America, ignoring prior histories of ownership and claim-making, and how Grotius transformed an act of piracy into a lawful form of taking. In a world divided between land and sea, the commons becomes a practice of dispossession. However, from the vantage point of the East African coast, this elemental distinction between land and sea is not so straightforward. Instead of the behemoth and the leviathan, locked in eternal conflict, we have the camel and the boat.

PIRATES IN A LAND OF PASTORALISTS

After a few weeks in Berbera shuttling between the fishery cooperatives, Musa's office, and the port, I finally received confirmation that my research permission for Puntland had arrived. I immediately made my way over to Musa's office to inform him that I would be flying out the next day to Bosaso, the largest port and commercial hub for Puntland. Now concerned, he said, "Puntland is so different: Bosaso is a war zone, with pirates and Al Shabaab— you should be very careful, it's not at all like Somaliland." Musa's warning did give me pause, and with some trepidation I departed his office and headed to the land of *harb* (war).

Bosaso at first glance felt no different from Berbera. This too was a town kept alive by the constant movement of goods between hinterland and ocean. Arriving boats unloaded their wares onto trucks that then screamed through town in predictable daily dust storms, transporting the goods from ships' holds to cavernous warehouses on the edge of town. Smaller trucks waiting hungrily at these warehouses would then be loaded up to rush down the coast with rice, pasta, tomato sauce, and the odd bag of wheat (not much bread was consumed in the cities of northern and central Somalia). Goats, camels, and charcoal would travel in the other direction, on their way across the Gulf of Aden.

Upon my arrival in Bosaso, officials at the newly created Puntland Ministry of Maritime Transport, Ports, and Counter-Piracy immediately took me under their wings. I appreciated this affiliation for the contacts, but also feared it would dissuade "real pirates" from speaking with me. The ministry's location inside the Bosaso port gave me ample opportunity to witness and begin to make sense of the comings and goings at the port, as well as providing me with daily contact with dockworkers, port security, merchants, boat captains, and others whose work lives were transformed in the wake of piracy. I was informed repeatedly by officials and other port workers that things had changed in the years following the increase in piracy.

Prior to 2007, World Food Program (WFP)–contracted ships, older bulk carriers,[4] and the occasional dhow would halt at the port of Bosaso. But in the wake of the upsurge in piracy, bulk carriers and WFP ships began to avoid Somali ports and coastal waters given the easy target they presented for pirates at sea. In their absence, dhows from South Asia, sensing new opportunities, started bringing goods, food-aid, and the Land Cruisers coveted by "pirate bosses" to Somali ports. The reduced cargo capacity of dhows meant that more boats would come in and out of the port, creating a constant buzz of work and movement, including an ever-present crowd at the port office. It was in this crowd that I met Dalmar, a local livestock trader, as he applied for an export certificate to transport camels to Saudi Arabia.

Following the establishment of Aden in 1839 as a major coaling station for British shipping, Bosaso and neighboring Berbera became ports of call for the British Indian Navy eager to secure supplies—primarily livestock (camels and goats) to feed booming Aden—thus giving this region the nickname the "butcher shop of Aden." This trade in livestock has ever since been a central node linking northern Somali port cities to their counterparts across the Gulf. On September 19, 2000, the Saudi government banned the export of livestock from the Horn of Africa, fearing health risks from Rift Valley Fever. The UAE and Yemen followed suit, though they had both lifted their trade ban by May 2001 even though Saudi Arabia continued its ban until 2009. Dalmar, I was to learn, had become a prominent trader during the nine years of the livestock trade ban. "I had contacts in Yemen and they would guarantee us re-export certificates, so I could still send cattle and camels to Saudi through Yemen . . . some people called this 'smuggling,' but to us it was just part of *seylad* [market trade]."

The next day, when Dalmar returned to collect his export certificate, he invited me to visit his boat that had just arrived from Salahah, Oman. As we sat in the hold of his motorized sailing vessel (MSV)–class dhow built in Mandvi, India, Dalmar likened the boat to a camel. As he explained, unlike sheep and goats, camels were both his individual wealth and a joint stock of his lineage (*summad*): "My clan has a claim on it because the camels bear the stamp of my lineage." This, for Dalmar, was due to the fact that no person

FIGURE 3: Fishing skiff in coastal Somalia.

individually raises a camel. "I share the milk and meat with others and in turn they help raise and maintain the herds," he explained, noting that while the prestige of ownership belonged to him, it came with an obligation to share. As with camels, whose milk and meat distributed to kin groups in turn obligated these groups to assist him in raising and maintaining the camel herds, ownership of the boat too was distributed: "My business success led me to buy the dhow that we are sitting in right now, but this boat is not just mine. Boats are like camels—they never only belong to one person."

In the anthropological literature on East Africa, pastoralists and their relationship to livestock occupy a central focus. Beginning with Herskovits's "cattle complex" (1926) through Evans-Pritchard's classic ethnographic account of the Nuer ([1940] 1969), anthropologists have long emphasized the "bovine mystique" of livestock (Ferguson 1985). Through ethnographically nuanced accounts, this scholarship has highlighted the role of livestock as a storehouse of value in multiple registers (Hutchinson 1992), a means for forging sociopolitical ties (Kuper 1982), and a mode of linking economies of production and exchange across local/regional and precolonial/colonial scales (Comaroff and Comaroff 1990). Somalia's "camel complex" fits neatly within this literature on pastoralism. The anthropologist I. M. Lewis (1994) has emphasized the ecological needs of pastoralism in a harsh and unforgiving climate along with the shared property claim to livestock as integral to social solidarity and clan cohesion. Together these works emphasize the central role of livestock in shaping institutions like clans, and their forms of sociality and moral engagements. What is often missed is that shared wealth in camels has historically also led to the emergence and perpetuation of raiding economies built around capture and systems of redistribution and incorporation. This pastoral logic of capture and redistribution also extends to the sea, creating a *pastoral commons*. In opposition to elemental distinctions between land and sea and a natural law vision of the commons, for Dalmar and his compatriots, the sea, as pastoral commons, is a set of desert paths traversed on boats. As Dalmar's analogy between boats and camels and the wider modes of exchange between land and sea in this trading world suggest, in encountering the sea, pastoral logics (and actual camels and goats) get transposed in ways that signify neither seamless symmetry and continuity between land and sea nor a radical disjuncture.

If boats were like camels, I asked Dalmar, then could one raid boats as one does with camels? "Of course, that's what the pirates are doing, but if anyone tried to take my boat, they would be in trouble," Dalmar replied, noting the limits of this analogy. In addition to being a discursive claim, the idea of a pastoral commons is one that emerges from an engagement with the saltiness and materiality of the sea. What do the sea and property-making look like for those tillers of the water (Rediker 2004) whose lives inhabit the *maraja*, the zone where fresh- and saltwater meet but do not dissolve?[5]

A SEA OF FISH

Ambergris is one of the more unusual varieties of flotsam in the sea. With one of the longest coastlines in continental Africa, Somalia is home to some of the world's richest marine resources. During the months from June to September, the warm southwest monsoon churns the waters off the coast of northern Somalia. Merging with the Findlater jet, a narrow low-level atmospheric jet stream that blows diagonally across the Indian Ocean, these currents combine to create a coastal upwelling that brings nutrient-rich waters to the surface, attracting tuna, snapper, and other coveted piscine delights. The northeast monsoon, which occurs from December to February, causes a reversal of the Somali current, moving the coastal waters southwest. As air from the north cools the water, more nutrients arrive at the surface, creating one of the most productive marine ecosystems in the world. These maritime currents also create a highway for ambergris jettisoned from whales to travel across the Indian Ocean and find their way up into its northwest corner, in the bottleneck formed by Somalia and the peninsula of southern Arabia.

In the nineteenth century, an ambergris craze developed globally as perfumes became central to a new olfactory regime of marking class and related ideas of taste and sensuality (Kemp 2012). This boom in the global ambergris trade led to the establishment of "ambergris villages" along the northern Somali coast, where communities earned their livelihoods by collecting the valuable wax as it was deposited on their doorsteps by the obliging waves. Ambergris was seen as a gift from the ocean, whose bounty tied these coastal villages to wider economies in the region. Indian and Arab merchants routinely visited these villages to purchase the substance, and the resulting cash provided villagers with access to livestock and other commodities.

The opening of the Suez Canal in 1869 and British imperial expansion into the Red Sea and the Indian Ocean incorporated northern Somalia into currents of global capitalism.[6] Within the world of ambergris collection, possibilities for profit and potential access to a wider world of consumer goods greatly increased alongside a rise in violence during this period. Colonial officials chronicled these violent contests as proof of the warlike nature of Somalis while seemingly ignoring both their own role in perpetuating conflicts and the logics of redistribution inherent in these worlds.

Echoing rules regarding the distribution of salvage from shipwrecks in the nineteenth century, this ambergris economy was built on a mix of capture, collection, and redistribution. Few restrictions existed at sea for its appropriation, and chance and risk were crucial to the acquisition of this bounty. Once the flotsam washed ashore, rules regarding property and ownership were strictly, and often violently, enforced within the local community. In one such former ambergris village, Sheikh Usman explained to me the principles of property allocation.

A native of a coastal village on the Red Sea and *qadi* (Islamic legal jurist) of the Bari (coastal) region of Puntland, as well as a self-proclaimed amateur historian, the Sheikh claimed to have visited every coastal settlement from Berbera to Mogadishu and was my guide to the ambergris villages in this region. According to the Sheikh, village elders (*oday*) allocated to each family in the village a section of the beach, with the sole right to collection. Like plots of precious farmland, these were zealously tended and handed down from generation to generation. The transformation of profits from ambergris into livestock or payments for laborers, such as *askaris* (guards) or cleaners for the sea frontages, created a redistributive network built around clan payment groups. Offshore, it was capture that determined ownership over ambergris. Some fishermen would go on boats to find the ambergris. As the Sheikh noted, this was a difficult way to procure this precious substance. "The color of ambergris is very dull, and it looks like rocks. If the fisherman had seen a [sperm whale] the night before that would give him a guess where to potentially find the ambergris." For the Sheikh it was this element of chance and skill that made capture determine ownership of ambergris at sea.

With the development of cheaper synthetic substitutes available to the perfume industry, demand for ambergris decreased. Additionally, starting in the 1970s, numerous countries prohibited the possession and trade of ambergris as part of a wider ban on the hunting of sperm whales. While ambergris continues to enjoy a niche market, mostly for its reputed properties as an aphrodisiac, the ambergris economy is no longer a mainstay in coastal Somalia. But, crucially, understandings of property implicated within the practice of ambergris capture and collection, and the circuits of redistribution that this has engendered, continue to be key in framing the practices of a variety of actors in this littoral space, from artisanal fishermen to pirates.

"Fish are fugitive," explained Ali, a fisherman with a fabled reputation for catching shark. "You and I can go into the ocean right now in the same area and I can guarantee we will come back with very different catch—actually, I will come back with fish and you will come back with saltwater on your face!" As with the economy of ambergris, within the world of artisanal fishing, capture at sea creates property. As Ali and other fishermen explained to me, chance, risk, and a mode of enskilment that echoes Pálsson (1994), where becoming enskilled entails the "whole person interacting with the social and natural environment" (919), are crucial in transforming fish into property. The mobile and migratory nature of fish requires a degree of immersion and engagement with the materiality of the ocean: a form of engagement built around practices of capture. For Ali, fishing was akin to a hunt that required chance and, importantly, skill. Echoing distinctions in the ambergris economy between collection and capture, Ali's framing of fish as fugitive foregrounded the importance of capture within practices of fishing, thus emphasizing his prowess and status. At the same time, Ali's understanding of fish as fugitive can be expanded in ways that resonate with idioms of property-making far beyond the shores of Somalia.

The notion of fugitive property has a long history within the annals of property law, especially concerning the status of foxes, whales, and (in the early twentieth century) oil and subsurface natural resources.[7] In a now classic case, *Hammonds v. Central Kentucky Natural Gas Co.,* the Court of Appeals in Kentucky turned to the rule of capture from common law doctrine in England in order to decide on ownership over natural gas extracted from the ground. In 1930, the Central Kentucky Natural Gas Company leased tracts of land above a depleted natural gas stratum and used this land as an underground storehouse of gas. But the geological dome of natural gas lay only partly under the land they were leasing and partly under someone else's land. When the company began extracting the gas, Hammonds, one of the other landowners, sued for trespass, claiming that some of the gas they were extracting came from beneath her land and this gas was stored under her property without her consent. Hammonds asserted that the defendant made illicit use of her property by introducing natural gas into the dome beneath her land. The court had to decide whether the company continued to own the natural gas once it was injected back into the ground, in order to adjudicate liability. Through analogy to classic common law doctrine on hunting, specifically fox hunting cases from the nineteenth century, the court held:

> In seeking for an analogous condition in the law, the courts, since the early Pennsylvania case, have compared natural gas and oil to that of animals *ferae naturae.* The analogy, as we have seen, formed the basis of the all but universal doctrine of property in these wandering minerals. So, we may look to that analogous law. From the beginning, wild animals have been regarded as quasi property of the entire human race. It is the recognition of land titles rather than of any individual property in the game that prevents its pursuit, and, barring all questions of trespass, exclusive property in birds and wild animals becomes vested in the person capturing or reducing them to possession. But unless killed, this is a qualified property, for when restored to their natural wild and free state, the dominion and individual proprietorship of any person over them is at an end and they resume their status as common property. [Similar for fish, foxes, and water.] We are of opinion, therefore, that if in fact the gas turned loose in the earth wandered into the plaintiff's land, the

defendant is not liable to her for the value of the use of her property, for the company ceased to be the exclusive owner of the whole of the gas—it again became mineral *ferae naturae*.[8]

By analogizing the status of natural gas to that of wild animals (*ferae naturae*), the court upheld a principle of first possession, or the rule-of-capture, in making property claims for fugitive property. First possession is a familiar concept in the realm of property law. Justinian's discussion of how things become property of individuals, for example, begins with the example of "wild animals, birds and fish, i.e., all animals born on land or in the sea or air, [which] as soon as they are caught by anyone, forthwith fall into his ownership by the law of nations: for what previously belonged to no one is, by natural reason, accorded to its captor" (Institutes of Justinian 2.1.12, transl. Sandars 1876). Enlightenment scholarship followed Justinian, and treated animals *ferae naturae* as the paradigm of the unowned thing—the commons.

But as the *Hammonds* case also highlights, wild animals (and natural gas) are a form of qualified property. As the court noted in *Hammonds,* "When gas is . . . brought under dominion and into actual possession at the surface, it, of course, becomes the personal property of the one who has extracted it under a right so to do."[9] Yet this right is limited, for once the gas is released back into the earth it returns to *ferae naturae* and once again becomes common property. Capture and possession, far from absolute, are contingent practices. Whereas the vision of qualified property envisioned in *Hammonds* is ultimately about the balance between public and private property, the moral economy of capture in Somalia is a mode of socializing and embedding property. The celebration and exaltation of the livestock rustler and raider—*xalaal iyo xaaraan, hadow xera galo midna kuma xuma* (whether through licit or illicit means, it matters most that you possess the camel)—paradoxically articulated alongside a critique of ill-gotten wealth—*hal xaaranihi nirig xalaal ah ma dhasho* (a stolen she-camel will not beget a licit calf)—works to regulate capture and embed rules framing property within a wider moral universe. These two ideals, the valorization of the rustler and the critique of ill-gotten wealth, are not oppositions resolved through the figure of the law (as in the case of *Hammonds* and fugitive property), but two faces of the same dynamic, namely a way of making claims on objects that are always already socialized.

In his classic text *Stone Age Economics,* Marshall Sahlins (1974) proposed a typology to understand gifts, capture, and other forms of credit/debit relationships. For Sahlins, theft and capture constitute an attempt to break the credit/debt relationship through the disavowal of debt that is co-constitutive of credit. In contrast to this neat typology, the capture of amber-gris and fish is located within preexisting ideas about reciprocity and return. "Fish are the bounty of the sea," Ali explained. "This means that I share with others, but also that my prize gives me the right to demand and expect things and respect from others." In Somalia and across fishing communities in the western Indian Ocean, the sea is the "gift of God," and cannot be owned or enclosed. In contrast, camels, wells, fish, and boats can be owned, stolen, or captured, and the boundaries of this ownership are often violently policed through references both to idioms of Islamic law—*xaalal iyo xaaraan* (licit and illicit)—and customary norms.

Mobility, as opposed to a fixed idiom of territory, is central in making and justifying claims to property. Fish, camels, and boats are constantly on the move: grazing areas transform through drought and other vagaries of nature; sea currents and upwells lead to a constantly moving fish stock. This mobility and contingency means that property claims do not emerge from enclosure, but through capture of objects and routes. Yet capture is always a form of qualified property: in order to be legitimate it has to be embedded within a social world of obligation and reciprocity. This vision of property, this *pastoral commons,* entails a politics of recognition. As Ali noted, capture (of fish in his case) gave him "a right to demand and expect things and respect from others." This pastoral mode of imagining property not only unsettles the elemental biases between land and sea but also usefully intervenes in understandings of common resource management, providing a way of thinking about the sea that brings together ruination and responsibility.

RETHINKING REGULATION

By emphasizing a logic of property that continues to shape engagements with the ocean across the western Indian Ocean littoral, the discussion with Ali described above allows us to reimagine the relationship between overexploitation and shared resource management: a relationship central to the ways in which global commons such as the oceans are conceptualized and regulated.[10] In his now-classic treatise on fisheries off the coast of California, Arthur McEvoy (1990, 9) outlines the fisherman's problem as the failure of the fishing industry to "respect the biological limits of its resource's productivity." He argues:

Fishing industries ... do not generally manage their affairs in a rational way. This is primarily because fishery stocks are common property resources; that is, although many different individuals or firms may compete with each other for fish, no one of them owns the resource so as to keep others away from it. As a result, everyone has an incentive to keep fishing so long as there is money to be made in the effort, whereas no one has an individual incentive to refrain from fishing so as to conserve the stock. (McEvoy 1990, 9–10)

As McEvoy notes, one of the first scholars to stress the importance of institutional and legal arrangements in managing fishery resources was the economist H. Scott Gordon. In a 1954 article, Gordon criticized the sustainable yield theory of fishery management. For Gordon, the fisherman's problem was the direct result of the industry's legal and economic organization as opposed to a problem of biology or population dynamics. Gordon's solution sought to transform fisheries from a common property resource to a limited entry regime, making fisheries into "private property or public (government) property, in either case subject to a unified directing power able to exclude outsiders and adjust harvesting efforts to maximum advantage" (Gordon 1954, 125).

In 1968, the biologist Garrett Hardin published "The Tragedy of the Commons," which expanded and canonized Gordon's argument about private property and common resource management. For Hardin, the tragedy of the commons, namely ecological degradation, is located in free and unregulated access to scarce resources. Hardin argued that freedom becomes tragic because individuals would rather maximize their own use of a shared resource than protect it from overuse. The solution to this tragedy implicit in Hardin's thesis was privatization, because individuals can only be expected to protect their own property. While admitting that this solution might be draconian and, at times, unjust, Hardin defended his findings by noting that the alternative was too horrifying to contemplate. "Injustice," he wrote, "is preferable to total ruin" (Hardin 1968, 1247).[11] Despite its popularity, Hardin's thesis has been subjected to many critiques and revisions.

In their analysis of Hardin's work and influence, Bonnie J. McCay and James M. Acheson (1987) highlight the individualistic bias central to Hardin's approach. The tragedy of the commons, they argue, "fails to distinguish between the commons as a theoretical condition in which there are no relevant institutions (open access), and common property as a social institution" (McCay and Acheson 1987, 12). They argue that Hardin's mistake is to conflate these two, and thus to ignore or underestimate the presence of regulatory institutions that manage the use of collectively shared resources. McCay and Acheson also point to the absence of a clear concept of community in Hardin's analysis: "Hardin assumed only a collection of individuals using a common resource. He did not recognize the existence of communities that dealt with conflicts and ecological problems associated with the commons by creating and enforcing rules about their use" (12). A rich interdisciplinary literature has developed in recent years, stressing multiple systems of governance, including polycentric forms of governance that complicate and indeed challenge Hardin's original tragedy of the commons.[12]

However, both these framings of the problem of the commons—overexploitation, on one hand, and a communitarian management of resources (i.e., an enclosure within limits) on the other—fail to adequately speak to the Somali case. Both approaches are underpinned by a notion of the commons as a distinct property regime, and by the question of scarcity. Additionally, Hardin and his critics operate within a system that presumes dichotomies between public and private, capture and redistribution. In Somalia, by contrast, the sea is a commons framed by interwoven maritime and land-based property regimes. At sea, capture creates property. But this property, like Dalmar's camels and boats, is embedded within claims that can be made by others on land. Capture thus works alongside redistribution and connects the coastal world to the pastoral hinterland through a shared idiom of property and ownership, but also through the material transformation of fish into goats and camels.

Land and sea, like capture and redistribution, are not incommensurable: capture allows one to make property at sea and to embed it within worlds of pastoralism. Fish and ambergris metaphorically transform into goats and camels, creating systems of interdependence as one moves between porous spaces (whether onshore or offshore). The next section focuses on how shifting claims to the sea brought together a host of actors, from the state to local fishermen and foreign trawlers, in contests over property and profit.

SCIENTIFIC SOCIALISM AND THE REMAKING OF PROPERTY

Fish and other seafood have rarely occupied center stage in the culinary traditions of those who inhabit the Somali Peninsula. I was telling Joole, a guesthouse owner in Berbera, about my meeting with Musa. Laughing at my missteps in reciprocity, Joole remembered efforts to convince people to eat fish from his time as a government employee working in Mogadishu during the heyday of the Barre regime. "When they started the fish factories [in the 1970s], the radio presenter would have a show where they would talk about the importance of eating fish and selling fish. They even had a jingle about it, what was it ... " Joole hummed a melody, "Ah yes, it was 'eat fish and make a profit!'" "Did it work?" I asked Joole. "The radio would say fisheries were important to the project of *hanti-wadaagga cilmi ku dhisan* (Scientific Socialism). This was surprising to us at first because most Somalis don't like to eat fish. The Ogaden, my mother's family, have a saying: 'Don't trust a man whose mouth smells of fish.' So, of course, it was going to take a lot more than radio to change people's minds."

Property regimes are seldom stable categories. Ambergris, camels, fish, and even the ocean acquire meaning and substance within specific historical, political, and economic contexts. The previous section focused on the centrality of capture in making property in ways that complicate boundaries between land and sea as well as those between public and private. This section turns to postcolonial Somalia and discusses various attempts at making (and unmaking) property at sea in order to highlight the temporalities and scales of property regimes—from local fishermen and state officials to South Korean trawlers and the UN Convention on the Law of the Sea (UNCLOS) (UN 1982)—which intersect at the transition from capturing fish to capturing ships.

On October 15, 1969, almost a decade after Somalia attained independence, the president of the Somali Republic, 'Abd ar-Rashid 'Ali Shirmarke, was assassinated by a disgruntled soldier. While the Somali parliament debated the election of a successor in the following days—a debate that revealed the "deep sores in the Somali body politic" (Laitin and Samatar 1987, 43), one divided along clan and regional lines—a group of army officers staged a coup. In the early hours of October 21, the army occupied key points throughout the capital, and members of the government and other leading politicians and personalities were placed in detention. The Constitution was suspended, the Supreme Court abolished, the National Assembly closed, political parties declared illegal, and rule by a Supreme Revolutionary Council (SRC) established. The membership of the SRC was announced on November 1, 1969, and the new president, as widely anticipated, was General Muhammad Siyad Barre. According to the historians David Laitin and Said Samatar (1987, 53), the early days of the SRC were focused on decrying the corruption of the old regime:

Drawing on an onomatopoeic expression from the poetry of the Sayyid, the SRC accused the politicians of *musuq maasuq*—of going in different directions at the same time. Politicians were also accused of *afmishaarism*—literally, acting like "saw mouths"—because they put praise singers on the government payroll. Government cars were being used as private taxis; government medicine was on sale in local pharmacies. The new government helped mobilize people's support through its campaign of *hisaabi hil male,* an "accounting without shame." The use of these colloquial political expressions lent a populist aura to the military junta's image.

Additionally, to bolster this populist sentiment, the SRC engaged in a discourse of anti-Americanism that resonated with a large segment of the Somali population who saw the United States as anti-Muslim and hostile to the unification of "Somalia's dismembered nation." This anti-Americanism was also fueled by closer alignment to the Soviet Union, and within a year US Peace Corps volunteers, along with other remnants of American foreign interest, were ordered to leave Mogadishu to be replaced by Soviet technical assistance and expertise. This realignment towards the Soviet Union was completed when, on the first anniversary of the coup (now reframed as a revolution), Siyad Barre proclaimed on Radio Mogadishu that Somalia would henceforth be dedicated to *hanti-wadaagga 'ilmu ku disan* (Scientific Socialism).

Somalia's Cold War shift towards the Soviet Union occurred within a broader chessboard-like trading of loyalties across the Horn of Africa and the Middle East in the period immediately following decolonization. From Libya to Somalia, newly independent countries moved back and forth between the Soviet bloc and the United States. These movements had significant political repercussions within the region and for the broader balance of power in the Cold War era, allowing local elites to consolidate and centralize their political power through arms transfers and economic subsidies funded by their patrons. Within popular memory and the scholarly archive on Somalia, Scientific Socialism is largely remembered for the ways in which the promise of the revolution unraveled and as a precursor to the process of dissolution of the Somali state. My interest here lies in the rescaling of the economy, and the remaking of property, during this period: the relationship between fish, property, and profit was transformed, even while retaining certain continuities with the past. Given the broader context within which Somalia's experiments with Scientific Socialism occurred, this section also seeks to locate this rescaling of property within a wider mode of imagining property under socialism.

Following the proclamation of Scientific Socialism, Barre's regime sought to quell criticism regarding the un-Islamic nature of the ideology. The criticism was not simply a theological critique of socialism as atheism, but one that focused on the compatibility of Scientific Socialism with an Islamic moral economy and communal rules regarding property and redistribution. Barre's socialism thus framed property reform and the wider management of national wealth as squarely within Islamic moral economies. In a speech marking the end of the Muslim holy month of Ramadan in 1974, Barre declaimed:

> Our Islamic faith teaches us that its inherent values are perennial and continually evolving as people progress. These basic tenets of our religion cannot be interpreted in a static sense, but rather as a dynamic source of inspiration for continuous advancement . . . If we decide to regulate our national wealth it is not against the essence of Islam. (Barre 1974, 24)

But more was at stake than moral economies. Property regimes and their associated legalism[13] were powerful political and economic tools for nation-building. Barre described the attempt to regulate national wealth as essentially a project of rescaling (i.e., shifting the locus from community to nation) rather than a complete transformation: "To help our brethren and our fellows, we must go beyond the concept of charity, and reach the higher and more altruistic concept of cooperation on a national scale" (Barre 1974, 24). Scientific Socialism thus echoes other postcolonial projects of refashioning the national economy. For instance, Indian nationalists, on the eve of independence, sought not to dismantle developmentalism altogether, but to scale it to the nation. As Manu Goswami and others have underscored, in the Indian case, "nationalists criticized a drain of wealth by colonial economic practices while sharing a broader epistemology with their colonial adversaries that emphasized the universalistic promise of development as part of national reconstruction" (Goswami 2004, 240).[14] The developmentalist project of Siyad Barre's Scientific Socialism involved a similar rescaling of a set of divergent local, regional, and transregional economic practices into the national frame as part of a project of Somali nation-building.[15]

Legalism was a central framework through which Barre sought to rescale these economic practices. Somalia's economy at the time of independence consisted of a thriving livestock trade centered primarily in northern Somalia and a small but profitable plantation economy in the riverine areas of southern Somalia. While trade in the North was controlled by the Berbera trading community and consisted mainly of Indians, Arabs, and Somali middlemen, the southern economy was dominated by Italian interests (the Filonardi and the Benadir companies) who had established a monopoly over property, export, customs, and tariff regulations. It was through property, then, that Scientific Socialism after 1970 sought to rescale this transregional economy— an economy that had been underdeveloped by both Italian and British colonial authorities—into the frame of the nation.

Bolstered by Soviet assistance and technical advisors, Barre's regime initially nationalized a number of institutions such as banks, petroleum distribution firms, and schools. Imports and exports were also controlled by government agencies, with the exception of livestock on the hoof. Bananas, the principal cash crop, were marketed and exported solely through government agencies. All grain grown privately was bought by the national Agricultural Development Corporation and sold at government-regulated prices. At the same time, government officials reassured pastoralists that livestock would not be nationalized and that they would continue to allow the private ownership of banana plantations, thus ensuring that the two major export sectors remained firmly in private hands. Nationalization was not simply a straightforward transformation of "private" property into "public" property, but "a process . . . of making and unmaking certain kinds of relationships" (Verdery 2003, 13).

Katherine Verdery's observations on property regimes in socialism are key to understanding property transformations in socialist Somalia. The definition of property under socialism in Romania contrasted with the distinctions between real and personal property, tangible and intangible property, and state commons and private property upon which Western economic and legal systems are based. As Verdery notes, "socialist property categories, by contrast, emphasized a different set of property types based on the identity of the owners and the social relations among them" (Verdery 2003, 49). In Romania these property types included the state, socialist cooperatives, and individuals or households; the role of socialist transformation entailed the distribution of property according to these three ownership patterns. In addition, and crucially for Verdery, what defined property and a theory of socialist property was not the status of ownership but rather "patterns of use, administrative rights and social networks of exchange and reciprocity" (Verdery 2003, 70).

In Somalia, the attempted transformation of a transregional precolonial and colonial economy into one scaled to the space of the nation-state entailed the redistribution and appropriation of preexisting forms of property and the creation of new structures and ownership regimes. Yet, these transformations were contingent and open-ended. Scientific Socialism's remodeling of property relations defies the easy teleology of private to public or clanism to developmentalism. As mentioned, the primary export economy remained in private hands, including key sectors such as livestock exports and the ownership of banana plantations. This private economy was organized according to lineage and clan logics, so that clanism was smuggled back in even as the state sought to eradicate clan and lineage as bases for political authority and legitimacy. And even the state itself, which quickly transformed into an extension of Barre's lineage, captured rents from this private economy, creating a clan-based patronage system while simultaneously disavowing the possibility of claim-making or access to property and resources through the language of lineage and clan.

Barre went so far as to criminalize clanism, policing even the ways people addressed each other. "Before Barre," recalled Abdi, a market trader in Mombasa, "a polite form of addressing a stranger was to say 'cousin' [*ina'adeer*]. Since this is a clan terminology, we were banned from using it, and instead told to say 'friend' [*jaalle*]. Of course," Abdi continued, "everyone knew that Barre was not calling people his *jaalle*. Nationalization was completely done in clan logic with everything divided between the MOD." MOD was the acronym used to surreptitiously refer to the three clans that were beneficiaries of the Barre regime: the Marrehaan (Barre's patrilineage), the Ogadeen (his mother's clan), and the Dulbahante (his son-in-law's lineage).

State appropriation was not simply a matter of seizure, but embedded, as Abdi notes, within structures of patronage and redistribution. In addition to rescaling economic practices on land, this attempt at appropriation/channeling had a significant impact in shaping the development of fisheries and transforming claims to the ocean. Beginning in the 1970s, a licensing regime sought to transform the capture/redistribution system highlighted earlier into a regime built on state appropriation. Yet, as I will show, state licensing was also a form of capture, where now the license (instead of the fish itself) became the coveted form of fugitive property.

In 1972, in Law No. 37 on the Territorial Sea and Ports, the Barre government decreed that the Somali territorial sea extended to two hundred nautical miles as opposed to the international designation of twelve nautical miles. This move was followed by the launch, primarily through Soviet assistance, of a deep-sea trawling fleet and the construction of fish factories and processing plants along the coast. The drought of 1974 that devastated large portions of the livestock throughout the region also created a new impetus for the establishment of fishing cooperatives along the coast. By 1975, new settlements along the coast were built for the resettled nomads at Eel Haamed, Eyl, Adale, and Barawa—stretching from the Red Sea to the Indian Ocean. With Soviet and later Australian and Italian capital and advisors, these settlements attempted to transform nomads into fishermen and create a vibrant fishing sector. Prior to the settlement program, fisheries accounted for less than one percent of the country's GDP. The Food and Agricultural Organization of the United Nations (FAO 2005) noted in its 2005 report on fisheries in Somalia that the introduction of mechanized boats in the early 1970s led to an increase in annual catch from five thousand tonnes to a peak of eight thousand tonnes. However, the absence of spare parts or repair facilities along the coast meant that, as boats broke down, "about two-thirds were out of operation after only two years, and, as a direct consequence, by the late 1970s annual fish production was back to 5,000 tonnes" (FAO 2005).

This short-lived development enterprise nonetheless created a pattern of licensing and concessions.[16] As the FAO report notes, Somali fisheries were both a small part of the country's GDP and, from the perspective of the global maritime regulation regime, considered "underexploited." Primarily emerging out of fishery management in the North Atlantic, the concept of maximum sustainable yield (MSY) was developed in the 1930s to manage global fisheries. A fundamental tenet of MSY is the assumption that it is possible to calculate the largest yield that can be taken from a species' stock over an indefinite period of time.[17] As long as stocks are being exploited under the MSY threshold, anyone has the right to fish off any coast, a principle enshrined within the international MSY treaty and the United Nations Convention on the Law of the Seas (UN 1982). Within this management system, coastal states like Somalia are obligated to promote "optimum utilization" of marine resources by giving third states access to the excess "allowable catch" (UNCLOS Article 62, in UN 1982) through a system of licensing.

Alongside the development of fisheries, the Somali government created a licensing regime based on principles of MSY that gave long-distance trawlers access to Somali coastal waters in return for a licensing fee. Even as equipment broke down and production in fish factories dwindled, this licensing regime continued to expand at a robust pace. Initially, Italian and Soviet trawlers were granted exclusive licenses and state concessions to fish in Somali "territorial waters" in return for a fee. But by 1986 the virtual monopoly of Soviet and Italian fishing was disrupted with the entrance of Norwegian and Japanese trawlers. Responding to the establishment of regional fishery management systems in the northern Atlantic and the Pacific and a growing global appetite for seafood, these trawlers utilized the MSY ethos of fishery management to force an entry into the western Indian Ocean. Specifically, licensing created "jurisdiction as property" (Lambert 2017, 115), where now licenses rather than simply fish were targets of capture.

At the local level, this form of licensing was mirrored in the interactions between newly resettled pastoralists and fishing communities that had traditionally inhabited the coast. A large number of pastoralists resisted the transformation into fishermen and instead loaned out fishing equipment and boats to *sab* and other coastal fishing communities, creating redistributive networks that were similar to the wider jurisdictional and property claims established over the sea by the Barre regime. The central government in Mogadishu and local elites both claimed the sea and then licensed that claim to a variety of clients, from long-distance trawlers to coastal fishermen. This recursive system both worked within and transformed preexisting understandings of fishing, bounty, and pastoral property relationships.

Benderbeyla, on the northeastern tip of Somalia, has been at the center of the recent upsurge in maritime piracy. A fishing village that was also the site of a major fishing cooperative in the 1970s, Benderbeyla is the perfect vantage point from which to understand the complex relationship between fishing, licensing, and piracy. Mohamed, a fisherman and clan elder, explained the licensing system that his village developed with the state-backed fishing cooperative in the early 1980s:

When the government wanted to fish near our village, they agreed to pay us $1,000 a month so that we stayed out of their way. They also hired a number of men from here to give protection to the trawlers and make sure no other vessels came into the area. Most of the time we were just keeping the area free from fishermen from Bosaso or other places around the coast. (Mohamed, interview with author, March 2011)

Villagers recalled that the trawlers began to arrive from other countries around 1986. While most of these vessels stayed away from the coast or were chased away by the local protection group, many interviewees recalled Norwegian trawlers attempting to make similar protection deals with the local community. A number of these trawlers had obtained licenses from the regime in Mogadishu and hired groups such as the local protection group in Benderbeyla to keep other fishing boats out of the water. As with the world of capture described in the previous section, appropriation and redistribution were intimately related in this system of making property at sea. This is not to suggest that this was a harmonious system or one geared towards sustainability or benefit for Somali fishermen.

Violent confrontations between local protection groups and foreign fishing vessels, especially those that attempted to fish in the area without official or unofficial "licenses," grew increasingly commonplace in the 1980s, especially after the fall of the Barre regime in 1991. In addition, foreign trawlers, in particular those using bottom trawling techniques, greatly harmed local fishing grounds, and impacted the artisanal fishing communities along the coast. Following the collapse of the Somali state, with the intensification of foreign trawling, this system of protection and licensing was transformed and rescaled when semi-autonomous regions, such as Puntland, turned to private security companies to extract rents from the sea. In this way, they created a commons from a pastoral commons and, in doing so, paved the way for the transition from licensing to piracy.

FROM LICENSING TO PIRACY

The national rescaling of economic practices under Barre engendered new property regimes, but also bolstered inequalities structured on clan and other divisions. The licensing system was not removed from the larger frameworks of the Barre regime. Siyad Barre's regime was built on a territorial logic of *Soomaaliweyn* (Greater Somalia). This vision of a unified country encompassing all the Somali-speaking regions in the Horn of Africa emerged in the colonial era and was mobilized by Barre to justify conflicts with neighboring Ethiopia and Kenya. By the mid-1980s the damage wrought by these conflicts and the regime's increasing authoritarianism led to the emergence of numerous insurgent groups. An increasingly violent counterinsurgency created "networks of dissolution" (Simons 1995), and by January 1991 Siyad Barre's regime was toppled.[18] From the vantage point of the coast, the collapse of the state in 1991 and the subsequent privatization of the maritime economy accelerated and reconfigured these already problematic systems of licensing and protection that had emerged following the establishment of fishery cooperatives in the 1970s.

The aftermath of state collapse was characterized by tremendous population upheaval, creating large refugee communities abroad from Norway to Kenya, as well as significant internal displacement. A number of these population movements occurred along clan and kinship lines, with many "returning" to ancestral homelands to establish subnational regions. The region of Puntland in northeastern Somalia, abutting both the Red Sea and the Indian Ocean, is one such entity that emerged in 1998 through a process of cohesion and concession amongst the Harti, one of the major clans within Somalia's kinship system. Maintaining a semiautonomous region of Puntland was part of a "building blocks" approach to reconstituting the Somali state. As the International Crisis Group (ICC 2009) notes, this approach was built on the argument that any attempts to recreate a unitary, centralized Somali state were bound to fail. Instead, each of the four major Somali clans was to form a "bloc" within a loose federal or confederal structure. The charter of Puntland recognized the in-between status of Puntland as a placeholder for a yet-to-come Federal Somali Republic.

Beginning in 2000, the government of Puntland, especially under the administrations of Abdullahi Yusuf Ahmed and Adde Muuse, turned to fisheries as an additional source of revenue. In addition to developing small-scale fish and lobster processing plants, the government attempted to exert Puntland's sovereignty over the ocean. Specifically, beginning in 2001 the Puntland government contracted international private security companies (often run by British and South African ex-military men) to establish coastguards. The coastguard initiatives of the newly emergent Puntland regime, along with a host of new technologies including mobile phones, global remittance systems, the proliferation of small arms, and access to skiffs with powerful outboard motors, further transformed this maritime world of licensing and rent-seeking. This was a key moment in the shift from catching fish to capturing ships. It is somewhat ironic that the coastguard was central to the emergence of piracy.

The arrival of coastguards helped (to some extent) to deal with illegal fishing, but crucially it also impacted the informal licensing systems that already existed in coastal communities throughout Puntland. Licensing itself became a matter of contestation. While a few Puntland coastguard initiatives attempted to create an inclusive and salaried employee pool, most attempts at coastal regulation were built on logics of capture tied to existing patronage networks and often led to violent confrontations at sea. Armed skiffs would intercept fishing trawlers at sea and "sell" licenses to boat captains. If a captain refused to purchase the license, the boat would be confiscated by the coastguards and released after the payment of "fines." Most of these trawlers operated in the shadow economies of global fishing and preferred simply to pay for licenses. The fees from these licenses would then be divided amongst the crew and authorities on land. These official licensing regimes often came into conflict with other unofficial systems that were themselves vying with official systems for access and license fees. The rise and fall of various coastguard initiatives was deeply tied to contestations over political power on land, and they underscore the close relationship between profits from the "sea of fish" and political authority on land.

In Benderbeyla, Mohamed noted that, starting in 2001, official coastguards consisting of militia groups with ties to the Puntland government in Garowe attempted to shut down their informal licensing system. Conflicts over jurisdiction often sparked armed confrontations between competing coastguards over the right to tax and issue licenses:

> When the Puntland government started issuing fishing licenses, the Thai trawlers that used to pay us to fish in our area stopped paying and said they would deal with the Hart people [Puntland Coastguard, which was trained by the British private security firm Hart Security Maritime Services Ltd.] instead. Since this was our right to issue licenses, we fought the Hart boats if they came close to our area. This was a time when even a fisherman had to take a gun when he went out to sea because everyone was trying to become a coastguard. (Mohamed, interview with author, March 2011)

The short-lived official coastguard initiatives also had a major consequence that is linked directly to the upsurge in maritime piracy. As official coastguards fell in and out of favor depending on their connections with the ruling elite in Garowe, these multiple and scattered attempts at regulation left behind a well-trained, armed, and unemployed labor force along the coast that took to the seas in order to extract revenues they felt they were due from fishing vessels, dhows, and cargo ships.

· · ·

On a map, the distance between Garowe, the capital of Puntland, and Eyl doesn't seem insurmountable; Google Maps claims the mere 200 kilometers can be traveled in about two hours. I traveled the road after the rainy season, meaning that my journey was twelve grueling hours that included a flat tire and a minor rockslide. The first thing one sees of Eyl is the old Dervish fort of Sayyid Mohammed Abdullah Hassan's forces, who fought the nineteenth-century British expansion into Somaliland. Past the fort, the Indian Ocean comes into view. Choppy surf breaking along a long uninterrupted coastline and howling wind greeted me as I made my way to the beach. Awaiting my arrival as the sky turned bright red in the dusk hours was Farah, the first pirate who had agreed to meet with me. Soon Farah launched into what turned out to be a fairly emblematic story about his transition from fisherman to pirate:

> I was born three houses away from where we are sitting on the beach. This is my home, this is my ocean. I grew up catching lobster, tuna, and snapper. One night a trawler cut our nets when we were fishing not far from the coast. A few of us decided enough was enough and we boarded the boat. We made the captain pay $1,000 as a tax to fish in our waters. We went back to the village and told everyone about it. Soon the boys started getting on the fiber boats and chasing trawlers to get money from them. This is how we became pirates. After a while, we started going after bigger boats. I used to capture small fish, now I capture a different kind of fish, a bigger fish. (Farah, interview with author, November 2010)

Over the next few days, I met numerous ex-fishermen who told similar tales of transition. But over the course of many interviews it became clear that these fishermen had been also involved in other practices of capture before turning to large-scale piracy. Many had worked as coastguards or "license protectors" beginning in the 1980s, when licensing emerged along the Somali coast, and then found themselves without a job once the coastguards disappeared. Hashi, a former private coastguard, exemplifies the experience of a number of Somali coastguards from the early 2000s, who found themselves without a salary when shifting political alliances left their employers (in this case Somcan)[19] out of political favor. Like Farah, Hashi was born in Eyl, though from a family that had been resettled there after the droughts in the Ogaden region. "We used to do some fishing, but my father was also an *adijir* [shepherd]," Hashi explained, describing his experience of traveling with the *aqal* (nomadic hut) during grazing season. "We used to walk to Garowe or even Galkayo with the goats, and then during the *jilal* [dry season from November until March] we would come back to Eyl and go fishing." In 2001, when Abdullahi Yussuf refused to step down as president of Puntland, a brief conflict erupted and Hashi was recruited to fight on behalf of Yussuf's group. "When the fighting ended, I was in Garowe as one of the protectors of the President. Xiif Ali Taar was establishing a coastguard with his brother who had returned from Canada, and they recruited me to become a protector of the sea."

In 2001, during the conflict between Yussuf and Ali Jama Ali, Hart Security, the British private security company hired by Puntland to patrol its coastal waters, decided to withdraw from Puntland. In its absence, the Taar brothers, who had close ties to Abdullahi Yussuf, stepped into the void and created Somcan, a Somali-Canadian company registered in the UAE to serve as coastguards for Puntland. Somcan followed the same model as Hart, namely a protection system built around license capture. For recruits like Hashi, this meant that they were trained in basic skills like boarding ships and reading GPS before being sent to sea. "I knew these waters," said Hashi as he described his first days as a Somcan coastguard. "It was easier for me because I had experience with these fishing vessels from before [when he was a fisherman]. We were trained on land to read GPS and also how to board ships with ladders and hooks. We would patrol the waters near Eyl and, if we saw a fishing boat, chase it down and get on board to see if they had a license." If vessels failed to produce a license, the coastguards would sell a license and charge a fine with the license fee going to the president's office in Garowe and the fine being distributed between members of the crew and the Taar brothers.

But soon Somcan ran into trouble. In addition to going after foreign fishing vessels, Somcan coastguard boats started targeting local fishermen. "The other fishermen would complain to me about the Somcan boats." Hashi recalled being attacked one day as he was returning home from the beach: "They [the fishermen] were very angry with us." In addition to local resentment, once Yussuf lost power in Garowe, the Taar brothers found themselves political pariahs, and their coastguard contract was not renewed in 2005 by the new administration. No longer possessing a boat, Hashi joined another group and attempted to start his own private security company. "We had to battle the Arabs [Al Habibi coastguard, a Saudi company given license after Somcan] for fishing boats. In those days [2006] people were telling stories about different possibilities, they said you could make $1 million if you went after bigger ships. A group from Hobyo had made that much money from a cargo ship [*MV Danica White*]." For Hashi and many like him, it was a straightforward calculation. "We also had the training and we felt brave," he explained, "so we decided to move from capturing fishing vessels to capturing even bigger fish. At this point, this is our work. Why would anyone go back to catching tuna when you can catch an oil tanker?"

Hashi's transformation from coastguard to pirate, from capturing fishing vessels to "even bigger fish"—like the 2009 hijacking of the *Sirius Star,* a Saudi-flagged oil tanker and the largest ship ever to be hijacked—highlights the scalar transformations of idioms of capture and bounty that this chapter has sought to narrate. Far from a story of failed states or disgruntled fishermen (though these are important factors), acts of maritime predation are extensions and breakdowns of contestations over property, access, and wealth in this oceanic space. Focusing on the transformations of property regimes provides not only an alternative understanding of the emergence of piracy in its current guise but also a framework to comprehend territoriality and fluidity, taking and giving.

———

TWO

Anchoring Pirates

GROUNDING A PROTECTION ECONOMY

A COMMON SIGHT THROUGHOUT COASTAL East Africa, from Djibouti to Bagamoyo, is the arrival of the khat trucks. Every day around noon when the calls of the *dhuhr* prayer have ended and the faithful amble out of the mosque into the harsh midday sun, the languid lethargy of the day is abruptly and loudly shattered by the honking and rumbling of white pickup trucks as they speed into town. These trucks are loaded down with bag upon bag of khat, known in parts of Somalia as *ubax jannada* (flower of paradise). Picked merely hours before from the mild, cool highlands of Ethiopia or Kenya, the arrival of the khat transforms the sensory landscape of cities across the Horn and East Africa. Most afternoons while conducting research in Puntland, when offices would shut down and most respectable people retreated into the shade of their homes, I would wander over to the central market in whatever town I was in and await the coming of the khat trucks. These afternoon breaks were usually spent sitting in shops with moneychangers and traders, and often led to some of my more productive moments of research.

An odd assortment of people—and occasional livestock—would gather at the market during these hot afternoon hours. Older men strolling out from teahouses and lunchrooms would take their seats on rickety plastic chairs strategically placed throughout the market area to maximize shade and observe the slow trickle of customers. Most of these customers were women, hurriedly picking up supplies for evening meals. The rest of the crowd was mostly hangers-on. Young men who load and unload supplies for shops would sit waiting around, taking naps. A few khat sellers would prepare for the arrival of the daily shipment, while eager customers would loiter about chewing stems and leftovers from the previous day's shipment. Khat loses its potency within 48 hours, hence the need for regular, daily shipments. The trucks would make their presence known well before arriving into view at the market with loud honks and the roar of the engine. This would be the signal for some frenzied activity as people would crowd around the khat stalls ready to get their first pick. Knowing next to nothing about khat, I would often walk over to a stall once the initial rush had cleared, pick up some easy-to-reach bundles, buy some cola and chewing gum, and make my way back to the moneychangers or importers I had befriended at the market.

One afternoon as the buzz of activity had faded and everyone had settled back into the shade to begin their daily chew, a khat wholesaler arrived at the moneylender's stall where I was sitting. Wearing a bright blue *garbasaar* (shawl) over a plain gray *dirac* (dress), the wholesaler stood out in the mostly male crowd that lingered at the moneylender's makeshift roadside office. As she handed over an envelope to Said, my moneylender friend whose stall I would sit at during the afternoon, he jokingly turned to me and said, "I'm her banker." Said then introduced me as a student writing a book about trade and piracy in Somalia. "You should talk to him," he said to Aisha with a grin. "You know everything about trade and piracy." Aisha looked at Said in mock horror and threatened to beat him for spreading lies. After a back-and-forth of jokes and jabs, Aisha turned to me and inquired, "What do you want to know about piracy?" As I started explaining my project, she stopped me and asked, "Who do you think these pirates are? They are people who are known to us, they belong to a *jilib* [group responsible for blood payments], a *reer* [clan]. They are normal people."[1] After a brief pause, she continued before I could respond, a pattern that would become a common mode of interaction between us: "That's why you can trade with them. If something goes wrong, they belong to a diya group."

Finishing this monologue in rapid-fire Somali, she left, insisting that she was very busy that day but that if I came to her office she would answer all my questions. It took many attempts and a few weeks before I met Aisha again. But I was reminded of Aisha's description of pirates a few days later on a trip to a lighthouse where the Red Sea meets the Indian Ocean.

Sheikh Usman, who had introduced me to the ambergris villages of northern Somalia, also promised a tour to the lighthouse of Ras Asir (Cape Guardafui). He regaled me with many stories of the sea over the course of a long, bumpy, and ultimately unsuccessful trip to the fabled lighthouse. As the bustling port of Bosaso faded into the distance, I asked the Sheikh about the pirates that had thrust this region into the global spotlight. "These people you call pirates," the Sheikh began, "I know them very well. In my home village, we have many of these guys now. The pirates have brought us much misery." He continued, listing a series of their vices: "Many young men have been recruited by them and go to sea and sometimes never return. Others have taken to drinking and drugs and made the area very unsafe. There is also a huge problem now with inflation." Somewhat exaggeratedly he added, "Food is too expensive because the pirates come with US$100 to buy one bottle of *biyo* [water]. There are also food shortages because why will a shop-keeper sell me pasta or rice when she can sell it to a pirate for so much more money? My friends joke that the hostages on the ship eat better than the people of our area."

As the car snaked its way between the shimmering Red Sea and the rocky mountains that hug the coastline, the radio crackling with the call to prayer, I asked the Sheikh if, as a *qadi,* he had declared piracy *haram* in his region. Instead of answering the question directly, he latched onto my use of *burcad badeed* (sea robber) to describe pirates and offered a corrective. "Yes, many of these people have done bad things, and as I said earlier they are 'pirates'—but they are not just robbers, they have a reason for doing what they do." Sheikh Usman had recently been involved in negotiating a code of conduct with pirates in a neighboring village. Wanting to return to the ethics of piracy, I offered the idea that piracy might be *makhruh:* falling into the grey area between *haram* (unlawful) and *halal* (lawful). Again, deflecting the question, he asked, "Why are you trying to be the *qadi?* Do you want me to lose my job?!" As he emphasized, "As long as they [the pirates] continue to fulfill their obligations to their communities and are guided by *mudarabah* [profit and risk-sharing contract],[2] people will continue to do this work."

In speaking of pirates as normal people, Aisha, Sheikh Usman, and others in the ethnographic encounters to follow allow us to engage with the forms of anchoring that are required to make the protection economy of piracy. While on the surface their claims to knowing pirates might suggest the con-ferral of legitimacy onto piracy as a form of acceptable "social banditry,"[3] I posit instead that it points to a distinct way to think about work and accumu-lation. Whether by locating pirates within networks of kinship that make trade relationships possible or by negotiating codes of conduct that emphasize principles of *mudarabah,* Aisha and Sheikh Usman turn our focus to the concrete processes through which piracy becomes *anchored* to land. Beyond legitimacy (although the ethics of piracy were often debated), this form of anchoring brackets the very question of licit and illicit through grounding it within economies of land. In addition to regulating piracy, this is also about profit and possibility. In Somalia, as we will see below, this anchoring happens through diya and khat, and their differing temporalities of accumulation.

ANCHORING ECONOMY

From the use of large stones to spade-like flukes, anchoring ships and other vessels requires a balance between fixity and flexibility. Some moorings are permanent, others—*sacram anchram solvere*—are anchors of last refuge cast in a storm. Each attempts a form of stability and grounding. As numerous boat captains reminded me, anchoring—whether for fishing vessels or large container ships—requires skill and a connection to the ocean. Here, I take anchoring as a theme to explain the work entailed in embedding piracy, emphasizing the interplay of flexibility and fixity that is crucial to anchorage as both a maritime practice and a metaphor for thinking about the relationship between piracy and the wider economy.[4]

As piracy expanded in the Indian Ocean, anchoring piracy was a way for pirates to protect themselves from the uncertainties of the ransom economy, and it was also a way for others like Usman and Aisha to govern this economy and to create profits, anchoring piracy into a world of protection. During fieldwork in northern Somalia, I was repeatedly struck by how pirates slip in and out of social worlds, how in their own world they are understood differently from the legal definition of an actor engaged in unlawful takings in international waters for private ends, or as the enemy of all mankind. For Sheikh Usman and for others we will encounter, pirates are neither reviled as criminals nor celebrated as social bandits, but are rather anchored within spheres of obligations that create possibilities of profit for themselves as well as their larger communities.

The triumph of *homo economicus* has been noted globally. From resurgent waves of populism to ever-expanding populations rendered precarious and superfluous, the logic of an economic globalization built in the image of *homo economicus* has radically transformed ideas of the public good (Bear and Nayanika 2015). This is a world of unmoored financialization and valuing profits over people—a situation exacerbated by the rise of the gig economy and mechanization. Central to this story is the idea of dis-embedding the economy—of ignoring the nested nature of economic practices within social worlds (Graeber 2011). However, as Julia Elyachar (2010) has noted in the case of Cairo and others have highlighted in the realms of microfinance (Kar

2013) and mobile banking (Maurer 2012), practices of financialization are built on older modes of accumulation. Drawing from this scholarship, here I emphasize what Hannah Appel (2012) describes as the *how* of economic practice. I explain how forms of accumulation are anchored to wider worlds, and thereby provide possibilities of extraction and profit.

The act of becoming a pirate in the western Indian Ocean is about being tethered; it is about becoming anchored to worlds of obligation that not only make possible a journey out to sea but also ensure a return to land and, sometimes, being ensnared within debts that cannot be paid. The morphing of piracy from an opportunistic targeting of fishing vessels and small boats to the capture of container ships required skill and chance, but also credit, collateral, and connection. It required moving from sea to ocean, but also returning to land.

FROM SEA TO OCEAN

In Puntland, whenever someone discovered I was an American, they would recount a version of the same joke: "When the Americans came to the Indian Ocean to look for pirates, they found none. The patrol ships flew the stars and stripes, and played the national anthem as they traveled along the Somali coast. Convinced that they had scared the pirates away, they organized a press conference where they brought the Mission Accomplished banner from Iraq and congratulated themselves on eliminating piracy." Then the narrator would pause and conclude with a flourish, "But the Americans came in June." The first few times I heard the joke, I was confused by the punchline, convinced my Somali language skills were too rudimentary to understand the nuances of this statement. One day, I finally asked my host to explain why the joke was funny.

"The Americans came in June, during the monsoon!" he exclaimed. "They didn't know the pirates were hanging out in their huts tending the goats. No one goes to sea then. When the waves calmed down, the pirates went back to work and captured many more ships than before."

This moment of humor built around knowing the monsoons, around knowing when a pirate would be at sea—a moment of humor built at the expense of the American navy—reveals the importance of seasonality and monsoonal time in the Indian Ocean. This seasonality is the central anchor grounding an Indian Ocean world of circulation and exchange. In addition to giving a seasonal rhythm to Indian Ocean life, knowledge of the monsoon

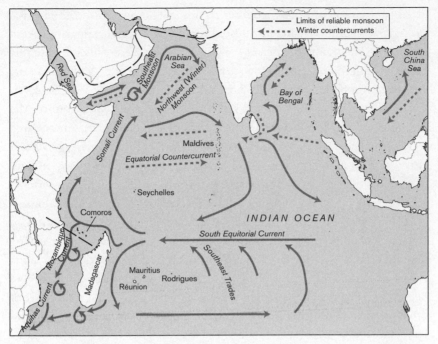

MAP 3: Map of monsoon currents in the Indian Ocean.

forged a pattern of transregional connectivity, creating repeated exchanges and encounters across the Indian Ocean rim.

The monsoon wind systems date back fifty million years to the collision of the Indian subcontinent with continental Asia and the subsequent uplift of the Tibetan peninsula. From the life-giving rains that feed more than half of the world's population, to the wind patterns that gave rise to an Indian Ocean society,[5] to the ravages of flooding and the destruction of droughts, the monsoons shape life and labor from Southeast Asia to East Africa. Along the Somali coast, the monsoons bring rain and respite from the heat to an otherwise parched land. They bring globally coveted fish drawn to the upwelling created by monsoonal currents. They bring ambergris and shipwrecks.

It was the discovery of monsoon patterns that also made possible European incursion into this oceanic space in the late fifteenth century. As Philip Curtin has noted, prior to the fifteenth century, European access to the Indian Ocean was limited to sailing along the coast of the Red Sea. "The European 'maritime revolution' of the fifteenth and sixteenth century was not so much a revolution in ship design as the discovery of the world wind system" (1984, 136). In the Indian Ocean this discovery was facilitated by local navigators.

In February 1498, after encountering a hostile reception in Mombasa—partly in response to having committed acts of piracy against unarmed Arab merchant ships prior to entering port—the Portuguese explorer Vasco da Gama's fleet found succor in the friendlier environment of Malindi, a port city situated one hundred miles north of Mombasa on the Kenyan coast. Credited as the first European to sail to India and the first to connect the Atlantic and the Indian Ocean, the Portuguese explorer circumnavigated southern Africa, sailing up the coast to Malindi before launching to India with the help of a mysterious local navigator, speculated by many to have been the famous navigator Ibn Majid. A forlorn, white coral pillar overlooking the Indian Ocean (and supposedly erected by Vasco da Gama on his return journey) is the sole reminder of his presence in modern Malindi, a town more famous today for its Italian expatriate population and a thriving narcotics shadow economy. Credited for inaugurating the "Vasco da Gama epoch of history"[6] in the Indian Ocean, these fifteenth-century voyages occupy a pivotal role in the supposed transition from an ecumenical mode of premodern Indian Ocean commerce to European domination at sea (and later land).

Knowledge of the monsoons is still a ticket into navigating the Indian Ocean, also for pirates. By 2007, navies had driven out the pirates from the relatively calm waters of the Red Sea to the monsoonal expanses of the Indian Ocean. This led to longer, riskier voyages, but also meant that pirates would now be hijacking more valuable cargo ships that sailed in the Indian Ocean. The possibility of greater rewards led to more people being drawn to coastal Puntland and longer, riskier voyages to capture ships. Badoon, a former fisherman whose village was transformed into a piracy base from 2008 until 2010, explained this transformation in organization and scale:

> We used to have some families that would go out to sea to find fishing trawlers or maybe even small dhows to hijack. That kind of operation had no major costs since it was fishermen who went to sea anyway for fishing. Maybe that family would spend $500–$1,000 for fuel and getting a weapon. After that they would come back and divide the money proportionally amongst each other after subtracting costs—just like with fishing. The pirates were now going out to sea for much longer and in more dangerous waters. Because of that the pirate groups had a more complex accounting system. First of all, instead of five or six men, you now had twelve to fifteen men go out to sea for many days at a time. So, whoever wanted to be part of the expedition would bring in money to sponsor the expedition, contributing something

like $10,000 each. The money collected in this way would be given to the leader, who would be responsible for organizing the group that went to sea. (Badoon, interview with author, May 2012)

These larger, more syndicate-like piracy groups, called *pirate action groups* by the EU and US navies, enjoyed unprecedented success in hijacking vessels. In 2007, Somali pirates captured approximately eleven ships, including the *MV Golden Nori*. In 2008 the number jumped to twenty-six ships, and in 2009 Somali pirates enjoyed record success, capturing forty-six ships (UNODC-WB 2013). These vessels ranged from large oil tankers—including the largest ship ever to be hijacked, the *MV Sirius Star*—to rust-bucket bulk carriers full of scrap metal and chemical waste. Given that Somali piracy is a monsoonal activity, most of these ships were hijacked during a six-month window, when waters are calm enough for small vessels to be out in the open ocean.

This transition of piracy into a monsoonal activity required, as Badoon noted, both navigational knowledge and a degree of capital, collateral, and connection that was not available to coastal fishermen. In opposition to the Red Sea, the Indian Ocean coastline is devoid of any coves or inlets. From late May until September this shoreline is battered by a near constant howling wind. This wind current (the Somali jet), annually produced by the monsoon, makes it almost impossible to go out into the ocean, especially using small fishing skiffs. The monsoons mean that no one is a fisherman (or a pirate) all year round. This inability to fish for months, to go out to the ocean amidst the monsoonal churn, meant that pirates, like fishermen, needed to anchor themselves to land—to limit their practices of raiding to the rhythms of seasonality and ground piracy within the solidity of the oikos. In the case of the Somali coast, this is the world of the diya.

DIYA: FROM REPAIR TO INVESTMENT

"Hostages require food and water," a shopkeeper in central Somalia told me. He was explaining how piracy had been a boon to his business. While he condemned the criminality of pirates, as a wholesaler he was regularly engaged in transactions to provide essential supplies to the people they held captive. In the aftermath of the *Nori* incident, piracy expanded dramatically both in number and scale. From 2008 onwards, it transformed from a Red

Sea practice targeting fishing trawlers to a multimillion-dollar hijack-and-ransom economy in the Indian Ocean. This shift required greater capital to finance the expeditions and provide for hostages. Regional entrepreneurs sought to profit from this expanding world by extending loans or provisions on credit. When I asked the central Somali shopkeeper how he ensured that pirates would pay him back—these were pirates, after all—he looked befuddled. "Of course they pay," he said. "Why wouldn't pirates pay? The men I'm supplying today belong to a diya group, like everyone. I can get payment from the group if they fail to pay."

Mentioned in three different verses of the Qur'an and noted in various Hadith, diya payment groups are central to wider questions of compensation within the juridical world of Islamic *fiqh* and its modes of restitution and retaliation. Belonging to the same family as *qisas* (retaliation) and *hudud* (restriction), the category of *diyat* (sing. *diya*) denotes a nonpunitive and socialized mode of dealing with harm (Hallaq 2009). Unlike *qisas* and *hudud*, where principles of retaliation and prohibition are anchored in the sovereignty of God, diya and the question of restitution are located within an everyday moral universe and the oscillation between injury and repair. Diya in this sense belongs to the "realm of private law and is the financial liability arising from a specific type of tort, i.e. unintentional homicide and wounding" (Peters 2005, 54).

In contrast to Western legal frameworks, diya blurs the boundaries between the realms of civil and criminal law as well as distinctions between crimes against individuals and crimes against the state. Instead of the state or the individual deciding and enforcing criminal punishment, diya enshrines payment as a mode of restitution, specifying in great detail how much is owed and to whom. This system thus shifts the locus of responsibility for adjudication and liability from both the state and the individual to the "community." Intisar Rabb (205, 35) notes that "as Muslim jurists understood the relevant Quranic verses, intentional or reckless acts that resulted in personal injury or death were subject to in-kind retaliation (*qisas*) which could be commuted to payment or financial compensation (diya) in case of pardon by victim or victim's family." Similarly, the financial compensation owed in the case of diya payments was often the responsibility of the *aqila*, or the male relatives, as opposed to the individual who had committed the act. In contrast to a logic of individual culpability, or one that reserves for the sovereign the right of leniency, diya payments distribute obligations to forgive and to pay within a broader social universe.

In the Somali context, diya payment groups are often known as *mag* paying groups. Existing at a level above the *xaas* (household), these groups are composed of a *reer* (lineage) or a small collection of lineages that trace descent back to a common ancestor in the span of five to eight patrilineal generations. Along with this *abtirsiinyo* (ancestral reckoning), diya groups are united in joint responsibility towards outsiders, specifically with respect to the burdens of payment and the distribution of compensation receipts. In addition, diya groups abide by a set of norms—often defined as *xeer* (customary law)—that govern relations between and within diya groups. In this sense, diya extends beyond what can be glossed as "blood payments" to regulate a host of interactions, from car accidents to fraudulent business deals. While seemingly fixed through kinship, diya groups—like other modes of genealogical belonging—are marked by a degree of flexibility. Over time, they expand and contract and echo what Pierre Bourdieu (1992, 167) notes regarding the politics of kinship: "Every adult male, at whatever level on the genealogical tree, represents a point of potential segmentation, which may be actualized for a particular social purpose." Additionally, while ostensibly belonging to one diya group—namely one's patrilineal group—the diya group of one's maternal relatives can also provide an alternate source of support. This expanded role of diya groups emerged repeatedly throughout fieldwork.

A common feature of driving in northern Somalia is the ubiquity of road accidents. All along the road I would see mangled metal remains of Toyota sedans and SUVs, with shattered windshields glinting in the mid-morning sun. Some would blame the reckless driving of pirates for these wrecks, while others pointed to the habit of driving while chewing khat, or the goats that constantly scurried across the road at the most inopportune moments. "But don't worry," my hosts would casually note as they observed me staring at car wrecks, "if anything happens we have my diya group; it works like car insurance."

During the heyday of Somali piracy, a certain "pirate style" came into vogue in the port cities of northern Somalia. This mostly consisted of young men, styled in gold-rimmed sunglasses, ostentatious watches, and English Premier League football jerseys, casually chewing stalks of khat as they sat about in tea shops, or driving recklessly around town in ostentatiously shiny Land Cruisers. These young pirates were a visible part of the landscape, though my attempts to approach them in public spaces were mostly unsuccessful. The merchants, government officials, and diasporic Somalis who had become my daily interlocutors would warn me from attempting to approach them. "They can be very dangerous," Timo, a Canadian-Somali I had befriended at a café due to our mutual affection for the Los Angeles Lakers, reminded me as we were driving out of town in his old Toyota sedan. A Land Cruiser had almost run us off the road. "They love fancy cars, especially the Land Cruisers. You know, they say the first guy who climbs aboard a ship is given a shiny Land Cruiser as a gift for his bravery." As he surveyed the torn upholstery of his car, he added, "but these guys are really bad drivers, man; they're crazy. They go to the beach and have races and break the gearbox in a week." He continued, "We call the cars *haram gaari* [illicit cars] because you can tell it's from piracy money."

Timo, like a number of people in Puntland, was deeply ambivalent about piracy. While impressed by the pirates' bravado and their ability to make lots of money, he would also often remark disparagingly that pirates brought shame to Somalia, and he was always critical of their driving and their hedonistic lifestyle, a mode of critique shared throughout Somalia (Gilmer 2017). That day, as we were driving to a sweet shop on the southern edge of town to buy *xaalwa kismaayo,* a sticky-sweet specialty of the region made of butter and sugar, Timo was a little too carried away by our conversation. In the midst of a rant about bad pirate drivers, he rear-ended another sedan sputtering along on the road. We were both slightly dazed but otherwise unhurt, and, after checking on me, he walked over to the other car. A small crowd had gathered and I decided to stay in the car. Five minutes of negotiations later, Timo ran back to tell me, "We're going to stay here for a little bit, let's have tea." As we sipped tea next to the silent, burly man whose car we had damaged, Timo explained that we were waiting for an elder from his diya group to come so they could decide on the amount of compensation. "No one is hurt so we can just agree on the spot what I owe him." An hour later, an older man arrived and within a few minutes a payment was agreed upon, a hastily drawn out contract signed, and we were on our way again. "See, I told you this is how we do it here," he said. "When it comes to accidents, the diya group is like insurance."

Soon after Timo had extolled the virtues of the diya group, he complained that as a diasporic Somali he was always expected to contribute a higher *qaaran* (obligatory payment to the diya) in addition to paying *sako* (*zakat,* Islamic compulsory alms) and *sadaka* (*sadaqa,* Islamic voluntary charity). "Every month there are lots of bills," he grumbled as we drove away from the accident. When I asked Timo about enforcement mechanisms or consequences for nonpayment, he simply shrugged. "People will call me all the time, I listen to them and pay mostly . . . I guess that's the general rule: pay your *qaaran* most of the time." After pausing for a moment, he added, "Sometimes I get tired and just switch off my phone. Then I don't have to pay." Pointing to the notebook on my lap, where I had been scribbling field-notes, he remarked, "You should write this down as the rule: pay your *qaaran*, unless you decide to switch off the phone. Then it's not necessary [to pay]." "What happens when you switch the phone back on?" I asked. "Well, some-times you still owe them a debt," he said stoically as we pulled into the *xaalwa* shop.

From Kant's "unruled regions" ([1795] 2003, 138) to the stateless societies foundational to early social anthropology, the question of "order without [state] law" (Ellickson 2009) is one that has befuddled theorists of political authority and sovereignty. In the absence of identifiable structures of govern-ance, scholars have argued that political organization in these societies—variously called stateless, acephalous, or primitive—could fruitfully be examined through kinship relations. Applying this model to Somalia, Ioan M. Lewis argued that "patrilineal descent (*tol*) is all pervasive: most corpo-rate activities are contingent upon it; in the veneration of local lineage saints Islam is interpreted to some extent according to it; and politics stem from it" (1994, 19). In Lewis's oeuvre, Somali society has been characterized as a pas-toral democracy organized according to the principles of segmentary lineage and the idiom of clan—a framing deeply contested and critiqued within both academic and nonacademic contexts for propagating a seemingly unchang-ing and primordialist vision of Somali society.[7] As the car accident illustrates, however, kinship ties and diya payment groups may function *like* insurance, but these obligations are not distributed equally and can, sometimes, also disappear when one switches off one's cell phone (though they might reap-pear once the phone is switched back on). This seeming flexibility underlines the dynamic aspects of kinship categories, in this case the diya, and how inequalities structure interactions within frameworks of customary law and kinship obligations. Neither incommensurability nor mere instrumentality captures this relationship of diya as insurance and the possibilities of restitu-tion and repair within this system.

If for Timo diya existed as a contract—a mode of guaranteeing restitution for injury—diya also emerges at times as a system of governing engagements, a composite actor engaged in the management of violence. Faisal, a livestock trader who made a daily trip to the port, helped facilitate my entrance to the port every morning. Even though I had the permission of the port manager, entrance into the port would be a daily negotiation with the guards. However, if I was in Faisal's car, we seldom encountered any obstacles. As a result, Faisal would pick me up on his way to the port most mornings.

One morning, he mentioned that his nephew had been in a car accident and we needed to stop by a house en route to the port. We arrived at a compound on the outskirts of town, in a neighborhood that sprawled on both sides of the Mogadishu highway. A group of ten men had already gathered at the gate. Soon we were welcomed inside, pleasantries were exchanged, and tea and samosas served. After an hour or so of sitting around, the group gathered and made a bit of a procession as we walked out and back towards the city and the port. This morning ritual continued for a week. Each day, Faisal would pick me up and we would stop by the compound, drink tea, and walk around the neighborhood in a large group before heading back. One morning, Faisal got into the car and said, "No stops for us today; we go directly to the port." I asked Faisal why we had been going to that house for the past week. "Oh, that was the man whose car had hit my nephew. He was refusing to pay the diya compensation. So we were going to his house as members of my nephew's diya showing him our strength and also shaming his diya group. Finally, they made the payment because they were probably tired of providing tea and samosas!" As this case highlights, the question of payment with respect to diya is not (just) a numerical mode of compensation. For Faisal and his nephew, diya specified what was owed, but also emerged as a composite actor—a mode of socializing the nephew's injury and compelling payment through a form of public shaming.

The protection of diya groups emerges inter alia from its retrospective ability to provide repair and restitution. This mode of restitution also meant that both colonial and postcolonial governments in Somalia sought to regulate these groups. During the British protectorate in nineteenth-century Somaliland, officials attempted to transform oral agreements for diya payments into written contracts with markedly mixed results. Another significant attempt to regulate the diya occurred in November 1970, almost a year after the Somali government of Siyad Barre came to power in a military coup, ushering in a series of legal reforms signaling the regime's commitment to Scientific Socialism. In addition to a number of technocratic innovations, these new laws also sought to establish a system of social security. Specifically, Article 6 of the 1970 Social Security Act (quoted in Adam and Geshekter 1992, 178) stated: "No one can be held liable to payment of compensation except the person responsible for a homicide or for material or moral injury." Seen as specifically targeting the widespread use of diya payments, the Social Security Act, along with the broader rhetoric of Scientific Socialism, was critiqued by the religious elite in Mogadishu, who sought to remind Barre that even British colonial rule had been unable to transform the (putatively religious) principles of collective responsibility enshrined within the diya system. The abolition of diya payments was seen as an attempt to shift the locus of responsibility from the familial to a relationship between state and citizen.

In addition, the protection of diya groups is also future-oriented as a source of credit and collateral. Diya and societies like the *hagbaad* (rotating saving schemes) are crucial reservoirs of private savings and collateral for credit. Beyond attempting a transition from diya to social security, Barre's regime also sought to shift this private credit and capital into banks. In 1971, the Barre government created two public commercial banks, the Somali Savings & Credit Bank and the Somali Commercial Bank, in order to facilitate and mobilize domestic savings (Mauri 1971). The government also nationalized a number of foreign commercial banks in order to encourage more domestic lending and borrowing. However, the banks were used primarily to fund public agencies. A negative interest rate on borrowing and savings meant that most domestic credit through banks went to public entities (Mubarak 1997), with private individuals continuing to turn to diya groups and *hagbaad* as sources of credit and/or collateral for investment. In opposition to shifting from "mutual aid to the welfare state" (Beito 2000; see also Shipton 2010), these technocratic reforms ended up reinforcing and eventually expanding the role of diya payments.

The absence of a viable state-run banking and credit sector—along with the oil boom in the Middle East that drew many Somalis across the Gulf of Aden to work in the economies of Saudi Arabia and United Arab Emirates from the mid-1970s onwards—forced Somalis to turn to private systems of exchange, transforming diya groups from spaces of repair to spaces of investment. My interlocutors described the importance of diya groups in facilitating mobility of people, goods, and money in the decade prior to state collapse. While there was a plethora of jobs in the Arabian Gulf, many companies and visa agencies required cash deposits from applicants to prevent worker abscondence or to restrict labor mobility. Diya groups, as the largest sources of capital, would provide interest-free loans to ensure visas and the ability to migrate during the oil boom. Faisal had worked in Saudi Arabia during the

1980s and recalled how his diya group provided both the capital to get to Saudi and a means of sending money back:

> It was difficult to send money in those days [the 1980s] because the state was desperate for dollars and would monitor foreign currency coming into Somalia. We had a shopkeeper in my diya who owned a tea and coffee shop in Galkayoo. I would buy tea and coffee in Saudi and send them to him via ship. I also gave him an invoice at a lower rate so that he could pay the difference to my family directly in Somalia without the government finding out. (Faisal, interview with author, March 2011)

Following the unraveling of the Somali state, a process that culminated with the arrival of US marines on the beaches of Mogadishu in 1991, diya groups emerged as reservoirs of capital, collateral, and connection, creating an infrastructure that allowed trade and business networks to expand across the increasingly transregional space of Somali commerce. Far from being an inward-looking "traditional" system, the diya group facilitates economic transactions across space and the ability to manage risk in insecure environments, transforming kinship into a form of collateral.[8] As the post-1991 Somali diaspora circulated across the globe, it was not only stitched together by cellphones, Internet connectivity, and private airline routes, but also through diya groups, which were central to creating a global Somalia.

This dual orientation of diya—its ability to retrospectively provide compensation for injury and its future-oriented credit function—is central to its ability to provide protection. As simultaneously past- and future-oriented, the protection of diya makes possible a whole host of transactions, including the exchanges central to Somali piracy. The ransom economy of Somali piracy meant that as pirates became more successful in capturing vessels at sea, they simultaneously became more dependent on the protection of diya groups on land. As one of the largest sources of capital, diya groups provided access to the credit required to organize a piracy expedition. They transformed kinship into collateral through distributing the risks of piracy before and, crucially, after capture.

Recruitment into a piracy group often drew on diya obligations, with aspiring pirates turning to diya groups to secure the men, weapons, and boats necessary to go out to sea. For those who took to the waters, it meant that the instruments of capture (the men, the boats, the fuel, the khat) were procured on credit—a system that both guaranteed and reinforced the diya. Beyond the credit required to go to sea, diya groups also provided crucial support during the waiting time before ransoms.

As Hirsi, a former guard for a pirate group, explained, "When we catch a ship, we have no idea if the ransom will come quickly or at all. All we are doing then is waiting." But waiting is expensive. "When I was a guard," he continued, "I could not leave the ship, so the food, water, and khat I had to get on credit, like all the guards on board. When we got the money from the ransom, the businessmen and the bosses would take their share. When we captured a ship, we knew already that a lot of the money would be used to pay the cost of being on the boat." For Hirsi, diya groups are a storehouse of credit in this period of waiting. The diya creates a space of obligation. Shared membership in this corporate entity makes future returns possible.

In other situations, diya membership also allows for engagements across groups, creating debts and payment obligations, along with networks of investors, entrepreneurs, debtors, and delinquents. Another ex-pirate explained this process:

> All the different people give us the money to go out to sea to find ships. [From merchants to khat dealers], they benefit if we catch a ship. When we are waiting for the ransom, they come to us and say things like, "Soon you'll make big money, so why don't you buy a Land Cruiser? I trust you; you're in my *mag* [diya payment group]." So they tempt us like that when we're waiting for a ransom. Because they belong to my diya, I trust them and buy lots of things from them. At the same time, the <u>diya</u> protects the businessman. The pirate is not going to run away; they have to pay or else the diya group is responsible for him. (Yasir, interview with author, February 2011)

For the investor and the pirate, diya makes possible a relationship that is not in fact predicated on shared membership in this group. You and I are not members of the same diya, but I know that if I cannot get my money back from you, I can make the diya, or other members of it, pay me back. Here, the diya emerges as a guarantor that enables transactions across unrelated groups.

Whether in setting the terms for an engagement or emerging as the guarantor for interactions across (kinship) difference, it is the protection of the diya that makes possible the investments necessary to become a pirate. The Somali pirate, whether he appears as a fisherman or a member of a pirate action group, is always a socialized figure, tied to the world of diya obligations and the ways they structure protection through governing the risks and rewards of piracy throughout the wider economy. If piracy is anchored to land in these modes of protection with longer histories and slower temporali-ties, there is also an element of fast accumulation within the anchorage of piracy on land. As Sheikh Usman would repeatedly note, "too many people were becoming too rich from piracy." Alongside its normalization into the world of diya, there was a spectacle to the economy of piracy—a spectacle made visible through khat.

KHAT AND CARRY: THE FAST ECONOMY OF PIRACY

It had been weeks of trying to contact Aisha. She had messaged me with a time to meet when I was away on my road trip with Sheikh Usman, and now I worried I had offended her. "She's a busy person," Said, the moneychanger, would remind me during afternoons spent with him learning about khat and money transfers from the local aficionados who gathered at his shop. "Aisha wants to become a dollar millionaire, she has no time for students," he would observe. One of the prominent market women, it was rumored that Aisha controlled most of the khat trade in town. One afternoon, as I arrived at Said's shop, he greeted me with a smile. "Good news for you—Aisha is not offended! She just came back from Addis and said she'll meet you at the lobby of your guesthouse this evening." Both relieved and a little concerned that Aisha knew where I lived, I eagerly anticipated my meeting.

True to her word, Aisha arrived in the evening and promptly began quiz-zing me on my business connections. Like many in northern Somalia, Aisha initially doubted that I was a student. Instead, she took my Swahili skills and knowledge of Kenya as proof that I was a Kenyan businessman looking for a new venture. "As long as you don't want to distribute khat, I'll tell you all about this trade," she remarked, as we settled in for tea in the lobby of the guesthouse. Like many market women, Aisha had initially sold camel milk in a highly gendered economy where women were central in the distribution of the milk at roadside stalls and markets (Anderson et al. 2012). "The civil war made women prominent in the market. Many women used to refuse to sell to other clans as a form of solidarity, and that's how we gained some power in the market." Aisha then explained how she joined a women's coop-erative that had been established through a development NGO. "I started selling other things instead of just camel milk." When I asked Aisha why women were so prominent in trade in Somalia, she somewhat straightfor-wardly remarked, "Well, the men were fighting so the business responsibility

FIGURE 4: Khat market.

fell to us. Also, in our religion, women traders are highly respected, like Khadija, the first wife of the Prophet."

Like many women traders, Aisha had diversified into khat in recent years. "Women have a natural advantage when it comes to the khat trade." Switching to English, she motioned around the room and said: "Look around at all these men chewing in the lobby, even when the sign says no chewing." She gestured towards the hastily drawn cross over a drawing of khat leaves that adorned the door to the entrance of the lobby. "Men cannot resist khat. If they became wholesalers like me, they would eat it all and have nothing to sell!" As we laughed at her joke, Aisha reminded me that it was funny because it was true. "You'll see," she remarked somewhat cryptically, and left me in a room full of chewers surrounded by the particular leafy smell of fresh Ethiopian khat that seasoned chewers note as intoxicating.

Praised as the flower of paradise, the tender shoots and leaves of the *Catha edulis*—an evergreen tree with a slender trunk and a white bark—produce a mild narcotic effect that leaves one alert and acts as a euphoriant. Writing in 1855, Baron Ernst von Bibra, "the early pioneer of drug studies" (Carrier 2007, 5), described the effects of khat as follows:

Khat seems to have a pleasant excitant effect on the organism. People who take khat become cheerful, talkative, and wide-awake. Some people also fall into pleasant dreams. The violent excitement caused by opium and sometimes by hashish does not seem to occur with khat. Khat more closely resembles coffee than those more violent excitants, although it is stronger than coffee. (von Bibra, quoted in Carrier 2007, 25)

The *Catha edulis* grows at an altitude of five thousand to eight thousand feet and is found in the highlands of Yemen, Ethiopia, Kenya, and Madagascar. Each regional variety has a unique smell and taste, leading to grades of khat as well as distinct markets and classes of customers. The earliest documented use of khat in Somalia dates back to the fourteenth century, when it traveled from Ethiopia to northern Somalia through religious networks (Gebissa 2004; Cabdi 2005). Until the early twentieth century, the use of khat was primarily confined to *dhikirs* (Sufi gatherings), and a rich poetic tradition from that era notes the centrality of khat to practices of piety (Cassanelli 1986; Warsame 2004). The union of British and Italian Somaliland and subsequent infrastructural transformations brought khat chewing to southern Somalia, where it spread amongst a newly emerging urban elite with time and resources to chew.

While it has slipped in and out of legality (Cassanelli 1986), khat is widely chewed throughout Somalia. Most of the khat consumed in Somalia arrives from elsewhere. With the exception of small parts of Somaliland, attempts to grow the plant in Somalia have so far been unsuccessful. This geographical separation and the fact that khat loses its potency within forty-eight hours of harvesting creates a particular temporality and a transregional network that links farmers in northern Kenya to street vendors in Mogadishu with millions of dollars transacted on an everyday basis. Khat comes to Somalia on regular flights and on heavily guarded trucks and, when I was there, sold for about $80 for a fresh kilo of *dardar* (organic highest-quality khat). This division between production and consumption, and its short-lived efficacy, create what Neil Carrier (2005) has termed a "need for speed." In addition to signaling a certain temporality, the idea of speed, I note, is also about the ways in which khat is framed, certainly outside Somalia, within discourses of danger and criminality.

Much like antimarijuana ads and media antipiracy campaigns, a certain rhetorical power is achieved in linking the unsanctioned circulation of certain objects/substances to terrorism in a post-9/11 imaginary.[9] Far removed from Baron Ernst's benign descriptions, khat today is clearly linked with piracy in ways that fit within this broader mode of representation. In 2010, the European Union Naval Force issued a pamphlet for commercial shipping vessels transiting the piratical waters of the western Indian Ocean titled *Surviving Piracy off the Coast of Somalia*. Printed in Arabic, Chinese, English, Hindi, Japanese, Russian, and Tagalog, the pamphlet consisted of a series of recommendations for crew members in the aftermath of a hijacking, ranging from being patient to seeking counseling upon release. One particular recommendation stands out in an otherwise straightforward list. Under the heading "Avoid Drugs," the pamphlet goes on to note:

> Khat is a common drug used in the Somali region. If the pirates onboard your vessel use this or other drugs, you should be careful to avoid any confrontations whilst they are under the influence of such substances. You should not be tempted to take drugs, other than for legitimate medical conditions, whilst in captivity. The taking of drugs may offer temporary relief, however the negative effects of withdrawal symptoms and increased tension due to cravings could result in unnecessary violence from your captors.[10]

This intimacy of khat and piracy has a number of resonances within Somalia as well. After I had become an apprentice of sorts to Aisha, I would spend my days learning how to identify the freshness of khat and other forms of assessment regarding texture and quality. In the evenings, eager to show off my newfound knowledge, I would find the *mafresh* (khat chew) at the various hotels in town. Most of my evenings spent conducting fieldwork in northern Somalia involved hanging out in hotel lobbies where men gathered to drink tea, watch the news, and, as the evening wore on, chew khat. This evening, I was trying to impress my companions with my understanding of *dardar*: organic khat not grown with any chemicals or pesticides, which was all the rage amongst the chewers of Puntland. Distinctly unimpressed, a younger man chewing next to me turned to me with a stalk of khat in his mouth and whispered: "Khat is piracy. Afweyne, Boyah [prominent pirate bosses] ... they all came up with the idea when chewing khat. We say that khat makes you think big ideas; piracy is one such big idea that came from khat."

While this man might have overstated its role in shaping the economy of piracy, khat remains as central to this world as the obligations of diya that govern its economy. In the spaces of sociality structured by khat, deals are struck and piracy expeditions planned. In addition to food, water, and fuel, khat is an essential ingredient when boats go out to sea. These initial supplies, acquired on credit, often represent moments of investment for a variety of local businesses, tying khat and pirates to diya groups. Finally, khat is central to the debts acquired in piracy. As many involved in piracy would remind me, "even before a pirate leaves land he is already in debt. The supplies, the boat, the khat they chew, it is all owned by different people. Becoming a pirate is about becoming indebted. That's why all these young men can never stop going to sea."

The story of khat in a world of circulation, of speed and waiting, of addiction and obligation, is thus a foil,[11] contrasting economies that circulate alongside piracy and helping us to navigate this sea of piracy both ethnographically and analytically. Like piracy, khat is characterized by ephemerality and seasonality. Like piracy, khat moves between the realm of acceptable and unacceptable. Like piracy, khat creates profits and losses, creditors and debtors. This cash-and-carry economy (Guyer 2004) is thus another vantage point, and a distinct temporality, from which to understand the relationships that structure and anchor the contemporary economy of piracy.

In Somalia and East Africa, khat circulates outside frameworks of terrorism, addiction, and piracy, though it is not completely removed from them. This is a world of millionaire merchants, aficionados who can smell the difference between varieties in the market, drivers, militiamen who provide security, politicians who debate the future of Somalia, Kenyan middlemen, Hadrami sheikhs who use khat in their weekly gatherings as a source of reverie and inspiration, Ethiopian and Kenyan farmers—and pirate bosses.

ECONOMIES OF SPECTACLE

After a few months of research in Somalia I had met a few pirates, but had never come across the elusive pirate boss. Every attempt I made was either rebuffed or I'd be quoted exorbitant figures for an interview. One afternoon, when I returned from a day of interviews, I was told by the guesthouse owner in a town in Puntland: "Absaame has agreed to meet you. We are going to a *mafresh*." Absaame was a pirate boss who had demanded $10,000 for a meeting, so I was stunned by this unexpected opportunity. I got myself ready quickly, and the guesthouse owner and I headed to the market to purchase some khat.

Arriving at the *mafresh* with some Meru Miraa (a variety of Kenyan khat) in the twilight hours with the sounds of the *isha* prayers in the background, I encountered a fairly mellow scene of seven or eight young men sitting around a table littered with bundles of khat and bottles of 7 Up. I wasn't sure which one was Absaame, so I added my bundle to the table and quietly sat down at one corner. Fifteen minutes later, a middle-aged man in an Egyptian-style *gallabeeya* stepped in and in Cairene-inflected Arabic introduced himself as Absaame.

"*Ana birate* [I am a pirate]," he said playfully, though it was clear he also wielded the status of his position. Absaame liked being called a pirate, not *buraad* (bandit in Somali) or even the more sympathetic rendering of *badhinta bahar* (saviors of the sea) popularized in recent Somali and Western journalistic accounts that recast Somali piracy as a local response to problems of overfishing and global exploitation. "Call me an *abaan* [protector] or just use the English word 'pirate,'" he told me. "Those are words that indicate *sumcad* [prestige]. I became a big man through this business, it's important to me." Absaame clearly saw importance in his status as a pirate/protector, a status he performed by hosting these daily gatherings.

Absaame remained fairly animated throughout the chew, holding forth in a voice that ranged between playful, stern, and bombastic, especially once the *mirqaan* (effect) set in. In a corner of the room, a Bollywood movie played and the smell of apple-flavored tobacco hung thickly. The khat ran through my system, its effect reminiscent of a first cup of espresso on a drowsy morning, just more intense. Absaame's father had worked in the Gulf and later moved to Cairo, where Absaame grew up.

> I was sixteen years old when we returned from Cairo. My father had an idea that he would build a plastics business in Kismaayo. The *Il-ittihad* [*ittihād al-mahākim al-islāmiyya*, or the Islamic Courts Union] had just come into power and we were hopeful for peace. During the Ethiopian invasion, we became refugees and ended up going to Moshi [Tanzania]. I was an errand boy there and even worked as a *matatu* conductor. My cousin wanted to become a pirate, but he didn't have the strength to become one. It's not easy . . . that's why we shouldn't hide from this label. I became a big man through this business. (Absaame, interview with author, March 2011, some details changed to preserve anonymity)

When Absaame finished speaking, Bole, a soft-spoken young man from the Ogaden region in Ethiopia who had been waiting for many years to cross the Red Sea before becoming a pirate, turned to Absaame and offered him a particularly green stem. "This is the *boqorka lanta*." The stem of the *boqor* (ruler) is the one customarily given to the elder within a group, emphasizing the importance of khat chews as places where hierarchy is performed. As he chewed the stem with particular relish, he said, "This is what piracy has given me."

As the reference to the *boqorka lanta* and the claim to being *abaan* show, in the space of the *mafresh*, Absaame sought to narrate piracy as something spectacular. He was known in Somalia as one of the few pirate bosses who went out to sea with his crew. In the *mafresh* he would constantly tell of the adventure and bravado central to hijacking a ship. "You cannot imagine how big some of these ships are when you are in a boat ready to capture them. We had been chewing all night to become brave; those who chew at night are said to be possessed with *isqarxis* [death wish]." Absaame was masterfully setting the scene for his tale. "The sea was wild, with the wind howling. At dawn we saw this giant ship and got our ladder and hooked ourselves to the ship to climb aboard and bring it back to Somalia."

Absaame's storytelling in the *mafresh* follows the style and structure of a rich poetic tradition in Somalia that exalts the raider as a heroic figure.[12] The *mafresh* brings into view the performativity and the affective labor[13] of inspiration, desire, and other nonnumerical modes of valuation that are central to becoming a pirate. Bringing out these distinct modes and disentangling the relationship between khat and piracy from stories of addiction and terrorism is not simply a question of refuting the connections that are implicit in the EU pamphlet warning of the dangers of khat-addicted pirates. It is rather to understand the different registers and temporalities through which the intimacies between khat and piracy are constructed. Doing so foregrounds the performative nature of both khat-chewing and piracy, as well as the poetics that frame this intimacy.

Thus, beyond the *mafresh,* likening khat to piracy emphasizes the spectacle that marks both these practices. Whether in the loud arrivals of the trucks or the kinds of sociality structured through chewing, the economy of khat is both quotidian and exceptional. Similarly, pirates are not only socialized figures legible within the networks of obligation of diya, but also spectacular ones.

Prior to arriving in northern Somalia, I had heard many stories of the lavish influx of wealth into Somalia due to piracy ransoms. In Mombasa, where I began research, rumors were rife of mansions with swimming pools and luxury cars in Puntland. The influx of Somali investment into the real estate market of Mombasa was also talked about in terms of whitewashing piracy gains. At academic conferences, researchers spoke of mapping the impact of piracy in Somalia through satellite images. Given this, my arrival in Puntland was a letdown. Everyday life in the port cities of Puntland seemed no different from Somaliland: potholed roads, incomplete brick and concrete buildings, and a layer of dust that seemed to coat everything in these towns. No swimming pools or extravagant wealth was on display. Slowly the subtle and not-so-subtle ways in which piracy was transforming Puntland started coming into view. From the "pirate style" practiced amongst a group of young men to the occasional glimpse of broken-down Land Cruisers on the beach, the detritus of late-night pirate parties, glimpses of the spectacle of piracy slowly came into view.

But for every story of lavish pirate parties and every Land Cruiser and occasional pink limousine that was unloaded at the dock, there were people who spoke of spectacular losses, of ruin and debt. Some were a result of failure. Hassan told me he always wanted to be rich. "When you are a young boy you are interested in football. All my friends wanted to be Ronaldinho, Bergkamp or Ronaldo. I wanted to be like Bill Gates or Donald Trump." Hassan was showing me his collection of American self-help books with elaborate plans from Trump and others about becoming millionaires overnight. "Piracy, I thought, would be a good business strategy." Hassan then explained how he had a cousin who had gone to sea and come back with $20,000. "It seemed like easy money, so I asked him to help me join a group." The cousin agreed on the condition that Hassan provide $5,000 as a guarantee. When his father refused to help, Hassan turned to his mother and her diya group for a loan. With this loan, he went out to sea. "We stayed out there for one week and had no luck. I came back and all of a sudden I owed $7,000." Since he had no money, he decided to go back out to sea—where he once more failed to hijack a ship. "Now, I owe my mother's diya $20,000 and my cousin $5,000. I have this job unloading things from a truck at the port. I don't think I will become a millionaire anytime soon." Hassan's was a story repeated by many. As I was walking back from Hassan's house with Hanif, my research assistant who had introduced me to Hassan, he too likened piracy to khat. "Did you notice he was chewing the entire time we were talking? It's nine in the morning . . . He's addicted so he has to chew to recover from his hangover. For people like Hassan, piracy is just like khat. It traps them and they become addicted and it ruins them."

Other stories of ruin were linked to deception. In addition to knowing a number of pirates, Hanif claimed to be friends with a woman who robbed pirates. As he explained, this woman would call pirates up in the middle of the night. "She likes to whisper nice things to them on the phone. Then [she] would invite them to a place outside town. She would say things like, bring my *yarad* [bride price] and I'll marry you right there." Hanif continued with a wry smile: "These fools show up with money and their fancy car in a *wadi* and then she robs them. It's great!"

These stories index the quick money and quick losses that are central to piracy. As Hirsi, a former pirate, noted, "We get all these benefits when we are guarding a ship, but it's never clear what someone's motive is in these situations." For Hirsi too, piracy was like khat, but in the way that khat deceives: "You think you're getting great ideas when you're chewing, but you're really just eating shilling and dollars. Similarly, you're dreaming of all the money you'll make with piracy when you're guarding a ship, but mostly in my case you're just going into debt."

The economy of khat becomes a way, then, to comprehend the excesses of piracy, including the way it produces ruin. If diya is about anchoring piracy within obligations of kinship and longer histories of risk-pooling, khat highlights that these forms of anchoring are also spaces of ephemeral opportunity, and equally of ruination. Both diya groups and khat anchor piracy to land. These forms of anchoring make piracy possible and socialize it within forms of obligation and exchange that both offer protection and govern the economy of piracy. The distinct temporalities of diya and khat—slow and fast—and the possibilities of profit and ruin that are embedded within them make clear the ambiguity of this protection. Anchoring piracy within an economy of protection is thus about channeling possibilities that come from moving between temporalities of accumulation.

FAST AND SLOW: DIYA, KHAT, AND PIRACY

Diya groups and khat also interact when anchoring piracy to land, as I realized one afternoon whilst sitting in a white Toyota Land Cruiser. I was attempting to listen to a news program on Radio Daljir, the local radio station in Puntland, as we sped north to the airstrip at the edge of town. Aisha was sitting in the backseat, talking on the phone; her *oud* perfume and conversation filled the space of the SUV. "Business," she said in English as she hung up the phone: "I'm finalizing my new business plan."

As we drove towards the airport, Aisha explained her business plan, one that was built on weaving together and accelerating the multiple velocities that define the circulation of khat. "They pick the leaves before the sun rises in Harar and send it by plane to Galkaayo." She paused so I could mentally map the journey from Ethiopia to northern Somalia. "I have to pay to offload the khat in Galkaayo, and it takes about three hours from there to get to here. In the middle there are five small roadblocks. I think I lose twenty to thirty bundles every day as *hadiyad* [gifts] for the checkpoints on the road, the guards, etc." Her plan was to cut the middlemen and bring the khat directly to the airport. "This deal I have with the Ethiopian company will soon make me the biggest trader in the market. My khat will get to the market first and freshest."

Aisha's ability to provide the first and freshest supply of khat shows the centrality of circulation time in shaping economies of exchange.[14] For Aisha, the ability to reduce circulation costs and increase income was the difference between a market woman and the khat tycoon, an aspirational status that Aisha sought for herself. Becoming a khat tycoon also involves navigating very distinct social, ethical, and biological worlds, both visible and invisible, from the speed of decay in the khat leaves to the speed blocks on the highway.

Upon arriving at the airport, I walked out onto the runway to watch her supervise the unloading. As soon as the plane landed, Aisha called out to a number of armed men who had been milling about, their AK-47s casually slung on their shoulders. *"Askari halkan* [guards come here], the plane is landing, time to work." Aisha was in the middle of inspecting the cargo and yelling out instructions when a phone call interrupted her. The ringtone, a discordant *nashid* (Quranic verse), punctuated the quiet efficiency of the unloading and loading. Aisha stepped away to answer the phone, but as she returned to the area next to the hold where I was standing, she remarked, "You have brought me luck today. A ship has been captured and the pirates called to secure some khat. They have ten guards on board and I just made a deal with them to supply fresh khat every day. Depending on how long the negotiations take, I'll be a rich woman!" As we headed back from the airport, I watched one of the pickup trucks speed north towards the coast, where I imagined a group of expectant pirates eagerly awaited its arrival.

The next day, arriving at the market right before the arrival of the khat trucks, I sat with notebook in hand waiting to observe Aisha's new business plan in action. As she had promised, her truck was the first to arrive at the airport. As she emerged from the Land Cruiser, I walked over to her and we watched as she sold out her daily shipment before the trucks from Galkaayo had even arrived. Once the frenzy had calmed and the buyers had retreated home with their bundles, or to the *mafresh* for a long evening of chewing,

I asked Aisha about the pirates she had supplied khat to the day before. "They were very happy to get the khat. I had sent them a *falad* [3/4 kilo], and since they were at sea for two weeks, I am sure last night they were really feeling the effects." Aisha continued: "Every day for the next month or so I'll send them a kilo or so while they are waiting for the ransom." At this point, I asked my usual question: "How do you trust pirates? What happens if they don't pay?" Aisha brushed off my concerns. "What do you mean by 'they will not pay'? Of course, they have to pay. The person who called yesterday, the *dilaal* [broker], is part of my *mag* [diya] group. I extend him credit and of course he needs to pay his debts! I have a claim on him if he does not pay me back." Turning to her notebook, Aisha showed me a page where she had scribbled in the debts owed to her with amounts ranging from a few dollars to thousands. "Some of these people are businessmen, others are poets and politicians and, of course, some of the biggest debts are those owed to me by pirates."

I was struck by this account book and Aisha's easy equivalence between pirate, poet, and politician. In addition to putting everyone literally on the same page, the account book also listed, next to the name, a brief genealogy or the name of a subclan. Far from the *hostis humani generis* (the enemy of all mankind—a figure removed from the realm of enmity and friendship), the pirate and piracy are anchored within this world of kinship, obligation, and debt. It is this entanglement that makes it possible for Aisha not only to find my concern incredible, but also to be confident in the fact that the pirates will pay their dues. After staring at the book for a while, I asked Aisha if I could take a picture. Snatching the book away from me, Aisha responded, "No! I don't know who you are. You could be CIA."

The economy of khat is structured around a particular geographical and temporal necessity. The spatial difference between production and consumption and the narrow timeframe of efficacy necessitates a move beyond the household oikos. As observed by Aristotle, with echoes in Marx ([1939] 1993b), and in everyday conversations across the Indian Ocean rim, necessity, whether geographic or temporal, begets mobility. We leave the solidity of land and traverse the sea in search of new opportunities and possibilities. This labor of mobility—whether in the form of the hunt or nomadism—was a natural mode of acquisition so long as the ends entailed the provision of the household. This is a world of constant returns: we travel not to conquer, but to return home.

Aisha's business, and the world of khat, makes visible the various exchanges and encounters that occur within this economy of circulation. Whether it is the quest to bring khat to the market—"first and freshest"—or an encounter at sea to capture container ships, circulation creates both obligations and potential sources of profit and connection. Who is included and excluded from these obligations and connections, as demonstrated by the notebook, is (often) a question of genealogy and kinship, creating a possibility where pirates can be trusted to pay back debts, but the solitary (unknown, unconnected to a kinship group) anthropologist cannot be trusted with a picture ("you could be CIA").

The collateralization of kinship and genealogy within the economy of khat through mechanisms like the *mag* (diya) group has been central to the forms of coping and private governance that characterize post-state Somalia and attempts to construct "governance without government" (Menkhaus 2007; Little 2003). This mode of embedding the economy (Polanyi 1957) can be seen as generating a form of value in "social obligations, connections, and gaps" (Tsing 2013, 22). In the transactions I observed with Aisha, an entire network of relationships was constructed through the sale of khat. From single purchases to gifts given in the spirit of charity, the economy of khat clearly defies the distinction between gift and commodity.[15] This is also a world that defies easy categorization into legal and illegal,[16] formal and informal.

The next day, over lunch, I was telling Sheikh Usman of my meetings with Aisha and how diya made it possible to engage in business transactions with pirates. The Sheikh's response surprised me. "If it were only diya obligations then you would not have all these problems with pirates. The khat merchants are in fact the real pirates in this system." Animated now, the Sheikh began explaining how khat merchants ensnare pirates. "They sell pirates khat at a higher price than the market, so they make money through that. But they also entice pirates. This lady you are speaking about, Aisha, I know she has her own network of spies. If a good ship is captured [one with potential for higher ransoms], she will send expensive khat and also more quantity than the pirate initially ordered." Gesturing towards my plate of biryani, the Sheikh continued, "You're enjoying your biryani. If the hotel guy comes to you and says, 'Instead of saffron color I've put actual saffron from Iran in your rice, and also you asked for goat, but I got you a Japanese cow.'" Sensing that I was a little puzzled, the Sheikh explained that he meant Kobe beef: "You know . . . the one they sing to sleep and wash every day." For Sheikh Usman, the answer was obvious. "Of course, you would eat the meal happily. Then you go to pay, and the hotel owner says 'Don't worry, come back tomorrow.' Imagine now this happens at every meal. For lunch, you get camel and for dinner cows from Japan. Finally, you go to pay and you get a very big bill. You can't say to the owner that you didn't eat any of the items. You may not have wanted them, but now you have to pay for them." After laying out these elaborate and luxurious meals and their disastrous financial consequences, Sheikh Usman returned back to Aisha. "That's what this lady is doing. Watch when the money comes for the ransom, she'll take a very big cut while the guards will be left broke and addicted to khat."

The Sheikh's story reminded me of the pirates who had likened khat to piracy. For them, as for the Sheikh, it was because piracy, like khat, had trapped them in cycles of debt to merchants like Aisha. For Aisha, khat provided a way to generate super-profits from piracy: first, as a percentage of the ransom for services rendered and then, due to the ephemerality of khat and the uncertainty of ransom time, as a payment for the khat chewed by the pirates while they awaited the ransom. The diya group then guaranteed these profits, both through a collateralization of kinship and through transforming accusations of unjust profiteering into an obligation towards kin. As Aisha (and other merchants) would repeatedly remind me, they were not profiteering from piracy: that would be *haram* (unlawful). In fact, I would be told that that framing wasn't even the relevant one. "What matters," explained Aisha, during one of our last meetings in Puntland, "is your obligation towards the diya group . . . that is all I am doing and asking others to do—be responsible to the diya group." "But this Sheikh I know," I responded, "he says merchants like you are the real pirates and in fact Interpol and the US State Department would also think you are a pirate as well." Somewhat ignoring my statement, she launched into a long critique of piracy for promoting what she termed "drunkenness" and "illegal sex." Immediately after, and without a moment of hesitation, she began an equally impassioned critique of financial interdiction and attempts to track money in general, which she argued fail to distinguish properly between "business" and "theft" and between *halal* (lawful) and *haram* (unlawful). "The Americans, I'm not surprised, but if a Sheikh doesn't know the difference between *haram* and *halal* . . . " Letting the statement linger in its incompleteness, she continued, "If you track money like this, we are all pirates; I am a pirate." "So are you a pirate?" I asked, to which she just laughed.

· · ·

As piracy went from sea to ocean, it ironically became more tied to land. Extended periods of time spent in negotiating for ransoms or waiting during the monsoons limited when and for how long pirates could be in the Indian Ocean. Through distinct temporalities, diya networks and the economy of khat helped anchor piracy to land. These modes of anchoring were less to do with legitimizing piracy as an acceptable practice—even while many in Somalia spent a lot of time debating this distinction—but rather about socializing piracy and pirates; creating possibilities of profit and prestige for some and ruin and debt for others.

In that sense, Aisha didn't have to answer my question about Sheikh Usman's accusation. Transforming the risk of piracy into an obligation to the diya group was, for Aisha as for the pirates, a way of converting risk into protection. For pirates, this was the protection to be able to navigate the monsoonal churn and the time of waiting after capturing a ship; for Aisha, it was bracketing discussions and accusations of unjust profiteering and converting them into obligations for kin, all the while ensuring super-profits through khat. These forms of conversion, this move between profit and protection, anchored the economy of piracy to land.

THREE

Regulating the Ocean

THE GOVERNANCE OF COUNTER-PIRACY

"WE'D BEEN AT SEA FOR ABOUT A WEEK at that point and, given our current speed, anticipated being in Mombasa in three to four days." Suraj, an Indian merchant mariner, had been sailing in the Indian Ocean for over twenty years and was accustomed to the ebbs and flows of life at sea. "I take comfort in mathematics," he told me as we sat in his office in Delhi, India. He had retired from life at sea and was now working for an import-exporter—"safely away from the ocean," he emphasized when we met. "I would calculate the possibility of hijackings. You hear all these stories about piracy in Somalia, so there's always a bit of anxiety when you get close to the western Indian Ocean. But on a daily basis so many ships with millions of tonnes of cargo, including oil, are going through the region. So, I would tell myself you only have a 0.3 percent chance of getting hijacked and hope for the best."

On this voyage he was telling me about, Suraj was on the *MV Enterprise*—an eight-thousand-dead-weight-tonne Roll-on/Roll-off carrier loaded with an assortment of second-hand vehicles—heading from Salalah, Oman, to Mombasa. Flying the flag of Mongolia, the *Enterprise,* like many in her class, was affectionately described as a "rust bucket" by the motley crew of Indians, Filipinos, and Syrians who manned the ship. Inside the bridge, an old marine scanner guided the ship through the soupy waters of the western Indian Ocean. Suraj remembered that it was a cloudy moonless night, where the humidity was only occasionally tempered by a faint southwesterly breeze. "We had Hafiz, our Syrian chief mate, who would have been watching the scanner for the AIS [Automatic Identification System] number of passing ships on the screen. On his screen, he would see fuzzy dots with unique registration numbers identifying the ship." But not all those fuzzy dots on the scanner have little numbers attached to them. Lots of little dots—fishing boats, Indian dhows, and other "rust buckets" with faulty AIS transmitters—also show up on the scanner screen without any identification.

"You try to watch, see if anything unusual shows up. If a dot is approaching too close, you get on the radio and get them to adjust accordingly. If it's a fishing boat or dhow, then it's their job to adjust; you just keep going." This night was different: three dots appeared on the stern side and started tailing the ship. Within minutes the boats were next to the ship. There was nothing Hafiz could have done. The ship was overloaded with cargo and could only go as fast as ten knots.

Suraj was on "pirate watch" that night, carrying the replica gun the owners had issued to the crew following orders by their insurance company. "We were not permitted by the insurance contract to have real weapons, so they gave us toy guns," he explained, also mentioning that the shipping company had cut corners and had not followed the recommended best practice list of the insurance company: a list that included installing barbed wire, water cannons, and other defensive measures. Given the darkness of the night and the loud hum of the ship's engine, drowning out any other noise, Suraj's pirate watch was as symbolic as the replica gun he was carrying. "I had no idea until I heard the alarm." The muzzled sound of gunshots near the bridge was what made him realize that the attackers were on board. "I threw my toy gun off the ship, because I didn't want them to panic and shoot . . . I knew at that point we had been captured. There was nothing more for us to do."

While there was nothing more for the crew to do as they were forced to endure the next six months in the cramped hold of the ship somewhere off the coast of Somalia, a visible and invisible world would come to life to secure the release of the ship. Hafiz had sent a mayday when the pirates entered the bridge, a signal received by a NATO warship patrolling the area as part of a counter-piracy mission. In London, the de facto headquarters of the global maritime industry, an insurance company was alerted to the hijacking of its underwritten ship. "All interested parties would be notified in that moment," Suraj explained. "Well, except for Mongolia," he said chuckling, at the peculiarities of shipping governance.

Contemporary counter-piracy—organized ways to protect against pirates in the Indian Ocean—has been studied as a global assemblage that brings together multiple state and private entities to regulate the ocean (Bueger 2018; Struett, Carlson, and Nance 2012). However, studies of counter-piracy operate under a distinction between policing and regulation. One either studies naval patrols and legal trials and their consequences for sovereignty and global governance or, less frequently, focuses on insurance and shipping companies as technocratic modes of regulating the ocean.[1] In essence we continue to operate on a distinction between force and contract. But as this opening vignette shows, with the navy and insurance company both getting involved in the immediate aftermath of a hijacking, force and contract are intimately tied together. An ethnography of counter-piracy, foregrounding both military bases and insurance offices, brings into view modes of regulating the ocean and economies of extraction built on controlling circulation (imperialism) as opposed to modes of extraction dependent on occupation (colonization). Counter-piracy blurs and spills over the boundaries between naval policing and insurance contract and reveals practices of discernment and distinction that make possible this system of governance and its claims over people and objects in global spaces, including over those understood as piratical. These practices have longer histories than contemporary piracy off the coast of Somalia. Let us begin within this rich, historical archive and one gruesome instance of raiding at sea.

MANHUNTING AT SEA

In 1695, the *Ganj-i-Sawai,* one of the largest Mughal trading vessels belonging to the emperor Aurangzeb, was returning to Surat, a major port in western India, with around six hundred pilgrims from Mecca and revenue from the sale of Indian goods at Mocha and Jedda. Given its valuable cargo, the ship was heavily armed with eighty cannons and four hundred muskets, and escorted by another ship, the *Fateh Muhammad.* As the ships sailed across the Bab el Mandeb, from the Red Sea to the Indian Ocean, a ragtag group of pirate vessels led by the notorious "King of Pirates,"[2] the Englishman Henry Avery, started chase. After sacking the *Fateh Muhammad,* Avery's crew pursued the *Ganj-i-Sawai* and, following a ferocious battle, boarded and ransacked the ship. The *Muntakhab al-Lubab,* a seventeenth-century chronicle of Mughal India written by the historian Maulavi Kabir al-Din Ahmad (Khāfī Khān 1869, 420–22), vividly details the treatment meted out by Avery and his crew to the hapless pilgrims on board:

> For a week, the pirates (*duzd darya'i*) tortured the faithful. Beatings and murder were commonplace and even the honor of women was not spared. So much so that many women jumped overboard in order to escape the fate that awaited them. After having remained engaged for a week, in searching

for plunder, stripping the men of their clothes, and dishonoring the old and young women, they left the ship and its passengers to their fate.

This act of piracy jeopardized the tenuous trading relationships of the British East India Company (BEIC) in Mughal India. Established almost a century prior to the *Ganj-i-Sawai* incident as a joint-stock company granted exclusive rights by Queen Elizabeth for trade in the Indian Ocean, the BEIC was a relative newcomer—a weak one at that—within the transregional world economy of the Indian Ocean. Dependent on local merchants for capital and an imperial *farmân* (decree) from the Mughal authorities to trade in India, the fragile relationship between the BEIC and the Mughals was further strained by Avery's capture at sea (Stern 2008).

When news of the attack on the *Ganj-i-Sawai* spread at the ship's home port—Surat—the *Muntakhab* recounts how angered and anguished residents, horrified at the attack on pilgrims returning from Hajj, tried to attack any available English merchants, acting on the assumption that Avery's attack was somehow sponsored, condoned, or facilitated by the East India Company. The Mughal governor intervened to prevent these attacks and also ordered his troops to occupy the East India Company's establishments in Surat and nearby Suwali, to incarcerate their sixty-three employees, and to stop their trade. In audiences with Mughal officials, the English governor of Bombay, Sir John Gayer, tried to distinguish Company employees from Avery, arguing, "We are merchants, not pirates" (Risso 2001, 308). The officials were unimpressed. After nearly a year of negotiations, the employees were finally released and trade reestablished—once the BEIC agreed to hire out two English ships to the Mughals as a protective convoy for the pilgrim vessels of Surat.

As the English governor sought to demarcate distinctions between merchants and pirates, the BEIC and Avery, he elided the fact that the "King of Pirates" had not always been a pirate. Like many English pirates, Avery's career began in the British Navy. Following his naval discharge in 1690, Avery was involved in the transnational slave trade, sailing frequently to the West African coast. From slaver, he transformed into a privateer working as a second mate on the *Charles II,* a warship that targeted French shipping in the Caribbean. Following a mutiny on board over failures of payment, Avery was elected captain and the *Charles II* renamed the *Fancy.* The now piratical *Fancy* sailed south en route to the Indian Ocean, soon plundering five ships off the West African coast before finding a home amongst the burgeoning pirate communities in Madagascar and the Comoros Islands.

This mobility between navy, slaving, privateer, and pirate was not unique to Avery. As Daniel Heller-Roazen (2009) has argued, between the sixteenth and mid-nineteenth centuries the legal categories of "piracy" and "privateering" emerged in close relationship to each other. Documents such as the letter of marque and reprisal—a royal license authorizing the bearer to attack and capture enemy ships—were the only distinction between an act of piracy and a legitimate form of plunder or reprisal at sea. For Heller-Roazen, this blurry boundary between piracy and privateering was crucial in "waging public wars by private means" (Heller-Roazen 2009, 81) and allowed states throughout Europe to demarcate the borders between acceptable and unacceptable violence as well as private and political ends, reserving for sovereigns the capacity to legitimize their violence while criminalizing the violence of rivals and those who resisted their attempts at monopoly.

In the Atlantic world, the "golden age of piracy" can be understood as the aftermath of a long oceanic conflict between free trade and monopoly protection. Privateering, initially financed by monarchs and later by private enterprises, and legally supported by both natural law and legal positivist claims to legitimacy, provided the ability for imperial newcomers (British, Dutch, Swedish, French) to effectively challenge Spanish and Portuguese monopoly in the name of free trade. When, by political or legal decree, privateers proved to be superfluous to sovereign requirements, they were transformed into pirates, and the same sovereign authority that had sought to channel them now sought to hunt them. In Avery's case, this resulted in a manhunt that spanned the Atlantic and the Indian Ocean. However, claims of legality and sovereign authority did not map onto clear demarcations between state and nonstate, public and private.

As noted earlier, the *Ganj-i-Sawai* incident threatened the tenuous relationship between the BEIC and the Mughals. In the immediate aftermath, Company officials were arrested, trade stopped in western Indian ports, and, equally troublingly, Company monopoly over trade—a monopoly granted by royal decree—was threatened by the presence of these British subjects at sea who operated without Company license. The movement of pirates from the Atlantic to the Indian Ocean was productive in manufacturing a "crisis" that transformed the relationship between public and private violence at sea in the Atlantic and the Indian Ocean. Representatives of the BEIC not only called upon the English state for protection and assistance against pirates in the Indian Ocean, but also had to construct piracy as a global problem tied to imposing British imperial hegemony. Rumors circulated of the patronage enjoyed by pirates such as Avery and William Kidd within American colonies. Additionally, pirate ports like Johanna and Saint Marie in the Indian Ocean were described as markets for unscrupulous (American and French) merchants attempting to circumvent provisions of the Navigation Acts. The BEIC capitalized on this anxiety, tying its difficulties with British pirates in the Indian Ocean to wider geopolitical currents and advocating for the creation of state bodies such as the Board of Trade and for expanding the powers of Admiralty Courts.

The *Ganj-i-Sawai* incident gave the BEIC an opportunity not only to call on the British state but also to transform its role. In an attempt to assuage the Mughal emperor Aurangzeb, Samuel Annesley, the BEIC president at Surat, accepted the role of providing escort and protection for Mughal shipping. For the historian Philip Stern, Annesley's acceptance of this role within the parameters of the "Lawes of Nature and Hospitality" highlights a particular vision of the East India Company as a sovereign sea power, "asserting a form of sovereignty over the sea lanes and, remarkably, over Mughal ships and subjects as well" (Stern 2008, 254). For Stern, a vision of the company as a "politie of civill & military power" is a corrective to the traditional understanding of the East India Company as a commercial body that only "'turned' sovereign—accidentally, haphazardly, and unwillingly" (Stern 2008, 254).

Avery himself, who started all this, eluded capture and was rumored to have sailed to Madagascar for a life of retirement with the captured granddaughter of the Mughal emperor. Many of his crew members and other participants in this wider world of "hydrarchy"[3] were not as lucky; the golden age of piracy (1660–1726) came to a harsh and conclusive end with trials and executions across the Atlantic and Indian Oceans.

This modality of governance—manhunts built on practices of discernment and distinction that deny past complicities—is central to the logic of global policing, from Atlantic pirates to the drone warfare[4] that characterizes the global present (Chamayou 2012; Dua 2018). In the case of Somalia, this form of governance transformed piracy into a global problem and established a multinational naval armada as the legitimate protectors against piracy.

THE USES OF FAILED STATES

"Do you know how much it costs to keep the navies out on the ocean patrolling against pirates?" I was sitting in the office of the Minister of Maritime Transport, Ports, and Counter-Piracy. Tucked away in the corner of the Bosaso port, the minister's air-conditioned office was a respite from the heat and port activity. Above the minister's chair, two nautical maps indicating water depths and approaches to the port were prominently displayed along with a portrait of the Puntland president. The portrait seemed to glare at me as I stumbled for an answer. Before I could come up with a number, the minister brought out a file folder and started listing facts and figures. "Right here it says the cost is $1 million a day for the navies to be out at sea," he said, pointing to an international NGO report on the costs of Somali piracy. "And how long have the navies been patrolling? And how many pirates have been arrested? How many ships saved from piracy?"

As we discussed the efficacy—or lack thereof—of the international naval response, the minister pointed to the practice of "catch and release" as a particularly egregious example of the failure of the navies. "When they capture pirates they just end up releasing them back to Somalia. So, many times if they capture some people, they don't know what to do with them. So they take their weapons, they give them enough food, water, and fuel to get back to Somalia, and set them adrift. They call it catch and release." Puzzling over the exorbitant cost of it all, the minister explained that he didn't understand why all that money was spent "just to catch and return pirates back to Somalia. If they gave us even one tenth of that money—actually, I've calculated that all we need is one twentieth of the annual naval budget for counter-piracy in order to solve the piracy problem for good."

I asked him why he felt so confident, given the increase and seeming sophistication of piracy attacks. "You have to understand," he replied, "we know the pirates; they're our cousins, our family ... our clan. We know where they live and what we need to do in order to fight piracy. We just need to be given the right amount of money to protect the world from piracy. Why can't we be given that money?" The minister's question, in addition to being a call for funding, reveals two distinct visions of piracy and, therefore, counter-piracy. Instead of the pirate as the enemy of all mankind, the minister locates the pirate within realms of intimacy, within bonds of kinship and the community. Counter-piracy can then be a localized affair, needing neither global jurisdiction nor a global armada. In contrast, constructing piracy and counter-piracy as global problems requires unmooring these figures from the ebbs and flows of the western Indian Ocean and shifting scales in order to produce pirates and regimes of counter-piracy. The creation of both is a process that involved the exclusion of Somali actors and was premised on an understanding of the exclusion of Somalia from the family of nation-states.

FIGURE 5: Naval antipiracy patrol.

Failure, specifically state failure, was productive in the making of these exclusions. To understand this process, let us move away from the littoral world of the Indian Ocean to the imperial capitals of Washington, DC, and London.

Over lunch at the Army/Navy Club in Washington, DC, Rear Admiral Terry McKnight, the former commander of the United States Navy's counter-piracy operations in the western Indian Ocean, described to me the precise moment when "the United States Navy and the global community got serious about Somali piracy." The admiral told this through the story of a ship, the *MV Danica White*:

> It was Friday June 1, 2007, 205 miles off the coast of Somalia, when pirates hijacked the *MV Danica White*. A twenty-year-old, 200-foot bulk carrier, the *Danica* was the perfect ship for pirates to capture. The ship was making six knots against a southerly wind and current. The five-person crew had no special watch or evasive measures in place to protect against piracy and the freeboard was less than five feet. The only thing missing, honestly, was a "welcome pirates" doormat! (Admiral McKnight, interview with the author, February 2012)

Once the ship had been hijacked, the admiral noted, the *Danica* drastically changed course and started heading towards land. The *USS Carter Hall,* an amphibious assault ship operating as part of Combined Task Force 150 (a multi-national counter-terrorism force established after September 11, 2001, to patrol and monitor the Horn of Africa), noted this erratic shift and started following the *Danica*. "After sending a private captain's message to the ship and contacting the ship's owners in Copenhagen, the *Carter Hall* realized the ship had been hijacked and began following *Danica* while awaiting orders from Bahrain." The admiral then proceeded to tell a riveting tale of hot pursuit at sea:

The *Danica White* did not change course or slow down. The skipper of *Carter Hall* had done everything short of disabling maneuvers and boarding the ship. When the shipowners suggested disabling the ship, the command center in Bahrain declined because they were worried about the safety of the hijacked crew. It's a risk and cost-and-benefit analysis for us, and endangering the life of the seafarer is never worth it. All the *Carter Hall* could do was fire warning shots, sink the skiffs attached to the ship, and watch as the *Danica White* inched closer towards the territorial waters of Somalia. Once the *Danica White* entered Somali waters, we were instructed not to violate Somali maritime sovereignty. The crew of the *Carter Hall* could only watch, even though it is a failed state. It was like a kid's game: they got past the line without being tagged, and they were free. (Admiral McKnight, interview with the author, February 2012)

In the aftermath of the *Danica White* incident, the spectral fiction of Somali sovereignty was gradually disbanded. Five months later, in October 2007, when the *MV Golden Nori* was captured—the tale of capture that began this book—US and German destroyers did not stop at the boundary of Somali territorial waters but instead blockaded the port of Bosaso in northern Somalia. A navy lawyer who had been involved in this event remarked to me that "no one at that point [in the *Golden Nori* incident] would dare say out loud that we were violating Somali sovereignty . . . In any case, the hijacking was a terrorist action in the making and we knew the question of legal authority would be moot in this ticking bomb scenario."

Within the framework of counter-piracy, the *Danica White* and *Golden Nori* hijackings gave the international community an impetus to move beyond what the admiral referred to as the "tyranny of borders" and transform an "over-the-horizon form of policing" into active engagement and intervention. These hijackings heralded the beginning—de facto if not de jure—of a new global war on piracy, one that traveled alongside and built on the legal and regulatory architecture of the ongoing global war on terror.[5]

To transform this de facto governance into de jure recognition would require the construction of a legal architecture. Almost a year after the *Nori* incident and following the hijacking of the largest ship ever to be hijacked (the US-bound, 1,090-foot, very large crude carrier (VLCC) *MV Sirius Star,* 450 miles southeast of the Kenyan coast) in June 2008, the UN Security Council adopted a series of resolutions to construct the legal edifice for the twenty-first century's global war on piracy.

Prior to 2008, international counter-piracy efforts were thwarted by the inapplicability of the international law of piracy in territorial waters. The legal definition of piracy as codified in article 101 of the UNCLOS emphasizes piracy as an act that occurs on the "high seas": that is, in maritime zones that are legally understood to be outside the control of any sovereign authority (UN 1982). Most acts of hijacking from 2007 onwards occurred in Somali territorial waters (Hansen 2009; Murphy 2011), thus providing hijackers a degree of freedom to operate in these waters.

Acting under the Chapter VII powers of the Security Council, which deals with the UN's authority to address threats to international peace and security, the Security Council adopted Resolution 1816 on June 2, 2008, to remove this legal safe haven. Through this resolution the Security Council authorized cooperating states to "take the same steps with respect to piracy in the Somali territorial sea as the law of piracy permits on the high seas" (Roach 2010, 400). The 2008 resolutions on counter-piracy (UN Security Council Resolutions 1816, 1838, 1846, and 1851) effectively dissolved distinctions between land and sea, territorial waters and high seas—distinctions that have been central to the construction of piracy as a legal category separate from armed robbery and smuggling (Heller-Roazen 2009; Benton 2002). In doing so it brought the definition closer to the one used by insurance companies, which do not distinguish between territorial and international waters.

In addition to respatializing piracy as an act that can occur in territorial waters and even on land, these resolutions placed the newly emerging coalition of national navies at the center of counter-piracy operations and gave them authority to take "all necessary means or measures at sea and on land to suppress piracy and armed robbery at sea."[6] By 2009, an international armada consisting of over thirty states operating under three distinct naval coalitions (Bueger and Stockenbrugger 2013) had assembled in order to police the waters off the coast of Somalia against these newly legally defined pirates.

Beyond transforming a set of diverse practices of taking at sea into "piracy," the counter-piracy regime relocated the field of operations for Somali pirates—pushing them from sea to ocean. Along with naval and aerial surveillance, the international counter-piracy coalition sought to construct a heavily patrolled transit corridor through the Red Sea. The Internationally Recommended Transit Corridor (IRTC) for shipping in the Gulf of Aden was envisioned as a "tightly controlled and centripetal disciplinary space" (Glück 2015, 649) to facilitate safe mobility through this region. Consisting of a 492-mile corridor with eastbound and westbound shipping lanes, the IRTC provided heavily armed group transits for ships traveling at differential speeds. These group transits were successful in eliminating attacks on ships traveling along the corridor, but ended up expanding the world of piracy from the Red Sea to the wider Indian Ocean. By 2010, attacks had occurred at places as far removed as nine miles off the coast of India and the Mozambique Channel. Ironically, counter-piracy ended up producing pirates in the international legal sense of actors engaged in forms of illegal taking on the high seas, and thus justifying itself as a global response.

SECURITY AND CIRCULATION IN THE GULF OF ADEN

Located in the quiet suburb of Northwood, a few miles from central London, the 1950s-style office block that serves as the headquarters of the EU counter-piracy mission conveys very little of its central role in operations in the western Indian Ocean. Walking into a building marked "Multi-National Headquarters," I navigated the complex maze of security protocols to enter the hub of the building alongside Colonel Pierre, a French naval officer working for the European Union's counter-piracy taskforce (EU-NAVFOR-ATALANTA). As we made our way past security, the colonel described the unprecedented logistical coordination that transpired on a daily basis inside this office complex. "On an average day, we have about twenty to thirty vessels patrolling the Gulf of Aden. Mostly it's EU, NATO, and US forces, but also vessels from India, China, Iran, Russia, and Thailand." When I remarked that it must be difficult to coordinate between all these countries, the colonel shrugged, "Well, I haven't even told you about the aircraft surveillance, and the manned and unmanned craft that patrol the Gulf of Aden. It's really an unprecedented multinational coalition. Here in Northwood we are coordinating between all these different stakeholders, keeping track of ships and personnel. As you can imagine, our job requires a great deal of coordination and engagement across all these different sectors."

The EU counter-piracy operation in the Indian Ocean spans three continents and employs over two thousand military personnel to provide what the officer described as a "24-hour manned response to the threat of piracy." Incidents of piracy, both attempted and successful, are updated on a live piracy map that circulates between navies, shipping companies, and insurance agencies. Regular fly-bys and aerial surveillance through manned and unmanned craft create detailed and often classified mapping of this oceanic space. In addition, naval ships and helicopters regularly patrol shipping lanes

with full authorization to board suspicious vessels through procedures ranging from friendly approaches—where small boats launched from the navy
ship will "meet" merchant ships and fishing boats—to full-fledged search-
and-seizure operations.

At the Northwood monitoring station these disparate "data" are visualized
onto maps and satellite images that function as "maps of legibility" (Scott 1998,
3), transforming a vast seascape into knowable grids and quadrants. As Colonel
Pierre and I watched the dots moving slowly across the map of the Gulf of
Aden, I asked him about life at sea. Leaning back into his chair, his gaze still
focused on the satellite map, the colonel spoke about the distance between
representation and reality. "These dots," he began, pointing to the screen, "they
can tell us many things, but I'm a sailor." Repeating this for emphasis, he continued, "For a sailor like me there is much more to navigating than a point on
the map." Turning to me, he asked, "What's your background, have you ever
manned a ship?" When I replied that I had no nautical experience, the colonel,
looking slightly taken aback, attempted to convey life at sea to me. "When
you're sailing, you want to feel the wind, to feel the roll of the ship: Is it choppy
or calm? How long before the next port? The sense of anxiety, anticipation:
that is part of sailing and determines so many decisions captains make."
Looking at the map, he noted, "I don't know what these captains are thinking,
what they're feeling. In case of a piracy attack, we can't anticipate how the
captain and crew will react. We just watch and determine if something out of
the ordinary is happening. We're *managing* from afar here."[7]

This form of management from afar becomes apparent in moments of
suspected attacks. Consider what happens when a ship reports a suspicious
vessel sighting:

Vessel Captain: We have suspicious vessels approaching us from the aft.
Please advise.

United Kingdom Marine Trade Operations [UKMTO]: Can you tell us
your location?

Vessel Captain: [lists location and weather conditions]

UKMTO: We have contacted the nearest navy vessel and they are heading
towards you. At this point we need you to follow our instructions. Begin
evasive measures. 1) Sound alarm, get crew to move to the citadel. 2) Increase
cruising speed. 3) Move in a zig-zag manner to create a greater wake making it more difficult for pirates to board. 4) If you have hoses or other active
deterrents engage them now.[8]

As the ship begins these procedures, another team is communicating with the navy patrols and making determinations about time and speed. One of the coordinators explained: "As we're watching the skiffs approach, we're making a decision whether this is a fishing vessel that's gone off course or indeed a pirate attack." Even pirate-infested waters, he reminded me, are not empty spaces. "We have fishing vessels, dhows, and other legitimate boats. So, step one is about excluding the possibility of a jumpy captain."

Once a determination is made that this is indeed a piracy attack, the coordinators step into a different mode of management. "At that point, we're figuring out if we can carry out a successful disruption of the attack. If the answer is affirmative, we have to keep guiding the merchant vessel and the naval ship. Sometimes we send out helicopters or launch small RIBs [Rigid Hull Inflatable Boats] to scare off the pirates. Other times the goal is to arrest the pirates. But if the ship is out of luck . . . you know, things like no patrol vessel in sight or it is too heavily loaded, then we prepare the crew and captain to be hijacked. That's the toughest thing to do. You're basically saying, 'Sorry, we can't do anything. Good luck with what happens next.'"

This kind of decision-making, of "managing" within a set of finite possibilities, is determined through deciding what are legitimate boats as opposed to pirate skiffs, and determining when to attack as opposed to suggest evasion. The kinds of decision-making that characterize who is a pirate versus who is a fisherman emerge in everyday practice within counter-piracy, a near-constant mode of management as vessels transit through these waters.

In Djibouti, one of the "forward-operating bases" for this counter-piracy regime, these everyday practices become starkly visible. Located strategically on the Bab-el Mandeb, allowing it to control access to the Red Sea and the Indian Ocean, Djibouti has, since its independence from France in 1977, engaged in a form of locational arbitrage in order to emerge as a key security and commercial hub for the Horn of Africa.[9] From the port run by Dubai Ports World to the foreign military bases, Djibouti—echoing James Ferguson's (2005) reflections on "enclave capitalism"—is perhaps one of the best examples of the transformation of sovereignty into contract for capital extraction.[10] After I had been in Djibouti for a few weeks, living with French legionnaires and observing antipiracy drills at the French military base, I finally got the phone call letting me know I had permission to board an EU vessel.

Intermingled with dhows and merchant ships, the counter-piracy naval vessels at the port of Djibouti seem both accessible and a world removed from the buzz of the port. Security barriers prevent easy access, although the soldiers allow stevedores to mill about next to the barriers on the docks. With my visitor badge, I was escorted onto a waiting SUV at the entrance of the special security area where naval vessels were docked. Once we got to the ship, a young midshipman walked me up the bridge inside the heart of the naval destroyer. Unlike the merchant ships I had visited until then, the destroyer was remarkable both for its order and for the fact that none of the instruments looked old or weatherworn. The mix of humidity, salt water, and smell of sweat I had come to associate with ships was noticeably absent. The combination of accents, uniforms, and air-conditioning conjured up a miniature version of Northwood, the headquarters of the EU taskforce.

Ships, as the historian Lauren Benton has highlighted, "played a dual role as sources of order in the ocean; they were islands of law with their own regulations and judicial personnel, and they were representatives of 'municipal' legal authorities—vectors of crown law thrust into ocean space" (Benton 2005, 704). This description of a dual role seemed to fit the EU destroyer itself as much as the era of European expansion that Benton writes about. Naval ships are disciplinary regimes par excellence, while simultaneously projecting themselves as islands of law in a sea of piracy.

During patrols along the IRTC in the Red Sea, mornings begin with the sound of the ship's public announcement system. The midshipman explained that on his previous ship, the broadcast often included the *Lion King* soundtrack, explained by the fact that "we are in Africa, after all." The days tick along with mechanical precision—the constant humming of the engines the only reminder that we're on a floating base. Within the world of vessels at sea, destroyers are the sturdiest: pitch and roll are almost absent. The ship was engaged in both escort and patrol duties. "We are the policemen of the Red Sea," remarked the captain one afternoon over lunch. "If we wanted to end piracy, it would be very simple: just go occupy Somalia. We have the intelligence reports, we know where all the bases are. All you need to do is attack them on land, but no one has an appetite for that. The EU is not about to occupy Somalia and the Americans got burnt with Iraq and also are in a mess with Afghanistan. So, we sit back and hopefully deter them enough to stop . . . there is no end goal to this operation, just potentially the end of the mandate."

Policing for pirates, I heard reiterated, was not about the elimination of all piracy everywhere, but the management of piracy incidents within an optimal range.[11] This entails not only a military response, but also creating and designating what Michel Foucault (2004) calls the "milieu" within which circulation occurs. The milieu for Foucault is needed to account for action at a distance of one body on another, "[the] medium of an action and the element in which it circulates" (2004, 22). Policing for pirates is not simply about finding pirates "out there," but rather constructing a physical and social seascape within which good circulation (shipping) is separated from bad circulation (piracy). It is within this seascape that an everyday form of distinction occurs to separate out pirates from other vessels. This involves staring at computer screens in Northwood, Dubai, Kuala Lumpur, and Bahrain, as well as on board patrol ships.

This management requires practices of seeing and surveillance, practices characterized by a host of technologies including drones and radar and an investment of hours and days of anticipation and waiting. On board the coalition patrol vessel, Karl, a member of a Danish boarding team, described standing on the bridge for hours on end scanning the choppy waters of the Gulf of Aden during his deployment with the naval transit corridor force. Even though naval ships come equipped with the most sophisticated sonar and radar systems, Karl explained the need for standing on the bridge with binoculars in hand. "Sometimes there is an echo on the radar, so we can't confirm if there is a boat or not without a visual check. There are also radar blind spots," he remarked, pointing to a diagram on the bridge that highlighted zones near the aft side where the radar often doesn't work.

In addition to visual surveillance, Karl and other officers on the bridge kept themselves busy, especially at night by calling vessels on the radio. Navy ships tend to switch off their AIS during patrols and thus don't appear on a merchant ship's radar. "If a ship is steering too close to us, we'll get on the radio and advise them to change course." Pointing to a "target" (the term used to refer to another vessel at sea), the officer explained, "see, if I click on the target, I can see its true bearing [horizontal angle between the direction of an object and another object] and can tell if it's on a collision course with us." In this case, the vessel was moving in the opposite direction, so we simply watched the dot gradually drift away. On the radar are also little electronic notes, including a geomapping of piracy incidents. For Karl, these notes were a reminder that "when you're escorting merchant vessels you realize that the threat of piracy is always present with you. For the days you're assigned to escort duty, you can never rest because you're constantly wondering when the next piracy incident will be and if you'll be close enough to respond. Most of the time, though, you're just waiting and watching . . . with the occasional burst of action."

These occasional bursts of action are documented in grainy cell phone videos that circulate amongst those involved in counter-piracy, and increasingly are also posted on YouTube. These videos, as well as the more "official" biometric and video surveillance that is essential to accounting every engagement with suspicious vessels at sea, share a similar aesthetic: that of the first-person-shooter video game. In one cell phone video that was shown to me, the clip began with a panorama of the vast emptiness of the ocean from the vantage point of the stern of the vessel. Suddenly, from what appears to be the break of a particularly choppy wave, a skiff materializes and seems to be accelerating towards the ship. As we watch the skiff approach from the side, a series of rapid and controlled bursts punctuates the ambient sound of wind and waves. A voice narrates, "Skiff engaged, warning rounds fired." The skiff now is much closer and, in the video, it's impossible to tell how many people are on board, but it is clear that there are at least six. The camera shakes and switches direction as a second boat appears and approaches the starboard side of the vessel. More gunfire. Another voice shouts, "Second skiff approaching, these are not fishermen, engage both skiffs." At this point, a hail of gunfire erupts as the two skiffs approach from the port and starboard side. The two skiffs suddenly change direction and stop pursuit. Offscreen, a marine jokes, "Can you believe it? They tried to capture a warship." His companion, also unseen, responds: "A bad day to be a Somali pirate, I guess."

If the global manhunt against Avery in the seventeenth century was predicated on effacing the history of complicity between BEIC and Avery and excluded him from the legal protections of the privateer, contemporary counter-piracy seeks to separate out "innocent" fishermen and "criminal" pirates. This process of sifting and separation is one that occurs within the everyday proceduralism of surveillance—practices of watching and waiting. This is a process that also occurs violently, as the video demonstrates. Force is key in shaping the global regime of counter-piracy. If navies are one actor in this world, an often-hidden actor is maritime insurance, the existence of which serves to highlight another aspect to this logic of counter-piracy: namely, the importance of counter-piracy as market-making in ways that combine regulation and profit.

RISKY TRADES: THE EMERGENCE OF
MARITIME INSURANCE

On January 23, 1977, during a routine voyage from the Italian Port of Chioggia to Hong Kong, the Panamanian-flagged but Dutch-owned freighter *Lucona* was sailing across the Indian Ocean when, without warning, a powerful explosion in the hold destroyed the hull. Almost instantly, the ship went down, disappearing into the deep blue waters two hundred miles north of the Maldives. Only six of the twelve crew members survived the explosion and were found, dazed and floating on the ship's life raft, about ten hours later by a Turkish oil tanker. Incidents like the *Lucona* explosion, while uncommon, are nonetheless part of the perils of being at sea. However, it became clear that something unusual was afoot in this matter when the cargo owner, an Austrian businessman, Udo Proksch, with political connections and a fantastically shady past, claimed the equivalent of $18 million in damages from the marine insurance company. Proksch had insured the cargo as materials for a uranium-ore processing mill that was to be delivered to an unnamed client in Asia. The high value of the cargo aroused the suspicions of the insurance company. As is typical in most marine insurance contracts, ship and cargo usually belong to separate owners and are insured under separate policies. The insurance company paid the Dutch shipowners, but refused Proskch's claim on the cargo. After years of suits and countersuits, an equally colorful private investigator hired by the insurance company, a Swiss man known as Dirty Dietmar, found evidence that Proskch had lied about the cargo—it was worthless wreckage from a broken conveyer belt—and had deliberately blown up the ship using a time-bomb. Eventually, divers for a search-and-rescue company found the wreckage of the *Lucona,* corroborating Dirty Dietmar's digging, and evidence collected from these dives was used to successfully prosecute Proskch (Mullen 1991).

I learned about the *Lucona* case at a seminar on marine insurance frauds in London. Organized by entities such as Maritime London and other trade associations for shipping and marine insurance employees working in London, events like this seminar are a vital part of professionalization for the thousands who work in London's maritime sector. In 2010, I conducted field-work within this maritime industry which entailed shadowing insurance underwriters, working at a risk analysis division for a marine insurance company, and attending seminars on various aspects of insurance. After this brief story about "coffin ships" (overinsured ships) like the *Lucona,* the seminar turned into a technical discussion on practices of due diligence for insurance underwriters.

From the frailty of ships and sailors to the perils of rough winds and jagged rocks, from unscrupulous businessmen on land to pirates at sea, oceanic voyages are characterized by omnipresent, yet uncertain, dangers. Yet it was precisely this risk that also provided the possibility of profit within the world of long-distance trade. In her discussion of double-entry bookkeeping, Mary Poovey (1998, 62) emphasizes that "early modern commerce *depended* on the excessiveness of risk to writing, for the fluctuations in pricing, production, and demand were the source of the profit that made commerce worth pursuing in the first place." For long-distance trade, risk was both peril and profit.

Given the risks entailed in maritime trade, it is little surprise that insurance originally emerged within the context of seafaring and oceanic commerce. Insurance contracts in their earliest form were agreements that entailed the transference of risk; one party agreed to retroactively compensate the other party for losses incurred. From the outset, however, questions of fraud and unjust profiteering framed the contract of insurance. The possibilities of large losses (and profits) meant that maritime trade required pools of credit, loans, or other ways of spreading risk. Within this system of risk pooling, the avoidance of usury or interest emerged as a central concern. The ancient Greek practice of bottomry is one of the earliest recorded forms of marine insurance and one of the first mechanisms of dealing with allegations of usury. Instead of a direct transfer of risk, bottomry can be likened to a mortgage whereby the master of the ship borrowed money against the bottom or hull of the ship. If the ship was lost at sea, the lender would lose the money advanced; if the ship arrived in the port of destination, the lender would get back the loan, along with a previously agreed-upon premium (Trenerry 1926). Bottomry became one of the most popular forms of insurance in the ancient Mediterranean world due, in part, to its simplicity and the ability of insurers to secure profits that escaped prevalent sanctions against usury. Merchants argued that bottomry was a product that could be exchanged and not interest on a loan.

Insurance contracts were also central to the world of Indian Ocean commerce. *Musharakah* (risk-sharing) partnerships and *mudarabah* (profit-sharing) agreements were common from at least the tenth century onwards. As it was for their Mediterranean counterpart, the question of *riba* (usury) was key to these contracts. Through complex forms of loss- and profit-sharing agreements, traders sought to insure cargo whilst avoiding allegations of interest-taking as well as *sudfa* (seeking profit from chance). Importantly, and in contrast to bottomry, these contracts often did not insure the value of the ship and only guaranteed cargo. As one commentary notes, a wrecked ship is like "a camel that lacks strength in the middle of the journey" (Al-Qarafi 2001).

By the thirteenth century, an incipient insurance industry had developed in the port city of Genoa, institutionalizing bottomry and other maritime loans. Merchants adopted complex systems of insurance and credit for sea voyages, especially those involved in the Indies trade. Land voyages and intra-European trade were usually not insured. Insurance at this point was still associated with "rich trades," i.e., trades in overseas commodities such as spices, silks, cotton fabrics, and semi-precious and precious stones and metals. These cargoes traveled long distances in well-armed ships and fetched high profits at port cities throughout Europe. In opposition, the intra-European bulk trade mostly included goods such as grain and hides; "the ratio of value to cargo space was not favorable enough to require insurance" (Ebert 2011, 102). While the problem of usury was easily discarded through the construction of techniques like bottomry that created spaces for profit beyond interest, the relationship between insurance and other (unethical) speculative practices like gambling was trickier to navigate and remained central to anxieties about the expansion and institutionalization of insurance.

What was needed to assuage these anxieties was both an epistemological shift and, closely tied to it, a form of institutionalization that legitimized insurance, transforming it into a system of protection and profit. According to Giovanni Ceccarelli, "as soon as the economic use of random events [was] no longer considered as a divinatory practice, insurance could be considered a form of collective defense from the threats of chance" (2001, 631). The more "modern" types of insurance contract that developed in Pisa and Florence in the fourteenth century involved paying a premium against risk to an underwriter or a group of underwriters. This expanded role of insurance becomes apparent in insurance manuals that started appearing from the fourteenth century.

As one such fifteenth-century manual on insurance underwriting noted, the insurance underwriter had a responsibility of "gathering all the news that comes from the sea and to pay special attention to them, to constantly ask for and inquire on pirates and other evil people, wars, truces, reprisals and all the things that may perturb the sea" (quoted in Ceccarelli 2007, 5). The manual goes on to highlight that the merchant/underwriter must be knowledgeable of "the seaports and the beaches, of the distance from one place to another and they must take into account the conditions of the captains . . . and they must consider the merchandise since all these elements are required" (quoted in Ceccarelli 2007, 5). This treatise, one of the most detailed medieval analyses of insurance premiums, was key to Mediterranean maritime practice.

Here we see insurance contracts moving beyond mere retrospective compensation to also account for future possibilities. This innovation transformed marine insurance into protection. Instead of a contract to compensate for loss retroactively, insurance became a defense against a future setback, whose contours were yet unknown, including the threat of pirates, thus recognizing the role of insurance as a form of counter-piracy. However, this transformation meant confronting questions around divination and profiteering from speculation.

The anxieties over divination and unethical speculation were resolved through both epistemological and regulatory shifts, at least in the context of Europe. The probabilistic revolution of the late seventeenth and early eighteenth centuries entailed a shift from prophesy to prognosis—the move from the unknowability of God's will to an "evental thinking" (Gigerenzer 1989; Roitman 2014; Koselleck 2004), where action in the present became a mode of governing a future. This mode of governance transformed the grounds upon which debates over ethical and unethical risk-taking emerged (Lobo-Guerrero 2012).

From the beginning, insurance was a decentralized practice that gave individual insurers (who were often themselves merchants) the possibility to generate profits through hedging the right bets. If ships successfully returned from oceanic voyages, insurers could reinvest those profits into other business ventures. As the market for insurance items expanded, the ability to profit also expanded, and so too did the possibility of loss and financial ruin. This expanding insurance market created a form of insurance mania, especially in the newly emerging realm of life insurance where people sought to insure everything from body parts to the lives of complete strangers (Clark 1999).[12] Necessitated in part by the need to regulate this expansion of insurance as speculation, a series of regulatory and institutional acts in England brought insurance within the fold of the early modern state: notably, through the creation of the Chamber of Assurances (1576); the Assurance Act of 1601, which established a Court of Assurances to settle disputes over insurance matters; the Bubble Act of 1720, which restricted the formation of corporations to those with royal charters; and, finally, the 1745 Maritime Insurance Act and the 1774 Life Assurance Act, which solidified England's role in the institutionalization and expansion of insurance.

Specifically, the 1745 Maritime Insurance Act, in its distinction between "passion and interest," created the element of "economic interest" as a necessary precondition to insurance. The Life Assurance Act went further and forbade "insurers to cover people or events where the insurer could not prove an interest in the person or event insured against" (Maurer 2005, 137) at the time of making an insurance claim (Hirschman 1977; de Goede 2003). Linking the ability to profit to a matrix of economic interest was thus a way of delimiting who could (and could not) profit, but it also set the stage for the development of an insurance industry, with maritime insurance at its helm. This insurance industry, headquartered in London, transformed insurance practices from mercantile strategies into storehouses for capital and investment. Knowledge practices, legal regimes, and commercial interests came together in this space of accumulation to "perform" the market (Bourdieu 1977; Boyer 2005; Callon 1998; Weber [1968] 1978).

Tying insurance to interests was a way of sorting out legitimate and illegitimate forms of profiteering as well as turning the insurance contract from an individual relationship between the insurer and the insured to a properly socialized relationship. Profit- and loss-sharing could now be understood as a group endeavor to transform "uncertainty into risk" (Knight 1921, 11), a legitimate, collective form of protection. The centrality of insurance to oceanic commerce meant that these questions often appeared most clearly with respect to the hazards of maritime trade, specifically in the case of piracy—one of the originals perils of the sea. Here we see the protection of insurance transforming into a mode of governing (and profiting from) counter-piracy.

LLOYD'S AND THE PIRATES:
COUNTER-PIRACY AND PROTECTION

In the summer of 2010, I conducted fieldwork at a maritime insurance firm affiliated with Lloyd's of London that was developing norms and policies to manage piracy off the coast of Somalia. As the oldest and largest of maritime insurance companies, Lloyd's of London has historically played an important role in shaping these insurance norms. From its origins as a coffeehouse run by Edward Lloyd on Tower Street in 1686, where merchants, sailors, and shipowners would gather to receive and exchange shipping news, Lloyd's has become the world's largest marketplace for insurance and reinsurance. In the labyrinthine atrium of its headquarters at One Lime Street is the massive underwriting room, where hundreds of "members" (underwriters) sit daily, drawing up insurance contracts that cover everything from celebrity body parts to damages from natural disasters and, given its maritime history, piracy.

The maritime echoes of Lloyd's Coffee House are found everywhere in this underwriting room, from the shipping bell used to announce major trades to the wood-paneled desks built from the wreckage of old ships. What is elided is the central role Lloyd's played in the transatlantic slave trade. In his powerful treatise on capitalism and slavery, the historian Eric Williams (1994) named Lloyd's as one of the biggest profiteers in this system. Insurance, underwritten by organizations like Lloyd's, was central in aggregating the risks of transatlantic shipping, including the risks involved in transatlantic slavery. These profits, which emerged in part from the transatlantic slave trade, were reinvested into a burgeoning industrial capitalism.[13]

In addition to this history of profiteering, Lloyd's—and maritime insurance in general—exerts a form of governance over shipping. The notion of insurance as governance has been productively used to understand the manifold ways in which insurance exercises control over institutions and everyday life, enacting a form of government beyond the state (Ewald 1991; Ericson, Doyle, and Barry 2003). Ulrich Beck (1992) has noted that the logic of insurance—namely, risk management—signifies a wider shift in the organization of society: the creation of a "risk society" built around discourses of safety and the future. Building on these insights, a rich scholarly literature has described the disaggregating effects of insurance or highlighted its continued moral valences (Knights and Vurdubakis 1993; Baker and Simon 2010; de Goede 2003; Golomski 2015; Kar 2014; Zelizer [1979] 2017). This scholarship has oscillated between the poles of disembedded or embedded, either emphasizing the historical transformation from informal to formal sectors or noting the salience, indeed necessity, of nonmarket forms of risk pooling in order to show how insurance reorients relationships of obligation from communities and the state to the individual and thus is key to neoliberal governmentality. Bringing maritime insurance—the original form of insurance—into this conversation not only adds an important dimension missing from this literature, but also accentuates the fact that the governance of insurance occurs not simply at an individual level, but across scale and space.

During my fieldwork, numerous underwriters told me that the larger question for marine insurance is how best to protect shipping. As Philip, an underwriter and Lloyd's member, put it, "When you look out from a port and see a cargo ship sailing away, what we [the underwriters] see is a common maritime adventure." Traditionally, ships are owned by one set of interests and the cargo by another. This means that each party has its own insurance, often taking on disproportionate risk and chance of loss. For example, if a

FIGURE 6: Lloyd's of London insurance underwriting room.

ship is unbalanced and the captain decides to throw out some cargo, then according to the common maritime adventure principle, the loss is divided equally. It is not the sole responsibility of the cargo insurance. The common maritime adventure principle underscores that the protection of insurance is not merely an individual contract between insurer and insured, but one socialized within circuits of obligation.

In addition, the question of how to protect shipping is explicitly about the division of violence globally, and cuts across the divide of sovereignty and biopolitics, of threat and security, that undergirds contemporary studies of regulation and governance. A particular feature of contemporary shipping is its international nature. As the Maritime Knowledge Center of the International Maritime Organization notes:

> Shipping is perhaps the most international of all the world's great industries. The ownership and management chain surrounding any particular vessel can embrace many different countries; it is not unusual to find that the owners, operators, shippers, charterers, insurers, and the classification society, not to mention the officers and crew, are all of different nationalities and that none of these is from the country whose flag flies at the ship's stern. (IMO-MKC 2008)

The international nature of the shipping economy and the policy of flags of convenience, a system whereby a ship flies the flag of a country other than the country of ownership as a way to avoid regulatory regimes and tax burdens, creates regulatory lacunas. Ensuring the seaworthiness of a ship ostensibly falls on the flag state. However, countries like the Marshall Islands, Belize, and even land-locked Mongolia, which account for the flags of most ships, merely provide the fig leaf of de jure control and exert few if any de facto forms of governance over ships registered in their name. As the anthropologist Bill Maurer (1997) has noted in the case of offshore finance in the British Virgin Islands, sovereignty for numerous "small places" is tied to a form of marketable identity. The open-registry system in shipping that emerged from the 1980s decoupled ownership of the ship from the ship's national registration and provided small states an opportunity for market sovereignty. By 1992, a few years after the implementation of open-registry, most companies had moved from the shipping registers of the United States, the United Kingdom, and Europe to boutique registries across the globe.

Open registries and flags of convenience transfer the role of governance onto maritime insurance. "There is an understanding all the way from IMO to flag states that insurance companies are now regulating this economy," I heard repeatedly in my first weeks at Ship Safe, where insurance agents described the insurance contract as a key document enacting governance over shipping. For Philip and other underwriters, the insurance contract was not only a guarantee of compensation for future loss, but a "tacit form of approval that the crew are hired properly and things like pollution controls are in place. When we insure a ship, we are vouching for that ship."

Another underwriter, Greg, decided to give me a quick lesson in contract underwriting in order to explain the specificity of marine insurance. Underwriting for shipping differs from any other kind of insurance, because shipping, he said, is about a "moving risk." As he explained, "We create a system based on a detailed risk profile." This detailed risk profile begins with a standard marine insurance contract; then, underwriters and shipping representatives create a set of exclusions—incidents that will not be covered by the insurance company. Handing me a marine insurance contract, Greg pointed to the regular exclusions in the document. "As you can see, there is boilerplate language here about exclusions such as negligence, inherent vice, delay in carriage, ordinary wear and tear, and lack of due diligence." After a brief pause, he added, "This is basic stuff. Where marine insurance [contracts] are different is that, more than any other [insurance] industry, we tend to have all-risk policies as opposed to named peril coverage."

Choosing between named peril and all-risk is about the transformation of the burden of proof in the event of loss and is common to most insurance practices. When policies are written on a named peril basis, the insured have the burden of proof that the loss emerged directly as a result of that peril. In the case of all-risk coverage, all losses unless explicitly excluded are covered. Given the moving risk of maritime insurance and the precarity of cargo and ship, marine insurance tends to be an all-risk policy system. "This means the underwriter needs to be smart," Greg emphasized. "I have to make sure I can protect the cargo and also my insurance company. Imagine the disaster if I sent out a ship to Somalia on an all-risk cover without a piracy exclusion. If the ship were hijacked, we [the insurance company] would be paying all of the costs out of pocket." He paused, and with a grin added, "We'd be screwed!"

In addition to the exclusion clause, insurance companies, especially in the case of piracy, are actively involved in forms of "indirect steering" (Habermas 1995) that touch upon the distribution of violence at sea such as approving the hiring of private guards or giving rebates for lethal and nonlethal forms of deterrent against piracy attacks. If insurance, as François Ewald (1991, 207) has argued, "functions as a *political technology* ... of social forces mobilized and utilized in a very specific way," then marine insurance is a political technology central to creating a system of protection and reparation for the shipping industry. As one underwriter noted, "Without maritime insurance, there is no justice for the seafarer." This form of justice includes the ability to compensate, but also crucially to redistribute the risks (and rewards) of oceanic voyages. The governance of maritime insurance is not simply a system of regulating and indemnifying individual ships or shipping companies, but a system of shifting protection costs across a global economy.

Protection against piracy has been a central aspect of this system of shifting protection costs going back to the earliest documented cases of maritime insurance contracts. The socialization and institutionalization of insurance saw an enshrinement of this principle of protection with the 1779 Lloyd's of London form that formed the basis of the Marine Insurance Act of 1906:

> Touching the adventures and perils which we the assurers are contented to bear and do take upon us in this voyage: they are of the seas, men of war, fire, enemies, pirates, rovers, thieves, jettisons, letters of mart and countermart, surprisals, takings at sea, arrests, restraints, and detainments of all kings,

princes, and people, of what nation, condition, or quality soever, barratry of the master and mariners, and of all other perils, losses, and misfortunes, that have or shall come to the hurt, detriment, or damage of the said goods, and merchandises, and ship, &c., or any part thereof.[14]

This language remained unchanged in major maritime insurance contracts until 1978, when the UNCTAD proposed a revised insurance clause, which has not been adopted by all insurers. While the Lloyd's form offered protection against "enemies, pirates, rovers, [and] thieves," most current maritime insurance policies do not include the losses of war, which are now exclusively under the purview of the war-risk cover. The status of piracy has oscillated between a varied set of insurance practices, each with its specific logics of obligation and accumulation, a logic that emerged clearly in the case of Somali piracy.

As Michael Miller (1994) notes, prior to 1983, underwriters at Lloyd's covered piracy as a war risk. In 1983, as global incidents of piracy declined significantly, underwriters decided to amend their clauses and included piracy under the hull and machinery policies as a generic "threat" that didn't require a specific technique of indemnity. A hull and machinery (H&M) policy is an insurance contract that typically brings together three parties: (1) a shipowner or one of the investors, (2) a broker hired to negotiate a contract by the party seeking insurance, and (3) a group of underwriters. The H&M contract covers the contents of a hull and the everyday running of a ship. An H&M policy is thus akin to other insurance policies and is negotiated on a time basis. Profit margins for an H&M insurer come from spreading the risks of trade as widely as possible. As an underwriter explained, "We want to make sure the ship is running, but beyond that, we have no vested interest in making sure it can go from point A to B."

In 2008, following the surge in acts of piracy off the coast of Somalia, the Joint War Committee (JWC), a group that comprises representatives from Lloyd's and other members of the International Underwriting Association in London, added the Gulf of Aden as a war-risk area, essentially requiring all merchant vessels to cancel their regular insurance policies and take out a war-risk cover policy that cost significantly more than the standard ship insurance. A key distinction between hull war-risk cover and regular hull-and-machinery insurance is that war-risk cover is a spatial practice that is based on the proposed itinerary of the ship. Certain areas of the world are constructed as high-risk areas, and ships transiting through that region have to pay a higher premium. Given the potential for high payouts, war-risk cover

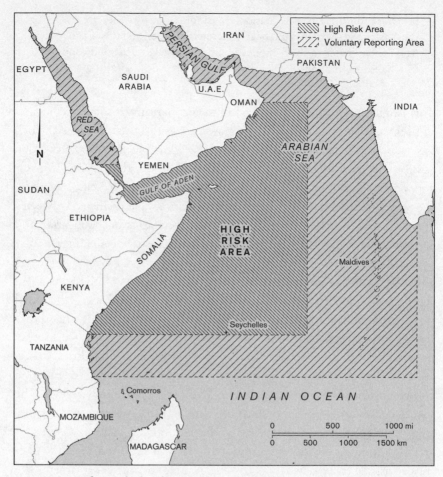

MAP 4: Map of piracy high-risk area in the western Indian Ocean.

is not calculated through standard actuarial models, but is a flat fee that is then negotiated down by individual shipping lines if they take adequate precautions.

In 2010, in addition to shadowing a number of underwriters who worked with Lloyd's, I also apprenticed with the intelligence department of Ship Safe, a private insurance company with offices across the world. The intelligence department was responsible for weekly reports on security threats at port and sea ranging from potential storms to acts of piracy in regions where ships underwritten by Ship Safe were sailing at any given moment. These reports were compiled using a mix of statistical data (often bought from private publications like *Jane's List*), and information gained from reading newspapers and surfing the internet. One morning, as I walked in—prepared for yet another day to be spent watching Simon, the head of the department, read newspapers while I read ship logs—an underwriter stopped me as I passed his office. "Today is your lucky day! You're coming with us for the war-risk cover seminar." Given the monopoly of Lloyd's in underwriting war-risk cover either directly or through reinsurance contracts, JWC's decision to mark the Gulf of Aden as a war-risk area had significantly impacted the London insurance market. While the actions of the JWC are nonbinding, most insurance companies follow the lead of Lloyd's, and through seminars and training the JWC creates informal regulatory standardization on war-risk policies.[15]

At the beginning of our seminar, Neil, a former member of the War Risk Committee and the facilitator, noted, "For many years, war-risk classification was simple and followed the outbreak of war and conflict." Stressing the "reactive rather than proactive" nature of war-risk classification, Neil proceeded to give a list of "crises" from the former Yugoslavia to Iraq where war-risk cover had been utilized in the aftermath of the outbreak of hostilities. "Of course, as you all know, 9/11 changed everything and today we have a proactive mode of ascertaining war-risk." Neil then began his PowerPoint presentation on Somalia and the impact of the JWC recommendations. After the seminar, I asked him why the World Trade Center attacks had impacted the war-risk cover market. Initially surprised by my naïveté, he remarked, "You must not be an insurance man to ask such a question." When he discovered I was an anthropologist, Neil proceeded to give me a long explanation for the shift in war-risk cover:

> Prior to September 11, war-risk cover was a relatively unproblematic system. Following the outbreak of a conflict—say, for example, the civil war in Yugoslavia—the JWC would add that region to its risk-list area, and once conflict ended the area was no longer considered a war risk. The World Trade Center attacks changed that system for good. Insurers and reinsurers reported a loss of over $8 billion from those attacks. Given that Lloyd's is the hub of the reinsurance industry, that impact was felt rather strongly here to say the least. The JWC realized that we can no longer be reactive but need to be proactive in understanding the security threats and the potential for terrorism, including maritime terrorism and piracy. A number of positive steps were taken in order to improve the accuracy of risk management *in order to predict and not just react to events.* But, numbers are only the beginning; we need human intelligence, maybe even anthropologists to help us anticipate the future! The utility of war-risk cover is precisely that it gives the insurance industry more

say in determining the present course of action . . . to make the future easier to fathom and understand. *We are dealing with the unknown unknowns here.* (Neil, interview with the author, August 2010; emphasis mine and edited for clarity)

Although presented here as a novelty, the idea of prediction has been at the heart of insurance from its inception in the city-states of the Mediterranean. The rise of probability and the probabilistic sciences legitimized these predictive practices and turned them into a technocratic regime of risk-pooling and risk distribution. War-risk cover represents the limit of these predictive practices. Since 9/11, war-risk cover has moved simultaneously in the direction of greater accuracy of risk management through mathematical modeling (often undertaken by private consultancy companies) and a renewed emphasis on "intelligence," which refers to classified information and data and also to the knowledge practices of underwriters. The shift from reactive to proactive risk management prompted by the JWC highlights the ways in which the contract of insurance spills over, both creating possibilities of profit and deciding the division of force and violence on a global scale—thus transforming insurance into the protection of counter-piracy.

In the contemporary world of counter-piracy, the negotiability of war-risk cover allows insurance companies an ability to shape the market they are supposedly providing indemnity for by distributing the organization of force. In its adoption of a proactive system for determining risk, maritime insurance seeks to instrumentalize risk as a tool of governance, and in so doing casts itself in an active role in determining the contours of counter-piracy, including the distribution of force and violence, as well as in getting to decides who counts as part of counter-piracy. With the steep increases in insurance prices due to war-risk cover (cover ranges from 0.5 to 0.75 percent of the cost of the ship, amounting to anywhere between $20,000 and $75,000 per voyage), marine insurance companies end up creating an exchange economy that governs counter-piracy.

As Simon, my supervisor at Ship Safe, repeatedly emphasized, "Once a company takes out the war-risk cover, we essentially owe them protection." This form of protection is built through a contract, but also through the collateralization of networks, reputation, and expertise. War-risk cover provides a moment of investment for numerous insurance companies. From 2009 on, Ship Safe has been providing war-risk cover for transit in the western Indian Ocean along with a kidnap-and-ransom package to provide what Simon called "a comprehensive policy of protection." This policy created an exchange economy involving lawyers, negotiators, pilots, and assorted "experts" who are paid a certain percentage of the war-risk fee when ships are hijacked. In addition, insurance companies had started licensing private security agencies to provide nonlethal measures for piracy prevention, such as equipping ships with loudspeakers, barbed wire, and high-pitched sound guns. By 2012, insurance companies had expanded this ambit of protection even further by creating kidnap-and-ransom packages and offering the services of security teams to travel alongside ships. As Simon explained to me, "We realized that shipping companies were hiring private guards, so we decided the best way would be to license [security] companies and then reduce the war-risk cover for shipping lines that used licensed maritime security companies."

Insurance companies and navies, contract and force, are thus clearly intertwined in providing counter-piracy in the western Indian Ocean, a form of organized protection against piracy, a fact repeatedly acknowledged by the actors within this governance regime. In his work on insurance and risk, Luis Lobo-Guerrero (2012, 110) notes the intimacy between navies and insurance when he quotes the NATO Secretary General Jaap de Hoop Scheffer's address to the 2007 Lloyd's City Dinner, the annual gala dinner for the insurance company. As de Hoop Scheffer noted:

> Like Lloyd's, NATO is in the insurance business. Like Lloyd's, we spend a lot of time assessing global risks—political, military, even environmental. We invest heavily in diminishing risk, for allies but also our global partners. And, like Lloyd's, when disaster does strike, somewhere in the world, often the first call is made to NATO to deal with the consequences.

Here, by noting this relationship between insurance and navies, I emphasize the ways counter-piracy functions as an *economy* of protection, creating obligations and possibilities for profit as well as reflecting more broadly on the nature of counter-piracy as a mode of regulating the ocean.

The ambiguities between public and private ends, between regulation and profit, specifically when it comes to the use of force and violence, resonate beyond the Indian Ocean. From Jean Bodin (1992) to Timothy Mitchell (1991) and more recent theorizations of global neoliberalism and austerity, the unitary or divisible nature of sovereignty has been a framework through which to pose questions about the shifting nature of actors, institutions, and policies involved in regulation. Privatization is either heralded as a more efficient use of resources or critiqued for usurping the legitimate power of the state. The ethnography of counter-piracy seeks to shift the contours of this debate. Extending Mitchell's (1991) idea of "state effects," I argue for a shift that foregrounds process.[16] Instead of assuming a priori the boundaries between market and state, between public and private, this approach underscores the need to focus on the processes through which these divisions emerge and its consequences for governance and regulation. In the realm of counter-piracy, it is the close relationship, and spillover, between force and contract that builds the legal architecture, economic market, and daily forms of policing that characterize this world. This spillover not only maps onto debates over public and private (importantly, deciding the legitimacy of certain actors) but also extends beyond it, thus eschewing single-explanatory frameworks such as neoliberalism in accounting for the shifting dynamics of counter-piracy.

. . .

When the crew of the *Enterprise* sounded the alarm, a NATO warship received the signal. The western Indian Ocean is vast, and even at the height of naval patrols it was impossible to systematically cover this region. By the time the navy ship could turn towards the *Enterprise*'s location, pirates were in control and the ship was en route to the Somali coast. "The insurance company handled our release," Suraj recalled. "But they had underinsured us and refused to pay more than $400,000." From the citadel of the ship where he and the rest of the crew were held captive, he listened in to occasional snippets of conversation among the pirates and the negotiators. "They sounded angry, and it looked like we were trapped in a stalemate. At that point, they [the pirates] started threatening us and pushing for us to raise money." Suraj, like the rest of the crew, was ordered to give his family's phone numbers. Initially resistant, a few weeks into the ordeal Suraj relented. "They called our families, and when the insurance companies refused to pay more, we had to ask them to raise money to get us out of there." The families were able to put together $100,000, and once the pirates received this ransom along with the $400,000 from the insurance company, the *MV Enterprise* was finally released. Visibly shaken as he remembered his ordeal, Suraj pointed to the office where we were sitting: "This place is not glamourous, but after twenty years of working on a ship, I realized the value of my life. As I said, I have faith in mathematics. I tell people now it's mathematically impossible for you to convince me to go out to sea."

FOUR

Markets of Negotiation

THE MAKING OF A RANSOM

"THAT HILL OVER THERE, do you see it? It's easier to call Europe from there. If you need to call Dubai or Singapore, it's best to go to the other side of town near the main road. For some reason the signal is better there." Badi was giving me the lowdown on his work. A former English teacher, for the past year or so—the finer details he deliberately kept hazy—Badi has been using his English skills as a negotiator instead. "I'm doing this to make sure the hostages can get home safe to their family." When I expressed some skepticism at this altruistic framing, he leaned in, his hand on my shoulder now: "Of course, I make some money. What's the problem with that?" We were sitting in a café in a small town in Central Somalia, far from the coast and even further from the insurance offices in London and Dubai that Badi spent most of his time talking with these days. "No one understands the pressure I'm under. The pirates want the millions, the shipping boss doesn't want to pay, and I spend so much time climbing these hills around town to get good cell phone reception!" In addition, Badi bemoaned, he was no longer the only English speaker in town. "A few boys have come back from the diaspora. Everyone is trying to make money from piracy."

The previous three chapters emphasized how claims are made over mobile objects at sea. They showed how piracy is anchored to the diya group and counter-piracy to insurance companies. This form of anchorage—through networks of obligation and exclusion—creates protection at sea. Market-making is a process of marking distinctions, of sifting between boundaries of legality and illegality, work and profiteering (Keane 2008). While highlighting the similar logics at play, piracy and counter-piracy have so far been located within distinct realms and locations: piracy as a problem of coastal Somalia and counter-piracy as a mobile geography between London,

Washington, and other capitals of empire. This chapter, by lifting the divide between these geographically and legally distinct domains, reveals a crowded and shared, if competing, world that emerges in the aftermath of capture.

As noted earlier, western Indian Ocean piracy operates exclusively on a kidnap-and-ransom basis. Instead of pilfering from ships, stealing containers, or making entire vessels disappear, Somali piracy entails interruption and, through this interruption, an alternative mode of connection. Kidnap-and-ransom is about holding crew and cargo hostage—within cell phone range from small ports in northern Somalia—until payments are received, often directly dropped onto ships from helicopters or small airplanes. This is a process that extends from as little as a few weeks to as long as three years. Capture is thus neither a guarantee of profit nor the end of an expedition. Instead, success in piracy is predicated on the ability to capture vessels and successfully negotiate a ransom.

This entails not only pirates and navies locked in an endless battle at sea, but also contractors, negotiators, pilots, consultants, and diviners. These various figures and their numerical and nonnumerical modes of valuation are essential to transforming capture into a ransom. Ransom payments represent a small portion of what counts as the "costs" of Somali piracy; the majority of expenses are in fact related to naval policing and increased fuel costs for vessels as they move faster through the Gulf of Aden. However, the ransom is a crucial moment that brings together the seemingly unrelated logics of protection that animate coastal Somalia and the offices of Lloyd's. Ransoms, specifically negotiations over ransoms, both make visible these competing forms of protection and show how protection makes possible the ability of Somali pirates to negotiate with risk consultants in London over the value of cargo and crew. It is also important to remember that a ransom payment is simply one possible outcome of a hijacking. The dynamic nature of piracy and counter-piracy means that intermediaries transform and are often replaced by others. This chapter will also trace the concomitant unmaking of the ransom economy.

From long-distance trading networks to the work of local human rights NGOs, intermediaries are central to a variety of projects and processes from the creation of markets, legal regimes, and other large-scale systems to practices of vernacularization and translation.[1] Drawing on this interdisciplinary literature on intermediaries, I note the centrality of these figures in the making of the ransom. Emphasizing the role of these intermediaries productively foregrounds the ways that violence and threat, as well as gendered and

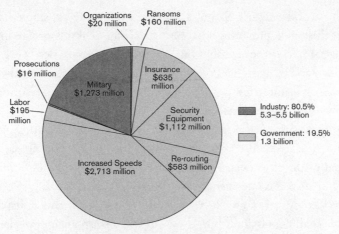

FIGURE 7: Estimated costs of piracy to shipping industry and governments. Source: Oceans beyond Piracy.

racialized ideologies and assumptions, shape both the quality and quantity
(Guyer 2004) of ransom payments, and economic interactions more broadly.
Focusing on how the ransom emerges through the work of these intermediaries also importantly lifts the analytic and epistemological divisions between
trade diasporas and financial markets, trust and actuarial science, piracy and
counter-piracy—divisions that continue to define our understandings of the
global order. Intermediaries are thus central in making the market for ransoms, but also crucially highlight the divides (of geography and legality) that
continue to shape our understanding of market-making. An intermediary-
focused understanding of ransoms therefore reframes piracy as an encounter
between worlds that are in fact mirrored and overlapping. This is a story that
asks: who is a pirate after all?

NAVIGATING EXPERTISE

A small office sits not far from Fort Jesus, the sixteenth-century fort erected
by the Portuguese marking their violent entry into the world of Indian
Ocean commerce, near the old port of Mombasa. Copies of *Seatrade* and
various other maritime trade magazines lie scattered around while an old
desktop computer displays the Baltic Dry Index, which tracks worldwide
international shipping prices for dry bulk cargo, as well as a website that
indicates the locations of thousands of container ships making their way

across the world's oceans. Salim, a former shipping agent, single-handedly manages this office, providing what he terms "logistical support" to individuals and organizations he describes vaguely as "interested parties." He explains, "About three years ago, I was one of the first people providing this service. Today there are quite a few people in London, Somalia, Dubai, Minneapolis, and a few others in Mombasa as well."

In 2009, as suspected pirates captured in the western Indian Ocean were being flown in to stand trial in the Kenyan port city of Mombasa, rumors circulated of the city's deeper connections to piracy. Stories of Somali men showing up at real estate agencies with bags of dollars and angry editorials warning Kenyans of pirates in their midst indexed a broader suspicion of Kenya's Somali population.[2] But, these rumors also sprang out of the understood intimacy—one that Salim's business relied upon—between Mombasa and economies of hijack-and-ransom offshore. Since the upsurge in maritime piracy, Mombasa, Kenya's second most populous city and home to the largest port in East Africa had been transformed into a "modern day pirate's port of call" (Dua 2010). A regular stop for naval vessels patrolling the Indian Ocean and the first port of call for hijacked vessels upon release, the Mombasa port was tied to an emergent global geography of piracy (and counter-piracy). Outside the port, neighborhoods that were once home to descendants of Baluch soldiers who served in the sultan of Oman's army had, in recent years, transformed into Somali neighborhoods lined with Internet cafés, tea and khat shops, moneychangers, and phone booths offering cheap international calls. Salim had worked as a moneychanger before his transition to "logistical support" and saw his role as a diviner, albeit one who sought the help of the Internet and the plethora of open-access online material about shipping movement as well as contacts at the port and the surrounding neighborhoods.

"There is a man in Puntland they call Computer[3] because he uses magic to tell people when to go to sea to capture a ship. I only use databases," he remarked sheepishly. "Magic is important for anyone who goes to sea," he continued as we stared at the somewhat mesmerizing map of shipping locations, thousands of dots scattered across the globe. "I use my computer to predict what can happen, others go to a Gosha[4] or people like Computer to find out what will happen." Salim's divination resulted in a printout of the locations of ships that were transiting through the Indian Ocean for the upcoming week. He would supplement this with a typed-up list of ships that had "attractive cargo." I found this puzzling, as everything I had read about the model of Somali piracy had emphasized the centrality of hijack-and-ransom. "Unlike Nigeria or Southeast Asia, pirates in Somalia only ransom crew?" I asked. "Ah, attractive cargo means ships that are fully loaded. You know, so it's easier to climb up using a ladder," Salim clarified, adding the concept of freeboard (height above the water) to my nautically uninitiated lexicon. "I make a note of ships that are slower. It's part of the special support I provide, the magic that is needed for them to do their work," he added with a somewhat conspiratorial look as he shut down his desktop, indicating that I had taken enough of his time.

In an insightful discussion on what she terms "capitalist divination," the anthropologist Laura Bear notes the importance of "technologies of imagination" on the Hoogly River in West Bengal, India. For Bear (2015, 414), these technologies, visible in figures such as "exemplary men, Kolkota Port Trust bureaucrats," are essential to explaining past events and planning future action within river-borne commerce. Salim and Computer—as well as security consultants—similarly produce technologies of imagination for ships as they navigate these pirate waters. Through printouts or Computer's divination, these men sought to explain why certain hijackings failed and how to ensure future success at sea. In addition, modes of logistical support through databases and magic are attempts to mediate in more quotidian ways. Logistical support is a world of payment.[5] Salim provided his service to the highest bidder, and Computer also sought payment for his divination.[6] Accepting payment is a way to make a claim on the profits generated through piracy in addition to being a reward for expertise. Through payments, men like Salim seek to become integral to the economy of hijack-and-ransom. This form of mediation is not limited to coastal Somalia. The upsurge in piracy also led to the emergence of the seers of shipping, the various intermediaries who protect global shipping as it transits through the Gulf of Aden.

Intermediaries of shipping—security companies, entrepreneurs, and inventors—claim special knowledge as well as technologies that are for sale at conventions and other maritime industry marketplaces. Vessel hardening is one of the common recommendations for ships transiting through "piracy zones" such as the waters off the coast of Somalia. Hardening measures range from crude techniques such as using barbed wire along the side of the ship to long-range acoustic devices (LRADs) that emit painful sounds to disorient and deter would-be hijackers. In its best management practices, the IMO recommends that ships transiting through the Gulf of Aden employ a range of these hardening measures. In the cutthroat world of cargo transport, with its very slim profit margins, vessel hardening was seen as a luxury until insurance companies started offering discounts for using these measures. This institutionalization created new possibilities for a range of security companies to market a variety of high-tech nonlethal fixes for vulnerable ships. These technologies are on full display at transport security expositions and shipping conventions where logistical support is marketed and sold.

In 2011, I attended one such convention in London. Looking over my registration card and noticing I had indicated an interest in "antipiracy measures" and "shipping and offshore platform security," the person sitting at the entrance booth remarked that I was in good company. "This year we have a robust showing from maritime security companies; I guess it's all the piracy in the news that's made the maritime sector very much in demand." After walking through booth after booth advertising "lethal and nonlethal modes of protection" ranging from the latest anti-IED jamming device to riot control lasers, I found myself staring at a photograph of a ladder, or, more precisely, two ordinary ladders tied together with string. A maritime security consultancy prominently displayed this intriguing "relic," as they called it at their booth.

I joined a small crowd of representatives from shipping companies as a middle-aged white man, like most of the representatives and audience at this convention, began his presentation. "This relic costs a million dollars," he began, theatrically gesturing to the photograph, which he later told us was a boarding ladder used by Somali pirates. After listing the horrific costs and risk statistics of hijacking in the western Indian Ocean, the representative began a slick video presentation that outlined the various hardening measures available through their company. They were debuting sticky foam and cannons that sprayed stinky water: "simple yet effective techniques to deter any would-be pirate." The foam, he explained, was sprayed on the deck of the ship in case anyone hopped over the rails and onto the ship. As sticky as glue, this foam would then ensnare aspiring pirates on the deck. "The stinky water cannon is something that is both environmentally friendly and a clear deterrent. No one wants to smell like a skunk—not even pirates," he added to laughs from the audience.

Other booths with less theatrical flair also promised a range of nonlethal techniques and logistics support for ships as they traveled in the Red Sea and the Indian Ocean. An Italian company that had been working in the Mediterranean on illegal fishing and migration detection emphasized: "Look, even in the Mediterranean it's difficult to do interdictions. The Indian Ocean is just bigger and wilder." Pointing to his amulet—a *cornicello* (devil's horn) tucked inside his shirt—the company agent likened the technologies they sold to this amulet: "We can't predict what will happen, but what we do is suggest [to] you technologies based on the area you'll be transiting and the kind of ship you have. I'm Catholic and sometimes I tell my clients that these technologies are modern-day *cornicellos*."

I was reminded, then, of Salim's assertion that magic was important for anyone who went to sea. For Salim and the Italian agent, the vulnerability and unknowability of life at sea—its possibilities and perils—frame their role and ability to mediate in this world. This mediation, the opportunity to become an intermediary within the system of maritime circulation and its interruption, is then an opening for profit and monetary gain.

NEGOTIATORS: RANSOM AS CO-PRODUCTION

The need for intermediaries and the possibilities that open up through mediation are equally important in the world of ransom negotiation. It is, after all, a successful ransom that transforms capture into piracy. An estimated $1.5 billion annually is globally transacted as ransom payments (Forest 2012). These include hijackings at sea as well as everyday kidnappings in "high-risk" regions around the world, specifically in Central and South America. The economy of ransoming has long been central to the world of trade, specifically seaborne trade, and is intimately tied to ideas of honor, prestige, and sociality. The rise of a professional security class and the emergence of insurance practices such as kidnap-and-ransom (K&R) insurance have further institutionalized the role of intermediaries, such as K&R negotiators, and security and risk consultants, in resolving these dramas of capture. The ransom economy of piracy is built on forms of agreement and infrastructures of exchange. How are these agreements constituted? What is the role of intermediaries in making these infrastructures of exchange?

Ransom negotiation is a secretive enterprise. Disclosing to anyone that you have K&R insurance is seen as a moral hazard and often grounds for the policy to be considered void (Lobo-Guerrero 2007; Economist 2018). As a security consultant noted, "if you are in a high-risk zone for kidnapping and let people know that if you're kidnapped a ransom is guaranteed, well you can see the problem with that." In addition to the secrecy over coverage, ransom payments remain legally ambiguous, given proscriptions on material support for terrorism within most jurisdictions. Negotiators and risk and security consultants also participate in perpetuating this secrecy, a fact that was made clear to me when I tried to get an interview with one. A contact at the IMO in London had suggested getting in touch with a company that offered K&R insurance. As I explained my research to the K&R division of this company, the security consultant politely declined my request for an interview, explaining that all his work was privileged for two basic reasons: "Information is value in our line of work," he stated, hoping that I would understand that he couldn't just divulge secrets for free. "Also," he added before hanging up, "we have to worry about information getting into the wrong hands."

The sense of secrecy and privileged information deeply shapes the social field of ransom negotiators and private security consultants. This is a homogenous world comprised almost exclusively of middle-aged white men with military backgrounds or extensive work experience with the political risks division at Lloyd's. Luckily, not all negotiators shared this devotion to secrecy, and I eventually managed to find a number of K&R firms willing to discuss their role in ransom negotiations involving Somali piracy.

James, like most in the ransom negotiation business, was a former SAS officer. We met in his company's office, a shiny glass building overlooking the Thames. James came down to the futuristic-looking lobby and escorted me through security and up to his office. "We have a host of risk management products for our clients," he offered, as we entered what looked like a law firm or accountancy company full of cubicles enclosed in glass—the only difference being the framed pictures of armed men on oil rigs or in desert landscapes that lined the walls. "We've started doing risk outlooks for climate change as well, but our bread and butter is personnel and asset protection," he continued, noticing me staring at the images of security deployments. We entered a windowless conference room equipped for teleconferencing: "This is usually where I sit to do negotiations for the ships. Let's chat here."

"I'm the second person on the phone with these guys [the pirates]. Once the pirates take control of the ship they instruct the captain to call the shipping company. As soon as the shipping company is informed, [the company] calls us immediately, day or night." James went over to the whiteboard and started drawing what he called the capture timeline. "At this point we take over. The shipping company has already called the UKMTO and knows if there is a warship nearby." He then mapped out scenario 1, which entailed warships, helicopters, and a dramatic rescue at sea. "Of course, I'm part of scenario 2. There is no warship in sight and the ship is making its way to

Somalia . . . that's when I'm involved." James wrote "NEGOTIATION" on the timeline and then sat back down.

"So how does it begin, the whole process of negotiating over ransoms? Do they suggest a price and you come back with a counteroffer?" I was drawing on an image of so-called "bazaar economies,"[7] a world of market traders—evocatively rendered in the writings of economic anthropologists and others who emphasize the "embeddedness" of economic life within social milieus—haggling through a series of elaborate ritualized offers and counteroffers. "Something like that," James replied, "though the first thing we do is to make sure I am the only channel of communication. We have to isolate the pirates and make ourselves the only communication point." For James and other negotiators, this channeling is critical to the production of ransom markets. If the space of the market has historically sought to "do away with the outside" and produce a set of "interior realms marked by greater control and greater autonomy from exterior conditions" (Callon 2012), the ransom market, from the perspective of James and negotiators for the hijacked ship, also seeks to shield itself from exteriority—in this case the exteriority of emotion.

MARKET-MAKING AS DETACHMENT

"You can't have emotions when it comes to ransom negotiations. When we are in scenario 2," James pointed back to the whiteboard and the capture timeline with the scenarios spelled out, "we start by making sure the shipowners and family members have no direct contact with the hijackers." An emotional response is seen as skewing the potential for a fair price. As James noted, "In an ideal world we never should be negotiating for someone's life. But those of us in this business don't have that luxury." James listed a few scenarios where emotions would harm as opposed to help. "Imagine you're a shipowner and the captain has been your friend for twenty-plus years. You like the guy, that's why you're trusting him with a multi-million-dollar machine, right? Imagine someone calling and saying, 'We have a gun to this guy's head, send us a million dollars.' Your first instinct is to say, 'Don't hurt him, I'll send the money right away.'" Pausing to let this situation settle in, James listed another equally difficult situation. "Now imagine you're the wife of a seafarer. You see your husband for six months a year. The rest of the time he is at sea. You get a call in the middle of the night. He sounds like he is scared and in pain. He tells you the ship is hijacked. These guys have guns, they are high on drugs and they want money now. What's your first instinct here?" Without waiting for me to answer, he continued, "You'll sell your engagement ring, you'll do what it takes to get him out of there. Now, why is your instinct wrong?" Without pausing, he continued, "paying up right away is no guarantee of safety or even that the hostages will be released. In fact, it signals to the hijackers that you have the money. We have evidence in those situations that the demand will just be increased." For James, detachment was key. "We tell all attached parties, look, we're the best in the business, we will take care of this. Your role is not to answer their calls, emails, or WhatsApp messages; we do the talking on your behalf."

Detachment emerges as a form of exercising jurisdiction over the transaction, a prerequisite from the side of those seeking the release of ships and, importantly, a theory of market-making.[8] James and numerous other negotiators would point to psychology textbooks and behavioral economics as central to how negotiators approach the ransom economy. Going back to the whiteboard, James outlined a payoff matrix: a description of the game for a ransom negotiation. "This is straight game theory, basically the chicken dilemma," he explained, mapping out the various possibilities. "First we have two outlier scenarios," he began. "If you don't pay the ransom, then the hostage is of no value and the chances of us protecting them are significantly decreased. Paying right away and at price means they'll think you have more, and good luck negotiating then."

Having eliminated the outlier scenarios, he began mapping the rest of the game. James explained that the first step involved establishing a channel of communication. "We usually do this by getting proof of life. I want to know they [hostages] are alive. We ask them to send a picture of the crew holding up a sign or a code." For James, the proof of life was part of establishing communication and also control over the transaction. "In our initial conversation, we're being firm and setting up the ground rules," he noted. "It matters that they understand we're professional. I will tell them at the beginning, 'Look, if you want us to take you seriously you need to call us on time, respond promptly, and such.'" As he underscored, "Jittery pirates are bad for business." Establishing what another consultant called "baseline professionalism" was stressed by a number of negotiators as setting the affective tone for conducting negotiations. Contact with pirates is as much about creating this proper tone—detached, businesslike—as it is about knowing the material conditions of the hostages.

Once this detached channel of communication is established, offers and counteroffers are made. "We tend to be aware of the established price for ransoms. For example, we were negotiating for an oil tanker last month, and I knew that an oil tanker had just been released for about $9 million. When the pirates asked for $14 million, we knew that we had a decent bit of wiggle room since the pirates also know the going price for a vessel." At that point, the negotiators take on the role of a cash-strapped firm and respond with a much lower figure, going back and forth until a price emerges. For James, what mattered was keeping control of the process so that he could steer the negotiations towards a preagreed price range. "The shipping companies will tell us how much they can pay, of course. We know the insurance situation, the wider going rate. The offer and counteroffer is a way of arriving at a mutually beneficial situation. As outsiders to the process, we are best placed to do this and get the fair price in this situation."

This "fair price" emerges as the end of the transaction—one that both gives a certain legitimacy to the economy of negotiation and becomes a marker of success and failure. And a fair price can only emerge through a practice of detachment. Unlike insurance markets, where establishing economic interest is essential to distinguishing between gambling and insurance, negotiators emphasize the virtue of detachment. Handling oneself with detachment is the affective space from which a gendered expertise can be established and proper decisions made, including what counts as a fair price for ransoms. At the same time, this claim to detachment brackets that what happens here is a process of bargaining over the value of life. Thinking of the hostage as someone enmeshed in ties of friendship and kinship is a deterrent to the ransom economy.

If detachment offers a possibility to control the transaction, in this "tournament of value"[9] detachment is also about the erasure of local knowledge. When I asked James if proficiency in Somali or the wider contexts of Somali piracy would be seen as a boon to negotiators, he again pointed to the problem of emotion. Turning to me, he emphasized, "You'd be too attached, for instance. You know these people and you'll be too soft. What is needed is a universal skill, not specific knowledge." In fact, when local knowledge is called upon in this world, it is a sign that things have not gone well: "Sometimes we have to call upon clan elders or other influential Somalis to put pressure on these guys . . . that only happens, though, if we've lost control of the situation, if we've failed."

"Ultimately, we're dealing with an opponent," James reminded me. "I think of them [the hijackers] as humans; focusing on anything else will muddy the waters." Such references to the humanity of the hijacker emerged repeatedly over my fieldwork with negotiators, but they clearly weren't directed toward crafting a form of sympathy or understanding. Instead, a specific kind of human is envisioned in this world of negotiation. If shipowners, family members, and anthropologists suffer from the problem of emotion, the pirate is also understood to be infected with interests—if only the self-interest of the *homo economicus*. Understanding the pirate as a profit-maximizing rational actor makes possible the back-and-forth of offer and counteroffer. As another negotiator explained, "We know they are motivated by money, so that makes us trust in the transaction."

This vision of the hijacker as homo economicus also furthers the expertise of the negotiator. If profit is what motivates the hijacker and is a universal motivator, local knowledge and language skills become secondary to this transaction. Rendering the hijacker as a rational actor brackets other concerns and other potential mediators, channeling the process of negotiation. As James mentioned towards the end of our meeting, "Today we're dealing with pirates, next week the big thing could be cartel kidnappings. We can intervene in all these areas and provide the best protection." For James, the best protection emerged through the negotiator as the detached party mediating between hijackers and hostages, thus legitimizing his role in the making of the ransom market.

Negotiation, however, is not a one-way street. On the other end of the phone lies a mirrored world that is seeking to transform capture into ransom. What are the logics of that world? What is the role of intermediaries in making pirates?

THE EMBEDDED RANSOM:
MARKET-MAKING AS ATTACHMENT

"I am not a pirate. I never go out to sea to catch a ship." Badi wanted to distinguish the role of the negotiator from that of the pirate. "I only come on board when the ship is in Somalia," he emphasized, making sure I knew his role in the whole operation. "In fact, I don't even go to the ship anymore. One of the translators will be on the ship and I tell him what to say. I only make phone calls. That's why I know where the best signal is in town," he joked as we sipped our tea.

Badi spent most of our time together distancing himself from pirates. However, unlike James and other ransom negotiators who emphasized distance

FIGURE 8: Water hose on the aft side of the container ship as part of vessel hardening against piracy, 2018. Photo by author.

as the requirement for a proper negotiation, distance for Badi was strictly about legal culpability. He agreed to meet with me only after I promised complete secrecy, and throughout our conversation he repeated the suggestion that international law enforcement should distinguish between "the bad guy pirates and people like us, those who are trying to resolve the situation."

This mode of distancing was not unique in coastal Somalia. Khat merchants, government officials, and village elders all sought to distance themselves from pirates while also emphasizing various connections and obligations to their world. As a negotiator, responsible for transforming capture into a ransom payment, Badi's intimacy with piracy had a different quality, one that required far more secrecy and multiple meetings over tea before he was ready to explain the process of negotiation. For Badi, the negotiation process began immediately after capturing a ship. In a typical hijacking, two fishing skiffs with six to eight armed men would approach the aft (rear) side of the ship in the radar blind spot and navigate their way to the side of the ship. As they made their way to the side, the navigator on board the pirate skiff would try to avoid getting caught in the ship's wake, which can often swell up to ten feet, as well as dodge water hoses and other boarding deterrent devices.

"We were rolling from one side to another." Adan, a former pirate, was telling me his story of boarding a cargo vessel. "The ship made a big wave and we could see that one side had barbed wire. So, we had to maneuver to the other side and hope they didn't see us on the radar. I had the ladder ready, and Dabhal over here climbed up first," he said, gesturing towards his mostly silent companion sitting on the bed in the small, tube-lit room where we were meeting. Ladders were essential equipment to board ships, and men like Dabhal, who went on board first, were given a bonus for climbing up a rickety and unstable ladder in the middle of the ocean. "Once Dabhal got on board, he secured the ladder and the fishing skiffs with rope and we all climbed up after him." Adan explained that as the *askari* (guard) on the expedition, his role ended soon after they boarded the ship. "The others [including the leader of the group usually chosen for his English language skills] would go to the bridge and switch off the communication system and the radar." Going offline signals to the ship owner or the company monitoring the ship that the vessel is no longer in the hands of the captain.

This is usually when negotiators get involved. "The negotiator talks to the captain and reassures him that everything will be all right. He will say things like, 'Remember you have a family. Think about them. Think about the crew members.' The negotiator is basically reminding the captain not to try anything funny and cooperate," explained Badi. The negotiator's strategy here is precisely the opposite from those who sit in London. Negotiation here entails an immediate recognition of and entanglement within various kinship relationships. While stressing their professionalism, negotiators seek to create worry, among both the shipping company and the captain, as a way to exercise jurisdiction over this process.

After a day of radio silence, the negotiator instructs the hijackers to reestablish communication through the captain. "At this time the ship is heading to Somalia; the shipowners know they have no other choice but to talk. The captain and crew also realize the navy will not save them." Badi paused, leaned in, and whispered: "Only then I know I will be busy with work." I asked him what this work entailed. "First we have to know we are talking to the right people." This process, he explained, was far from simple. "Ships are very confusing," he complained as I nodded along in agreement. As I started to tell him about flags of convenience, Badi shushed me with an annoyed look. "Anyway, there is a simple solution. We ask the people we are speaking with to send us a fax of the company logo. If it matches the ship manifest letter we know we have the right person." Akin to the proof of life demanded by James and the security consultants, the letterhead is key to establishing a connection between pirates and ship owners.

Throughout this initial process, most communication occurs between ship captains and owners. As Badi said, "We want the captain to do the talking so he can put pressure on shipowners." The captain becomes the figure through whom the negotiator initially engages the shipping company. The captain as the face and voice of the negotiation is crucial in transforming the hijacking into a plea for help from the crew to the owner. This plea requires a quick and sympathetic response, or at least so the hijackers hope. "If we can keep the situation between the captain and the ship owners, maybe we get the money within a week. But it's not so simple," he continued: "too many people can get involved and then it's complicated." When I inquired about these complications, Badi listed a range of people from greedy pirate bosses and absent shipowners to private security consultants who make things difficult. Mentioning the security consultants, he complained, "Those guys are a headache, they always want to underpay."

For Badi, a successful negotiation relied on keeping visible the obligations and kinship ties that linked crew members to life on land, including the captain as the face of the negotiation for at least the initial offer. It also entailed seeking out family members and pressuring them to help ensure a quick resolution. These moments, when hijackers rifle through personal belongings and cell phone contact lists are mined for connections, are remembered by crew members as moments of incredible violence and anguish. For negotiators, however, using cell phones and going through personal belongings is part of a strategy of embedding transactions. In a strange echo of James, Badi insisted on seeing the hostages and shipowners as humans. But instead of the profit-maximizing homo economicus, the human envisioned here is the "family man."

BETWEEN HOMO ECONOMICUS AND
THE FAMILY MAN

So far, the world seems to be divided between the disembedded homo economicus of K&R consultants and the embedded family man of coastal Somali negotiators. However, if we see the transaction as unfolding in time, these boundaries appear less rigid, less located in the divides between the Global North and the South, between finance and trade diaspora. As this encounter unfolds, the homo economicus and family man blend into each other, both emerging as strategies of extraction and modes of moral calculation.

During a particularly busy month for piracy in 2011, an old cargo ship was hijacked near Seychelles. As the ship trudged back to Somali waters, the group responsible for the hijacking hired a negotiator. "As we got close to Somalia, the people who had taken the ship went away and this new group came on board." Rajesh, a crew member on this ill-fated cargo ship, was recounting his ordeal in a hotel lobby in Mumbai. I had first heard the story of this hijacking from an ex-pirate in Somalia who claimed to have worked as a cook on this ship during his time as a pirate. When I asked Rajesh about him, he paused for a minute and replied, "The cook was in that new group . . . I remember him. They would stay to themselves mostly. But the first negotiator, I remember him quite well." Rajesh described him as young man with a fondness for walking around with a pistol.

"He came up to us and took away all our cell phones and personal belongings before sending us back to our rooms." For Rajesh, the next few weeks were marked with deep anxiety and fear, a situation exacerbated by the "glaring incompetence" of the negotiator. "He came to our captain and said, 'I'm going to get $9 million for this ship.' The captain repeatedly pointed out that we were an old fifteen-hundred-TEU ship and nine million was at least ten times the value of the ship."[10] As he recounted more tales of the negotiator, Rajesh noted that "It would be funny [the negotiator's incompetence] if it wasn't the worst moments of my life."

The shipping company had hired its own negotiator as well. Bob, a security consultant with a London-based K&R firm, was making little headway with his counterpart. As Bob described the situation, "We had been authorized a number well below $1 million for the release by the shipping company. The negotiator was refusing to budge from $9 million. I told him, 'Look this is no oil tanker. You have an old ship on your hands, take the money we're offering.'" As weeks turned into months, the families of the crew members in India grew more anxious and vocal. At that point, Bob advised the shipowners to hire an Indian facilitator to work with the families.

In the meantime, the young gun-slinging negotiator was fired and replaced by an older man with more experience. Rajesh recounted numerous conversations with the new negotiator. "He was quiet, knew a little about ships, and promptly convinced the hijackers to lower the asking price. He would also spend time with us too, at one point telling me that he was not from the hijackers' clan and was an outsider like me." Badi had mentioned the flexibility in hiring negotiators, emphasizing a form of meritocracy over considerations of family, clan, or other obligations. "What matters is someone who is trustworthy and good at their job. A group based in Puntland can even hire a translator from Somaliland." To underscore this last point, he added, "Hiring a person from Somaliland is the same as someone from Pakistan hiring you [an Indian]."

Ransom negotiation is also one of the few places where women often play a crucial and public role. The world I inhabited during research was highly gendered. Seafarers, shipping executives, navy and private security personnel, as well as insurance brokers, are mostly men who form a tight-knit community. Piracy in Somalia, while similarly gendered in terms of who went out to sea, was one of the few places in this transregional economy where I regularly encountered women. As we saw in chapter 2, a number of women, mostly khat traders like Aisha and other high-powered financiers or negotiators, are key in making and anchoring the ransom economy. Hodan, a young woman and aspiring café owner, had negotiated with shipping companies and described the surprise that would follow when she first called the London-based negotiators. "When I call them, they're shocked to hear a woman's voice. I don't think there are any women that work for shipping companies." While it's impossible to verify the claims of Hodan, personal interviews conducted with K&R negotiators and scanning the webpages of companies offering these services in London have shown the K&R world to be one deeply connected through gender, race, and occupational kinship. As a K&R consultant explained to me, "We are a group of people who trained together and would take a bullet for each other. That's how this industry is forged." If the hiring of negotiators in Somalia and London does not correspond to the boundaries between the embedded and disembedded, as the transaction unfolds, other logics also become apparent.

As soon as the new negotiator stepped on board Rajesh's ship, he would have realized there was a big problem. The cargo ship was small and old. The bridge room had an old automatic identification system (AIS) and other equipment that looked as if it was barely hanging on. The ship had been hijacked when it had engine trouble and was carrying general cargo. Walking down to the crew quarters confirmed his feeling that this ship was not going to land a big payday for the hijackers (or for the negotiator). The crew was mostly Indian and a smattering of African nationalities. Nine million dollars was far too much to ask for this crew and cargo, and he immediately contacted the hijackers and suggested restarting the negotiation at $1 million.

One of the first jobs of the negotiator is to assess the potential value of crew and cargo. The agreed-on value—the ransom—depends both on the skill of the negotiators and on preexisting ideas about the differentiated value of life and labor at sea. Badi liked to compare ships with khat. "There are many kinds of khat. You have the more leafy Yemeni kind, the slightly bitter one from Ethiopia, and then the sweet stems from Meru [Kenya]." Each geographical region corresponds to a particular effect—Badi preferred Ethiopia's "exciting effect that lasts the longest"—and each khat carries a widely different price tag. "Ships are not very different from khat, they come from different places, and importantly where they are from also tells you how much they are worth." Telling the value of good khat is a visual and sensory exercise. "You pick the bundle and see, based on the leaves, where the khat is from. You smell the bundle. Does it have a distinctive sharp smell of freshly cut grass? You touch your fingers through the bundle: is there a slight stickiness? Finally, if you're a real connoisseur and the seller isn't looking, nibble a little. Does it immediately burst into bittersweet flavor?" The system for evaluating a ship's value is not very different, as Abdullahi, a retired negotiator, explained: "You get on a ship with a list. The first thing we must do is find out what kind of ship it is. If it is carrying oil or gas, then it's a good day. If it's lots of containers, then also it can be okay. Then you have to judge if the ship is in good maintenance—does it look old or new? Finally, is the crew European or Indian, Filipino? All these will determine the price."

While Badi's comparison to khat naturalizes the differential value of crew and cargo, Abdullahi's list shows that assessment is embedded within the wider logics of global capitalism, specifically the racial hierarchy of labor. Up until the 1970s, most merchant ships were crewed by nationals of the flag state in which the ship was registered. This changed in connection with the global financial recessions of the 1970s and 1980s (ILO 2004). This downfall hit the so-called "embedded maritime nations in Europe and Japan" (ILO 2004, 58). *Embedded maritime nations* refers to those nations that had large merchant ship fleets that were registered under the nation's flag and were crewed by that nation's citizens. They were embedded because both trade income and employment in the trade were linked to the same national economy.

In order for ship owners to save on labor costs, national legislations were liberalized, and it became easier to crew ships with maritime laborers from other countries. The Philippines emerged as the largest supplier of global maritime labor in this period of liberalization. The International Labour Organization (ILO) writes: "In 1987 alone, the employment of Filipino seafarers on European-owned ships increased from 2,900 to 17,057 people . . . Almost all the displaced seafarers were domiciled in the embedded maritime nations of Europe" (ILO 2004, 58). Instead of being hired directly by shipping companies, most non-European crew were hired through recruiting agencies with drastically different contracts. This led to the development of distinct pay scales as well as amounts of time spent on board ships with non-

European crew being paid significantly less and spending anywhere from six to nine months at sea, in contrast to the two to three months spent on average by crewmembers employed directly by the shipping company. These differentiations echo a long history of racial capitalism (Robinson 1983) at sea and significantly shape the ransom market for piracy. The labor recruitment for shipping continues to operate on a racial hierarchy, with most captains and chief mates being European or American. The majority of mid-level officers are from India, the Middle East, and Eastern Europe. Finally, the majority of ratings (mariners without certification) are from South Asia, the Philippines, and Southeast Asia. Given that payouts for K&R insurance are based on shipping hierarchies—specifically, higher-ranked officials have higher ransom coverage—racial differences get inscribed (and naturalized) into the payout structures, with European hostages often worth twice or three times as much as non-European hostages.

Rajesh's ship with its non-European crew and bulk cargo was, thus, not worth much in the valuation of global capitalism. The hijackers were dismayed. When Bob relayed the final amount the shipping company was willing to pay for release, the negotiator called him back angrily. "We told the negotiator, 'Look, this is our final offer'. The next day he calls back practically yelling at me. At this point it had been over six months of negotiation and the hijackers were in debt to people who were providing supplies to the hostages. They were yelling at the negotiator; the previous guy had convinced them they would get a nice payout. I was sympathetic to the negotiator, but we had our limits." It was six more months before a deal was struck and the ransom airdropped to the ship. "This is another part of our service," Bob explained. "We hire pilots who make the airdrop. It's not straightforward, transporting a million dollars."

Markets for ransom thus emerge through these negotiations over price. Within the temporality of these encounters we see gendered and racialized ideas about attachment and value as key to shaping who and what counts. While these forms of valuation exceed the framework of the transaction and are anchored within more enduring and unequal frameworks, the actors are part of a contingent and ever-shifting cast. By 2011, this ransom economy had become well established, and quite profitable, for everyone but the seafarers. The only way to stop this market of negotiation, and the various intermediaries—pirates and negotiators—who were benefiting from it was preventing ships from being hijacked. This was not through the success of the navies, but through the emergence of a new intermediary, the private security consultant (PSC).

FIGURE 9: The making of a ransom.

"Let's meet at a bar in Place Menelik [Djibouti]. Come to this place called La Mer Rouge; it's a fun spot." Mildly annoyed by the cliché of the private security contractor wanting to meet in a seedy bar, I nonetheless agreed to meet Jack, an operations manager for Oceansecure, a UK-based private security company. With his shaved head, large build, and intricately tattooed arms, Jack, a former royal marine, certainly looked the part when we met later that evening at La Mer Rouge. Seated at the bar, surrounded by a motley crew of French foreign legionnaires and their evening companions, Jack proceeded to recount the relatively short history of Oceansecure. "Private maritime security is the wave of the future," he began, above the din of synthesized Euro-pop. "Most of us involved in private maritime security companies [PMSCs] started off working in the private security sector in Iraq. There are a few guys with more experience who used to do security details on luxury yachts, offshore oil drills and undersea cable–type stuff, but this is a brave new world."

Beginning in the 1990s, private security companies (PSCs) and private military companies (PMCs) emerged with growing prominence in a number of post–Cold War conflict zones. With names like Executive Outcomes and Sandline, these companies distinguished themselves from the mercenaries of the 1960s and 1970s with their promise of corporate, market-driven solutions to intractable conflicts. The 9/11 attacks and the 2003 invasion of Iraq marked a watershed in the contemporary privatization of the military. A month after the 9/11 attacks, US President George W. Bush gave a televised news conference promising a new and different war, reminding the world that "the attack took place on American soil, but it was an attack on the heart and soul of the civilized world. And the world has come together to fight a new and different war, the first, and we hope the only one, of the twenty-first century. A war against all those who seek to export terror, and a war against those governments that support or shelter them" (Bush 2002). The premise that this deterritorialized global War on Terror was new and different was built on a certain historical amnesia that imagined all conflict prior to 9/11 as interstate. Premised on the erasure of colonial violence and the irregular wars of the Cold War, this fiction of interstate conflict is central to the project of sovereignty itself that excises the blurry boundaries between state and nonstate in telling the story of political authority and legitimacy.[11]

If the global War on Terror was, and remains, altogether familiar and legible within recent violent histories of empire, the invasions of Afghanistan and Iraq can nonetheless be seen as "new and different" in their attempt to reverse what has been referred to as a strong antimercenary bias in Europe and North America (Percy 2007). As early as Machiavelli (1961), we see a strong critique of the hired gun. In *The Prince,* he warns: "If a prince bases the defense of his state on mercenaries he will never achieve stability or security. For mercenaries are disunited, thirsty for power, undisciplined, and disloyal; they are brave among their friends and cowards before the enemy" (Machiavelli 1961, 77–78). This critique extended to the American Revolution and beyond. Mercenaries are repeatedly portrayed as morally suspect and dubious, a categorization that also has the effect of producing the state as the virtuous and honorable actor in the international arena.[12]

The neoliberal rhetoric of privatization and efficiency sought to rehabilitate the mercenary, this time in the guise of the private security contractor, a process that reached its apogee with the 2003 invasion of Iraq. By 2008, in an unprecedented degree of privatization, the US Department of Defense employed 155,826 private contractors in Iraq—and 152,000 troops. In Afghanistan there was a similar distribution, with approximately 94,413 contractors in 2010, compared with 91,600 US troops (Schwartz 2010). A report on private military contracting by the RAND Corporation (ironically itself a private contractor for the US military) noted that "the Army spent roughly $815 million ($163 million per year, or about $200 million per year in 2012 dollars) to employ contractors under its Logistics Civil Augmentation Program between 1992 and 1997. But between 2001 and 2010, that expenditure grew to nearly $5 billion per year" (Dunigan 2013). In addition to these burgeoning costs was the expanded role of private military contractors in all aspects of combat, including guarding installations, protecting convoys, and acting as bodyguards.

A veteran of this surge in PSC employees, Jack's previous job was in Basra, in southern Iraq, for a large UK-based private military contractor, the same contractor that now operated as a PMSC in Djibouti. When the Iraqi government exercised its sovereignty over PSCs and PMCs by denying them immunity from prosecution in Iraqi courts in 2009, contractors like Jack looked for more lucrative and legally permissive markets.[13] Somali piracy was one such potential market. In 2008, Erik Prince, the head of Blackwater, one of the biggest and most controversial names within this private military world, docked in the port of Djibouti with a luxury yacht retrofitted as an antipiracy vessel. Prince did not find any takers there for his private mercenary navy, but as piracy incidents skyrocketed in 2009, a number of shipping companies started looking to private security to ensure safe passage through the Gulf of Aden. Private security was also suggested as a solution to piracy more generally, with observers recommending a return to the world of letters of marque and armed escorts.[14] Governments and insurance companies cautioned against these moves. In a brochure distributed to maritime underwriters by Allianz Insurance, insurers were warned of the "potentially costly" implications of hiring private security guards for transit through the Indian Ocean: "Insurers should be very wary of insuring any vessel that carried arms or armed guards on board. A potential liability claim for shooting a pirate— or causing a crew member's death—could be very costly, as could the resulting damage to the hull" (Allianz 2011, 2). Given this risk, private security companies found themselves operating at the margins of the counter-piracy world from 2007 until 2011. Ironically, this margin meant that private security companies were geographically closer to piracy than the ships patrolling the Indian Ocean. A number of companies established coastguards and informal "navy colleges" in some of the mini-states in northeast Somalia, echoing the 1990s when private security companies were inadvertently instrumental in training what became the first generation of Somali pirates.

Jack, whose company Oceansecure had been involved in "under-the-radar" protection from 2009 onwards, recalled the complicated legal terrain in the early years of counter-piracy. "The legal environment, unfortunately, doesn't allow us to operate freely. A number of ports, like Mombasa and Jeddah, don't allow weapons on merchant ships. But we're resourceful and have found some ways around it. We'll dump our weapons when we arrive near port or often just have a boat stationed in international waters with our weapons stash." In spite of the complicated legal terrain, piracy, as Jack noted, was "good for business." Throughout the evening Jack had laced his complaints of the tedium of being at sea with tales of bravado in Iraq. "You could say I've dusted the sand off my boots and jumped onto a skiff," he slurred, grabbing the bill from me as we concluded a long evening of many whiskeys.

Almost suddenly, the legal landscape around the use of PSCs in counter-piracy transformed. In December 2011, the British shipping minister Mike Penning released a statement acknowledging that the UK had reversed its position on private armed guards on board ships:

The word 'pirate' can conjure up cartoonish images of eye patches, parrots and wooden legs, but the reality is much more serious. Modern pirates are dangerous, organised criminals who have shown they are not shy of using violence to achieve their goals. We have not taken this decision lightly. It is clear that we must offer those flying the Red Ensign every opportunity to ensure the safety of their crews and vessels. By allowing the use of armed guards in a structured, legal framework we can move to a system where ship owners can provide an adequate deterrent against this scourge on the maritime industry. (UK Department for Transport, 2011)

Within days, the US State Department also withdrew its objections to private security escorts, and Jack and his fellow mercenaries were now the central providers of protection in the western Indian Ocean, with all indications that the mandate for the EU and US navies would be severely curtailed.

So how did private security come to win? I want to suggest that private security at sea was not simply a product of "neoliberalism," given the heavy critiques of privatization following Iraq and Afghanistan. This world had produced a surplus population of armed men whose "war making" (Tilly 1985) skills could easily transfer to policing the restive waters off the coast of Somalia. But before this could happen, it had to exorcise the ghosts of Iraq and Afghanistan. Doing so required transforming private security into a legitimate intermediary.

MAKING INTERMEDIARIES

"The problem with PSCs in Iraq was simple. They were asked to do too much." I was attending a series of trainings on the Montreux Document organized by private security contractors for the shipping industry in early 2012.[15] Speaker after speaker had sought to allay the fears of shipping companies by noting that private contractors were coming together to produce a document that actively welcomed regulation. A central theme involved distancing themselves from the misadventures of Iraq: "We had been asked to be soldiers," one speaker remarked. "That's not our job. We are in the business of protection, not building states." The language of work was crucial in rehabilitating the private security contractor. In the buildup to the Iraq War, Blackwater and other companies emphasized their deep relationship with the state. However, now they sought to emphasize their role as intermediaries outside the state. It was neither sovereign power nor profiteering that was the goal of private security, but salaries. As one speaker put it, "We're in the oldest business in the world for men."

When I suggested in interviews with contractors in Djibouti that they were perhaps profiting from piracy, most companies uniformly sought to deflect the charge back to navies or other bureaucrats. "We are the ones who can actually provide protection; the navies are the real profiteers." When I asked if his company was perhaps unfairly making money from piracy, Ron, an American contractor, responded angrily, "Look at how much they [naval forces] spend per day to do something we can provide for a fraction of the cost." Pointing to a medal on his desk, he sought to clarify: "I'm not saying the navies have no role. I'm an ex-marine, I respect the institution, but it makes no sense to have one-hundred-fifty-plus people in a warship patrolling the sea when you can have seven people attached to a merchant vessel." Uncomfortable with his cost-benefit logic, I quizzed Ron on the problem of trigger-happy security guards and indicated that I had heard first-hand accounts from fishermen in places as diverse as Lamu and Somaliland complaining of being shot at from commercial vessels with PMSCs on board. Ron, surprisingly, acknowledged the problem, but indicated that his company adhered to rigorous standards that made such incidents impossible. Ron posited bureaucratic accountability as a key mode of enforcing these rigorous standards. Pointing to a rather bulging file cabinet in the corner of his office, he noted, "We account for each and every bullet used by our teams. If there ever is a live-fire incident, they have to document in great detail, and, honestly, we drown them in paperwork—it's quite the deterrent." "So, then, who is shooting these fishermen?" I asked. "Oh, it's the upstarts. The problem is the upstarts, you know, all these new companies that are coming up. We need a good regulatory system, and all these issues will be sorted out." Instead of seeing themselves as outside the law, private maritime companies actively sought legal regulation as a mode of recognition. From firing on fishermen to allegations of bribery and illegal weapons purchases, the problems of private maritime security were easily explained as stemming from an absence of legal and regulatory oversight.

Consider the everyday life of private maritime security: often described in language of tedium and routine, this dull orderliness was nonetheless what gave it a form of legitimacy. "It's slow work most of the time." Jeff, an American private contractor, was describing the journey from Suez to Dubai. "We get on board in Suez. There is a hotel where we stay, and when we need to get on a ship, a small boat takes us so we can board from the gangway.

Once we're on board, we spend most of our time on the bridge or up front. It's quite boring. You're scanning the sea, checking out fishing vessels. Mostly, we sit around. When we get close to the HRA [High Risk Area], we advise the crew to stay inside while we carry out live fire exercises. We don't interact much with the crew. Imagine ten days where you don't really talk to anyone. Then finally you get to Dubai and slip out at a mobile base due to weapons restrictions before the ship docks in Jebel Ali." This customary description emphasized a broader way of engaging a life at sea, one that unites pirates, shippers, and other itinerant sojourners. But, for private maritime contractors, the idea of tedium was also a way of working against the idea that they were somehow undisciplined cowboys, shooting without consequences on a lawless ocean. "It's boring because we're the most regulated profession. Everything has a rule. Think about it. You got many different boats at sea. If they come close to us, we don't just shoot them. First, you give a warning. Then you give a second warning. After that you show your weapon and then and only then do you even get to shoot in the air. Forget about shooting at pirates. That's just media bullshit."

The rising tide of legalization did not, however, lift all boats. If Jack and his fellow "corporate warriors" in Djibouti looked the part of mercenaries, Farah, the fisherman-turned-pirate we met in chapter 1, had very little about him that suggested a warrior. Short and unassuming, he nonetheless had a serious reputation. "We've never been *buraad* [pirates]." Shaking his fists and waving his AK-47 towards me, Farah joked about his shooting abilities and his desire to be known as the most famous *abaan* (protector) in Somalia. "As I've said, I've never been a pirate; it's a dirty word. When you use it, you make me angry. What if I came to your country and asked you if you were a pirate? You could shoot me and that would be legitimate. I'm a fisherman, a coast-guard. I'm a businessman. I'm many things, but not a pirate." He ended his admonition, and we sat in silence, the buzz of the fan the only sound as I tried to regroup. "Stop fidgeting with your pen." I had been nervously playing with my pen in our awkward silence. Incredibly self-conscious, I turned to my research assistant and attempted to signal that we should try to extricate ourselves from this situation—but he too seemed struck silent. Farah got up, rewrapped his *mavis* (sarong), and started walking towards the door. Strangely relieved at the failure of my interview, I mumbled, "*Maalin wanaagsan* [see you later]," and got up to leave. But before I could take a step, Farah headed over, grabbed my hand, and started telling me about his new business plan:

You know you came to see me because I am a person who is an important person. Everyone must have told you to talk to me. So, I'm thinking that I will use this importance to help the foreigners. I want to think about my children and our future and have decided to create a security team to help ships pass through Somalia. We will go to sea and guide the ships. If someone tries to attack them we will fight. I will fight personally to guarantee their safety. I think it is a good business idea. (Farah, interview with author, November 2010)

When I returned to Somalia a few years later, I called Farah's number to inquire about the success of his new venture. When no one answered the phone, I asked a few people in town about Farah and his private security company. "He is gone." "Gone where?" I asked. "He decided to make his company, but they had no clients. One day he decided to go to sea like the coastguards used to in order to sell licenses to some ships. They tried to approach a ship to negotiate a license, but the ship had private security guards on board. They shot at Farah's boat. His boat was damaged and he decided to try and go to Yemen or Dubai . . . he left, I don't know where."

This chapter has focused on the world of intermediaries in the making (and unmaking) of ransoms. Moving between coastal Somalia and offices in London, we saw how transactions are structured and the gendered and racialized forms of numerical and nonnumerical valuation central to market-making. These forms of valuation shaped what James and other negotiators called detachment; they determined who negotiators trusted and the networks that link people like James and Bob, the American private security consultant, within the economy of counter-piracy. These forms of valuation are not only part of the extraordinary moment of ransom negotiations, but structure the mundane practices of life at sea, including the division of labor that brings people like Rajesh onto underinsured vessels. Ransom-making, then, reveals what is an everyday reality for the millions who labor on sea (and land). However, this is a world constantly in motion: by 2012, PSCs had transformed this world of piracy and counter-piracy by replacing negotiators and offering armed escorts to ships transiting through the western Indian Ocean. Ships protected by PSCs traveled through the region unscathed, in many ways bringing an end to the ransom economy of Somali piracy.

FIVE

Captivity at Sea

PIRATES ON DHOWS

"*WARYA, HINDI! KAISE HO? WARYA, KALEY, YAHAN AAO.*" This strange blend of Somali and Urdu at first seemed incomprehensible. Without turning back, I kept walking along the dock, dodging bags of rice and cement that were being unloaded in the harsh midday sun at the port of Bosaso in northeast Somalia. "*Urdu nahi samajthe yar tum?* [You don't understand Urdu, man?]" This time it was clear.

Hearing Urdu at the port wasn't necessarily a surprise. For the past few weeks, I had watched wooden dhows glide in and out of Bosaso daily. Bringing everything from daily staples to dentist chairs, Land Cruisers, and the occasional pink limousine, these boats make the circuit from Kutch and Gujarat in South Asia to Somalia via the ports of Dubai and Sharjah. They create a world of trade abutting the container ships (and, since 2007, naval vessels and pirate skiffs) that regularly ply these waters.

These dhows are manned by a diaspora of seafarers from western India and Pakistan, and therefore the sounds of Urdu, Gujarati, and Kutchi are as familiar in this sea of trade today as they were in the nineteenth century (Simpson 2006). Following the establishment of Aden in 1839 as a major coaling station for British shipping, Bosaso and neighboring Berbera became ports of call for the British Indian Navy. Eager to secure supplies—primarily livestock to feed bustling Aden across the Gulf—these naval vessels anchored into a preexisting world of trade and exchange. Then, as now, the northern Somali coast stretched outward—across the hot, salty Gulf of Aden—connecting these seemingly desolate port cities with worlds of exchange far beyond their hazy shorelines.

But the Urdu that accosted me on this day was not from the portly Rashid, a captain from Gwadar in Pakistan whose hometown was being transformed into a deepwater port financed and constructed by the Chinese, nor from Abdallah, a cook from Jam Salayah in India who constantly complained about the lack of chicken in the local market. Turning around, I saw a young Somali stevedore running towards me. Without further introduction, he immediately launched into a long narrative in almost flawless Urdu complaining about his current predicament and asking if, as his kinsman, I could help him get out of Somalia. I was puzzled by both his linguistic proficiency and his claim to kinship.

When I asked Jafaan, as he turned out to be called, why he spoke Urdu, he replied that he had grown up in Pakistan, a reminder of the wide scattering of the Somali diaspora. When I asked why he considered me kin, his answer was more mysterious: "I have eaten your food, you gave me protection, we are now kin." Following him around for the next few days, I noticed—to my slight disappointment—that the Urdu and claims to kinship were extended to every South Asian–looking visitor at the port—from boat captains to inquisitive and somewhat out-of-place anthropologists.

Over the course of our regular portside encounters, I would learn that Jafaan had an ambivalent relationship to the sea. One day, as we took shelter from the ever-present, glowering sun in the hold of a recently arrived boat, Jafaan explained, "I am *madhibaan* [a leather worker] and had never even been on a boat until two years ago." After being approached to join a pirate group, Jafaan decided to step aboard a skiff and found himself in the Indian Ocean. Wincing, he muttered "seasick" in English. Our conversations usually moved between Urdu and Somali, so the sudden English word stood out. "Seasick," he said again, before continuing in Urdu, "I got sick as soon as we left shore. I could not eat or drink anything." Still wincing in recollection, he settled into his story. "The money was good and it sounded like an easy job. I was told I would be a guard for the ship and get paid $20,000." But things did not go as planned for Jafaan. "I was sick all the time and the other guys on the boat were very upset. They even threatened to throw me overboard or shoot me if I didn't stop getting sick in front of them." He shook his head as he recounted his predicament. "But that wasn't the worst part. The navigator was a fool and we got lost." Trying to keep up the banter, I asked if they also threatened to shoot the navigator. Looking at me with puzzlement and some annoyance, he asked, "Why would someone shoot the navigator?" Then he continued: "We all thought we would die. Luckily then we saw a *vahaan* [Indian dhow] and made our way towards it and captured the boat. Once we got on board, I was better. It was bigger and there was no smell of diesel all the time. It was the best part of my time at sea. That is why I call an Indian my *aboowe* [brother]."

As we sat in the cool darkness of the hold, amidst the odd jumble of cardboard boxes filled with spaghetti packets, and rows upon rows of cheap plastic lawn chairs destined for tea stalls and restaurants from Bosaso to Mogadishu, Jafaan's tale hung heavy. Somewhat foolishly, I asked, "So are all pirates and Indians *walaalke* [siblings]?" Instead of answering my question directly, Jafaan simply noted, "Many of the people here who went out to sea [to become pirates] think of Indians as the enemy because the Indian Navy arrests and sometimes even kills their family members and friends. At port, we can be brothers; at sea, enemies—though sometimes we are also brothers at sea. Things are different at sea; a pirate can also be a *marti* [guest] on a boat."

Within a maritime world of violence and seizure, Jafaan's language of kinship and the claim that pirates can sometimes appear onboard as guests is an opening for a reconsideration of the boundaries of enmity—central to understanding the figure of the pirate and piracy—in the context of economies of capture. Neither a denial of violence nor an erasure of force, the pirate as guest points to an alternative genealogy of piracy—where piracy is a trade of no dishonor and the pirate is a fellow traveler along liquid paths. This comingling of intimacy and violence provides a way to imagine sociality and connection, through encounters that are fleeting and abrupt, though built on longer histories. A shape-shifting vessel that has been central to stitching together a world of trade and mobility as well as one of captivity, piracy, and escape, the dhow is the central ship through which I tell this story of hospitality in captivity. Unlike the network of mediators previously discussed, the dhow is both essential to piracy, especially as the geographies of piracy shifted from the Red Sea to the Indian Ocean, and also an unwilling partner. This ambiguity brings to the fore the slippery nature of capture and captivity.

Capture as act is central in the anthropological archive; it is a mode of engendering and sustaining forms of sociality. From the reciprocal raiding of livestock (Evans-Pritchard 1969) to practices of bride capture (Barnes 1999; Herzfeld 1985; Pitt-Rivers 1977), the anthropological record makes clear that the act of capture gives status to the captor while also allowing for the establishment and continuation of a social relationship between captor and (the kin of the) captive. Captivity, on the other hand, is the state of being held. The prison and Atlantic slavery often serve as models for captivity, revealing institutionalized ways of producing abandonment, social death, and precarity (Allison 2013; Povinelli 2011; Sharpe 2016; Standing 2011). But captivity is also a place for forging new intimacies. It is central to the dynamics of hospitality, with its ritualized modes of engagement between guest and host, as well as being a state of incarceration. The dhow as mothership sutures these two literatures together in productive ways, showing that a vessel employed in the capture of other vessels can be both a means to an end and an end in itself. The mothership as a space of captivity and technology of capture thus emphasizes forms of social relationship that emerge specifically out of states of confinement: relationships built not on freedom as the opposite of captivity but on protection as the opposite of isolation.

THE WORLD OF THE DHOW

Central to trade and mobility in the Indian Ocean, dhows initially operated at a far remove from piracy. They traveled between ports from South Asia to East Africa, connecting locales otherwise excluded by the itineraries of container ships. However, this shape-shifting vessel eventually became key to the world of piracy as pirates transformed it from trading vessel to a veritable technique of captivity. From 2008, as naval vessels started patrolling the Red Sea and interdicting suspected pirate skiffs, pirates had to launch themselves farther offshore in search of cargo ships. Piracy transformed into a floating diaspora scattered across the western Indian Ocean with attacks occurring as close as forty nautical miles off the coast of India. Central to the making of this new diaspora, like the older diasporas of the Indian Ocean, was the dhow, transformed this time into the contemporary form of the nineteenth-century mothership.

During the height of the whaling boom in the nineteenth century, motherships were central in expanding the reach of the whaling trade by functioning as a base from which smaller, faster cutters could be launched to chase and kill whales. The whale meat was then processed and stored on these larger ships—a practice that continues to this day in the fishing industry, where motherships are now called factory ships and are used to store and process catch. For whalers, motherships were not only little floating factories but also ways of domesticating the sea, of extending intersubjective space-time in these watery domains (Munn 1992).

Instead of a vessel that allowed whalers to travel far and wide in search of the lumbering giants that illuminated the nineteenth century, the dhow as mothership enabled pirates to chase a different beast: the oil tanker that fuels contemporary globalization. Dhows promised a modicum of stability in the monsoonal open waters of the Indian Ocean, an ability to traverse long distances and to extend the amount of time one can spend at sea. This made it possible to transform Somali piracy into a western Indian Ocean practice and to evade naval patrols. Additionally, attaching themselves to the dhow was a way for pirates to blend into maritime traffic. The sea, as we've repeatedly seen, is not an empty space. From pieces of ambergris to schools of tuna, from small fishing boats to post-Panamax cargo ships, a variety of objects and living beings circulate, float, drown, and are washed ashore constantly. The dhow was yet another way to blend into this crowded world at sea, providing camouflage and cover. In addition to the protection of diya groups on land, dhows became an unlikely and unwilling ally to piracy in the Indian Ocean.

In early 2010, seven Indian dhows were hijacked off the coast of Somalia and over a hundred seafarers held captive over the duration of a week (Hindu 2010). These dhows were not captured for their cargo, but instead were refashioned into what the European Union (EU) called "motherships" (a term very quickly adopted by seafarers, dhow captains, and even pirates). By hijacking these trading ships and using them as a mobile base for their activities, pirates transformed dhows into motherships. In response to a steady increase in the capture of dhows, NATO and the EU launched a "Dhow Project" in 2011. As the description of the Dhow Project states,

> It is known in the Maritime Security industry that Somali pirates use hijacked ... dhows as "Motherships" in order to operate at extreme range from Somalia, carrying attack craft (skiffs) and weapons. NATO has received reports of Somali pirates using common local ships in piracy attacks. They will board the ship and hold the original crew hostage. A local ship enables the pirates to blend in among the boating traffic and present itself as a fishing or trading vessel. (Officer of the Watch 2012)

The Dhow Project sought to understand the dhow trading routes in the western Indian Ocean as well as to provide seafarers with dhow recognition charts in order to make visible to cargo ships the threat of motherships that lurked adjacent to their sea-lanes. In spite of this surveillance system, by 2011, dhows had become central to the story of piracy and counter-piracy.

The transformation of the dhow into the mothership is the latest transformation of this most Indian Ocean of vessels. Referring to a range of ships of differing sizes with names such as *sanduqs*, *jahazis*, and *vahaans* that crisscrossed the western Indian Ocean before the advent of steam, the dhow, with its single lateen sail and wooden construction, is both an embodiment of the dense trade networks of the western Indian Ocean and, since the advent of European incursions, the object of its regulation. As the historian Abdul Sheriff (2010, 1) poetically notes:

[The dhow] is often imagined as an uncouth leaky vessel with a triangular lateen sail, carrying a motley crew of Arabs. Its holds were filled with a miscellaneous cargo of Arabian dates, dried fish, Indian and African timber, food grains, Indian cotton goods, Indonesian spices, Chinese pottery, and African ivory, as well as passengers or slaves in every direction.

For Sheriff and others, the dhow embodies the cosmopolitan ethos of Indian Ocean commerce, a polyglot world built on the circulation of objects, peoples, and ideas in the leaky holds of these wooden ships that sailed according to the timeline of the monsoon.

Unlike European vessels, dhows take their names not from rigs (the combination of sails), but from the shape of their stern (the back part of the ship), and are often divided between coastal and oceangoing vessels.[1] The very term *dhow* emerged from British attempts at classifying this range of "native craft" into one unifying legal category. In the nineteenth century, as colonial empires sought to consolidate their hold on the Indian Ocean littoral, regulating dhow traffic became the maritime counterpart of this extension of colonial sovereignty.[2] As the historian Erik Gilbert (2004) notes, the dhow trade was part of a larger colonial discourse of modernity and tradition. For the British, the dhow exemplified the traditional, premodern trading world of slaves and spices, and was therefore an anachronism in an era of free trade and steamers. The dhow economy was recast as piratical in the late nineteenth century, with European warships regularly patrolling these waters in search of pirates and assorted traders of disrepute amidst the wooden boats that circulated between South Asia and East Africa.[3]

This project of illegalization unfolded within a broader global shift from sail to steam. Prior to the opening of the Suez Canal, European clippers and other sailing vessels competed with a variety of other ships to create a multinational trading economy. Numerous Asian and African seafarers sought employment on European and American sailing ships, often rising in rank due to their skill in navigation and intimate knowledge of the monsoonal patterns of the Indian Ocean.

The opening of the Suez Canal in late 1869 transformed this world of sail. In addition to dramatically reducing the sailing time between Europe and

Asia, the canal quickly made European sailing vessels obsolete in the Indian Ocean. Transporting clippers across the narrow canal required tugs, a process that was both impractical and expensive. By the following year, the era of clippers was over and steam vessels reigned supreme over the lucrative Indian Ocean routes. This transition was a deeply racialized project. Employment on steam vessels for non-European workers was limited to various unskilled categories and to jobs that were often the most dangerous and difficult, such as coal-making. This led to exploitative employment patterns, as well as setting up the racial division of labor that continues to shape global shipping.

In addition, the steamship, as the historian Tamson Pietsch (2006) notes, radically changed ideas about the self and the world in Britain, and indeed elsewhere. Through close attention to the journeys of the young Scottish medical student J. T. Wilson who, between 1884 and 1887, made three voyages to China and one to Australia, she highlights how, in the space of the ship, Wilson forged a particular kind of British identity that collapsed the spaces of empire, elided differences among Britons, and extended the boundaries of the British nation. Similarly, for societies of the Indian Ocean rim, steamships, and later railways, loosened these places from the rhythms of the monsoons in ways that made new kinds of mobility possible. Steamship service integrated distant reaches of the ocean, such as KwaZulu-Natal in South Africa, within older trade networks, effectively expanding the Indian Ocean region. Additionally, steamships required coaling stations along the route from Suez to India, which led to the revival of old port cities (such as Aden) along the Red Sea coast. Just as important, as Jeremy Prestholdt notes, "railways stretched far inland, linking port cities with small communities and burgeoning cities across the interiors of Indian Ocean and Red Sea coastal states" (2015, 443). The temporalities and spatial geographies of steam, like those of sail before it, created new forms of mobility that spun together "places, texts and persons in meaningful narratives of travel" (Ho 2006, 28).

The transition from sail to steam was, however, not a totalizing project. The dhow continued to operate at the margins of the Indian Ocean economy, primarily transporting goods that were not profitable to steamships and going to places excluded from the new geographies of steam. While the dhow survived these nineteenth- and early twentieth-century attempts at regulation, the onset of decolonization and the transformations wrought by the rise of oil—what Timothy Mitchell (2011) has called "carbon democracy"— seemingly struck a death blow to this transregional economy. Bulk carriers, with larger cargo capacity than dhows and fueled by cheap diesel, reduced

FIGURE 10: Port security guard on board Indian dhow in Bosaso, 2012. Photo by author.

transport costs and spurred a period of port-building and expansion in the region. In addition, nationalism along the oceanic rim, built on claims to land, earth, and soil, turned its back to the Indian Ocean. This postcolonial lockdown led to the dhow, and with it the sea, receding from view, fading into the realm of the nostalgic and the artisanal. But the rise of containerized shipping and ever-increasing ship sizes ironically brought back the dhow in the 1970s, transformed this time into the motorized sailing vessel, or MSV.

Before the rise of containerization, the hold of a ship consisted of a jumble of objects tightly packed together, secured by rope and the ingenious spatial awareness of stevedores and other cargo loaders. Bags of cement would sit cheek-by-jowl with tins of soup, cars next to hospital beds. Loading and unloading ships was time-consuming and slow. The container and the rise of containerization both made cargo invisible and sped up time in global shipping.[4] Containerization was a process of streamlining and standardization. The uniform dimensions of the container make loading and unloading, including the transportation of goods from ships to trains and trucks, seamless and straightforward, at least in theory.[5] However, not all ports transformed into container terminals—due to location, or often, infrastructural limits. Containerized shipping thus created a parallel economy, a world of cheap trade operating in the shadow of free trade that connected these out-of-time ports.

The reverberations of containerization, the rise of Dubai in the 1970s and 80s, and the first Iraq war (1990–91) created a transregional trade network that operated in the underbelly of the logistics revolution. Primarily transporting bulk goods such as rice, cement, foodstuffs, and charcoal on wooden dhows and other small bulk carriers, this shipping network can be understood as an economy of arbitrage.[6] "We pick up things from Dubai, Sharjah, and Oman that are unloaded from container ships," I was told by a boat captain, who explained the logic of this trade network as he waited for his ship to be loaded in Bosaso in July 2013. "We get tea from Kenya, cement from India, sugar and wheat in Oman, and bring it to Somalia. Some boats also go to Iran. Twenty years ago, we started this job. At that time, we picked up things to take to Iraq from Dubai, because ships were not going to Basra in those days [due to trade sanctions and insurance costs]." For the captain, and many others, the logic is simple: they travel to places where container ships cannot or will not go due to expenses, port capacity, or security. Profits are made and lost in this economy due to price and time differentials (selling livestock from Somalia instead of Australia or New Zealand) or through regulatory arbitrage (going to places where other ships cannot go due to insurance and hazard pay costs or legal sanctions). In the case of Somalia, war (and, from 2007 onwards, piracy) pushed out container ships, and dhows eagerly filled up the vacuum left by these vessels (Dua 2016).

THRESHOLD: THE MOMENT OF CAPTURE

The homeports of dhows lie on the west coast of India and Pakistan, in the port cities of Gujarat and Kutch. While these towns provide the infrastructure (the people, boats, and credit) for the dhow trade, most of the cargo is picked up in the major transshipment ports[7] of the Arabian Peninsula. In 2012, during my research in Sharjah (one of these major transshipment ports for the dhow trade), numerous boat captains remembered their surprise when pirate skiffs sought to commandeer their vessels to search for container ships. "*Bhai* [brother], we had heard scary things about Somalia." Shafiq—a captain from Pakistan—and I were chatting during a break from a particularly animated game of cricket played in the shadow of a container that was being unloaded and reloaded inside the hold of his dhow. "It was late at night, some *gandu* [asshole] was playing the Indian national anthem on the radio as we traveled in the pitch dark towards Mogadishu." Shafiq explained how other ships often used the shortwave radio to play music or hurl obscenities at each other. "It's boring when you're sailing, so we play around with each other," he said in English. Shipboard radios are a constant source of chatter at sea. As Shafiq explained, "Most of the time people are cursing each other or playing bad music, but we also inform each other if anything is suspicious. I was looking at the AIS screen, lots of dots, each a boat late at night, when suddenly I see two dots following us. Nowadays everyone will know this is a pirate attack, but those days [2010] it was a little different. Pirates were going after big ships and would leave us alone." Shafiq described how gunshots rang out and, before he had time to react, pirates had boarded the ship.

This unexpected arrival of armed pirates at the threshold of the dhow resonates with their entrance onto other vessels. Comparing these scenes of arrival on various ships highlights not only the centrality of violence in shaping capture but also the distinctions between cargo ships and dhows.

Let's start with the capture of a cargo ship, which is the better-known version of a piracy hijacking and told in many movies, most notably the 2013 Hollywood film *Captain Phillips*. Based loosely on the high-profile hijacking of the big container ship *Maersk Alabama* in 2009, *Captain Phillips* renders this incident cinematically and is the most visible narrative of Somali piracy in popular media. It begins on land, where the white American title character is on his way to Oman to take command of the *Maersk Alabama* for its journey to Mombasa, Kenya, through the pirate waters of the Red Sea and the western Indian Ocean. As the captain and his wife discuss the perils of school tuition and the everyday anxieties of neoliberal life in the United States, the scene shifts between rainy New England and the bright, unblinking sun of coastal Somalia, where a pirate expedition is being organized. Young men speaking mostly untranslated Somali are volunteering to hijack ships. We know little about the motivation of these young men as they prepare to board rusty skiffs, but the tattered clothes and the general poverty of the surroundings seemingly give us all the information we need.

After this general introduction on land, the rest of the movie takes place at sea. As the *Maersk Alabama* travels along the pirate-infested waters off the Somali coast, two skiffs suddenly appear alongside the ship. Evading one of the boats, the large lumbering *Maersk* is unable to escape the climbing ladder of the second boat. Within minutes a pirate foursome has boarded the ship, and taken the captain and his crew hostage. "Don't be afraid, I'm the captain now," declares the young leader of this ragtag gang, thus setting the stage for capture.

The sudden and violent arrival of armed pirates sets the theme for the rest of the movie. As in the movie, in reality seafarers on big cargo ships also talk about sudden arrivals. They share their stories with each other and with the curious anthropologist in their midst in social spaces, like seafarer clubs. During fieldwork conducted from 2010 to 2012, Mission to Seafarers (MtS) clubs, which dot major port cities around the world, were important sites for meeting seafarers employed in global shipping. Established in 1835 by the Anglican priest John Ashley, in the port town of Bristol, MtS clubs now operate in over two hundred ports globally, providing spaces of both reflection and companionship for seafarers in transit. In the port city of Mombasa, in addition to providing a space of spiritual counsel and mundane forms of entertainment, the MtS club had also become a place of solace and recovery, since 2009, for seafarers who had been held captive by Somali pirates.

A short distance from the Kilindini Harbour (home to the Mombasa port, the largest port in East Africa) and tucked away from the bustle of Moi Avenue lies the Mombasa branch of the MtS club. Upon entering the somewhat modest 1950s concrete building, one walks past the Anglican chapel and towards the common room. Here, amidst the TV screens showing football and a small bar serving samosas, chai, and beer, seafarers from all parts of the world mill about as they rest and recover before journeying onward from Mombasa. In 2010, the common room was abuzz with tales of encounters and near misses with pirates. An Indonesian mariner working for over ten years in the global maritime industry, Johan, had been held hostage for over six months and had just arrived in Mombasa when we met at the Mission restaurant. Over the course of a long meal he told me his story of capture in the Indian Ocean.

As Johan described it, his ship was the ideal prey for pirates. A chemical tanker, like the *Nori,* his ship was loaded down with cargo and cruising slowly through the Gulf of Aden. "Our ship doesn't have the best of security systems. We had some water hoses, but no fences or any other physical barriers. I'm first mate, so the night we were hijacked I was actually on the bridge with a cadet looking at the navigation scanners." Johan said that he reassured himself that things would be fine: "It was a clear and bright night, almost a full moon . . . We know that pirates prefer dark, cloudy nights or early mornings. I told myself at 0600 hours we'll be near a coalition vessel [navy ship]— just get through the night." Unfortunately, four dots appeared closer and closer on the AIS. "I had a sinking feeling when I saw them on the screen. I don't think I even got on radio to confirm their identity. I knew it was pirates." Within ten minutes, the pirates were on the bridge and Johan's ship was hijacked.

Johan's story, like that of Captain Phillips, is one of sudden interruption and rupture from the mundane, everyday life at sea. Piracy, as the unexpected arrival at the threshold, is a process of violent disruption—of itineraries and lives—but also a space "betwixt and between." Anthropologists have long observed the crucial role of the threshold as a symbolic space of transformation. For Arnold van Gennep (1960) and others (Shields 1991; Turner 1967), the threshold (*limen*) is a crucial space in demarcating individual and social transformation. Importantly, for van Gennep, the threshold is also a physical space: as he notes, "the passage from one social position to another is identified with a *territorial passage,* such as the entrance into a village or a house, the movement from one room to another, or the crossing of streets and squares" (1960, 192; emphasis mine). The moment of arrival is thus a space of (temporary) reversals. "I am the captain now," utters the pirate to Captain Phillips when the *Maersk Alabama* is captured.

These arrival scenes also echo Maurice Blanchot's (1995) writings on the disaster as that which has no history—a sovereignty of the event. For Blanchot, disaster is linked to what is unthinkable and thus cannot be written. This sudden and unexpected arrival is crucial in shaping piracy as without either history or context. The drama of hijacking is premised on beginning the story with the arrival scene, through a disavowal of any previous histories or other forms of relationality. It is here, though, that a fruitful contrast can be made between the hijacking of the container ship and the capture of dhows as motherships. While dhow capture is also defined through sudden and violent arrivals, this crossing of a threshold, unlike rites of passage, is located within other encounters and more mundane histories.

Like most dhow captains, Shafiq had a small amount of cash and boxes of cigarettes that are often essential "gifts" during encounters with customs officials, inspectors, and the occasional pirates. But in this case, something unexpected happened: "I offered them the money, but they said no. One of the guys, who was their navigator, pointed to my AIS and said 'Let's go find a big ship.'" For the next two weeks, Shafiq's dhow operated as a mothership guiding pirates through the western Indian Ocean shipping lanes. However, the pirates were unsuccessful in coming close to a big ship. "They tried for a while, but then gave up and slipped out at night right before we arrived in Mogadishu."

While the capture of container ships and the capture of dhows both begin with a similarly unexpected arrival of pirates, these moments of capture are located in two distinct scales and histories. For those on board big cargo ships, pirates arrive out of nowhere, inaugurating a story of capture and violence. The transformation of the dhow into the mothership necessitates a different relationship. As Shafiq's tale highlights, the arrival on board is a moment of violence: there are gunshots, and Shafiq and other dhow captains described the fear they experienced. However, Shafiq immediately tried to make them familiar through the offer of "gifts." And in contrast to the capture of container ships, pirates boarding dhows do not claim to become captains: instead, it is the vessel and the skill of the dhow captain that are essential. Unlike a moment of rupture, then, capture harkens back to an older anthropological archive of making and sustaining relationships through forms of taking (without apparent giving). If we move beyond the threshold into life in the hold, we see the forms of social relationship, on land and at sea, that are central to making and sustaining captivity.

THE HOLD: LIFE IN CAPTIVITY

What kind of relationship is possible with someone who arrives at the threshold, armed? What kind of relationship is possible with someone who takes without giving? The encounter between pirate skiffs and dhows is an encounter effected through violence. In response to the hijacking of the Indian dhows in 2010, the Indian government attempted to limit the circulation of these boats in the Indian Ocean and banned dhows from sailing south of Oman. Yet a steady stream of boats continued traveling from Gujarat to ports on the Arabian Peninsula, and from there onward to Somalia.

For Rahimullah, the decision to continue sailing despite the ban was straightforward. "This is our work. It's always dangerous. There were many times when a big wave almost wiped us out. Anything can happen when you are at sea. When the government restricted travel to Somalia, we had to keep going. Otherwise, some other boat would make that journey." Rahimullah and I were chatting on the deck of his dhow as he awaited his cargo of livestock to take across the Gulf of Aden to Dubai. After a long description of the market for goats and the change in trade since the 1990s, our conversation faded into silence. As we sat on the deck watching the longshoremen load hay, he told me his boat had been used as a mothership on at least two separate occasions.

Recalling the moment of arrival when pirates appeared at his threshold, Rahimullah explained, "We had just left the port of Salalah [in Oman] when

[we] heard on the radio that the *ali babas* had been seen by someone not far from where we were." As Rahimullah described it, they left the port late at night—a practice common in Red Sea ports during the unforgiving summer, when loading and unloading livestock occurs during the relatively mild nighttime hours. "All of a sudden, before we could head back to the port, a small boat came alongside us and fired shots." Alarmed at the gunshots, Rahimullah slowed down the ship. "We didn't know where they were and didn't want to get killed. I cut the engine and they boarded us." "Were you scared?" I asked. "Of course! The *ali babas* had come onboard with guns."

As I sat chatting with Rahimullah, his story was interrupted when another captain joined us for tea. "He wants to know about pirates," Rahimullah said to Haji Ali as he introduced me. A native of Kutch who was in Bosaso unloading a cargo of air conditioners, Haji Ali was significantly older than Rahimullah. Bespectacled and sporting an immaculate gray beard, Haji Ali wanted to know if I had any connections to the Indian government and dutifully studied my letter of invitation from the Puntland Ministry of Ports before settling in for tea.

"Life has no value for them [pirates]," he began, echoing a common sentiment I heard from seafarers on both cargo ships and dhows. "I've had many experiences with them. Just twenty minutes from Bosaso in the middle of the day, once, our ship was taken." Staring out at the hazy blue water, deceptively calm for a May afternoon, he continued: "We were sailing away empty because it was almost the end of the season. There were some fishing boats not far from the dhow. I was inside the bridge when all of a sudden two of these boats started following us. I looked from the bridge and saw they had grenade launchers." Having described the violence of arrival, Haji Ali continued his tale of being captured by pirates. "After they had taken the boat, it was clear they wanted for me to take them out to the Indian Ocean."

"What happened after they came on board?" I asked Rahimullah and Haji Ali. "*Hum sab gharib log hain* [we are all poor people]," Haji Ali cryptically replied to my question before continuing. "They are *gharib* like us, we had to live with them. What else was supposed to happen?" He explained that after the first sleepless night, when pirates pointed their weapons at him and his crew all night, things gradually calmed down. The next day, weapons were put down and pirates gradually transformed into faux crew members. On dhow journeys crewmembers live and sleep in close proximity within the small hold of the boat. "As you can see, we have no separate rooms here." Rahimullah pointed to the somewhat cavernous main room of his boat. The room had one main window where the helm and navigational equipment was located, and one corner converted into a kitchen. In the opposite corner were piled a number of mattresses and other bedding. "At night we spread out the mattresses and sleep in the center of the room," he explained. "The pirates also slept here, just like crew," he added. Beyond this close physical proximity, the operation of the mothership required pirates and crew members to turn into (unwilling) accomplices in ways that unsettled the distinctions between captor and captive.

Unlike other spaces of captivity, the mothership is simultaneously about being held in place and also about a mobile meandering through watery domains. In order to capture cargo ships, motherships need to constantly travel, farther and farther away from coastal waters. Navigating open waters, especially the waters of the Indian Ocean where no land is visible on any side, is a far trickier prospect, and one where dhow captains have more experience than pirates (who often had been fishermen working close to the coast and have little experience of going to open waters). A standard refrain amongst dhow captains I spoke with was the recognition that pirates often appeared clueless about the operation of ships far from shore. Both Haji Ali and Rahimullah described how helpless pirates appeared on board dhows. Haji Ali recalled the *khauf* (terror) when he started turning the dhow towards the Indian Ocean. "As I started turning the ship, they [the pirates] panicked. They were convinced I was taking them to Djibouti to the navy ships! I had to explain to them that we were going in the right direction. When I showed them where we were on the radar they had no clue how to read the screen. Finally, I had to take one of the pirates outside on deck and show him the location of the sun. Only then did they believe me." Haji Ali narrated this story with a certain amount of bravado and took pleasure in noting the lack of navigational skills on the part of pirates. This register of bravado is not out of place in the dhow economy. Captains would often refer to novice sailors in similar ways. An important part of crew sociality on board involved telling tales of basic errors and other accidents caused by apprentices (or heroically averted by the intervention of the captain). Beyond the boat, this mode is also prevalent in shipyards in Gujarat, where the mistakes of novice craftsmen are used as fodder for taunting and chiding these boat makers and sailors in training as well as reshaping their bodily habitus (Simpson 2006).

These stories of cohabitation and the rendering of pirates as somewhat inept, in a sense, is a mode of domesticating the violence of pirates into a practice of hospitality. As anthropologists like Andrew Shryock (2004) and Matei

Candea (2012) have shown, beyond an abstract scale-free system of rights and obligations, of citizens and noncitizens with clearly defined roles and notions of reciprocity, hospitality exists as an "object of contention, concern, and debate" (Candea 2012, S42) in everyday practice. As Rahimullah and Haji Ali's stories signal, whether lost, hungry, thirsty for water, short on fuel, or just looking for a mobile base from which to attack ships, the pirate arrives at the threshold. This is clearly a moment of violence, as the pirate arrives armed and holds the crew hostage through the threat and enactment of force. Yet in the coming hours, days, and sometimes months of capture, hijackers and hijacked sleep in the same place, guns are put away, and pirates become dependent on the navigational skill of dhow captains.

Like the parasite as depicted by Michel Serres (1980), the pirate takes residence in the system and engages in a form of taking without giving. Mothershipping rechannels the dhow towards the world of containerized shipping in whose underbelly this arbitrage economy already operates. It both makes apparent the ways in which channeling and rechanneling create value at sea and at the same time makes possible a brief, temporary form of relationship. The AK-47 put away in the corner, the meals shared, and Bollywood DVDs watched are the material objects that mediate this relationship of protection. Instead of the move from sympathy to disavowal or even what Achille Mbembe (1992, 3) calls the "conviviality of the ruler and the ruled," we have forms of acknowledgement, of temporary living together in the rocky hold of a ship. "*Hum sab gharib log hain* [we are all poor]" transforms the enemy of all into a fellow traveler. Like Aristotle's (1962) oikos, piracy in this watery expanse is a natural mode of acquisition. These everyday encounters are moments when identities of hijacker and hostage—of pirate and merchant—are transformed and reconfigured though not dissolved.

This recognition of cohabitation is one shared by pirates as well, who also acknowledge their own lack of navigational skills and dependency on dhow captains. In their narratives of time on board dhows, pirates would often refer to being dependent on dhow captains and liken this dependency to that of the *marti* (guest).

THE PIRATE AS GUEST

In 1331, the venerable Moroccan traveler Ibn Battuta reached Somali shores and landed in the northern port of Zeil'a in present-day Somaliland. Within a day he had set sail again, glad to have left behind what he called the "most desolate and smelliest place in the known world," a condition he attributed to the presence of a large fish market in the center of the town and the blood of numerous camels that were slaughtered daily. Traveling south for fifteen days and fifteen nights, he finally arrived in Mogadishu, a city far more to his liking. Ibn Battuta's recollection of his arrival into this cosmopolitan and urbane port city is a chronicle of the slippages between cosmopolitan hospitality and the policing of this hospitality through coercion. In describing the practice of *jiwar* common in cosmopolitan Mogadishu, Ibn Battuta (cited in Dunn 1989, 123) noted that the following occurred immediately upon mooring:

> Boatloads of young men came out to meet [the ship], each carrying a covered platter of food to present to one of the merchants on board. When the dish was offered the merchants fell under an obligation to go with the man to his house and accept his services as broker. The Mogaidshi then placed the visitor under his "protection," [transforming the visitor into a *mustajir* (protected guest)] sold his goods for him, collected payment and helped him find a cargo for the outbound passage – all this at a healthy commission deducted from the profits.

Through the acceptance of food, a social relationship of protection is constructed. Framed in a language of *mujir* (protector/host) and *mustajir* (protected/guest), this practice then temporarily ties the stranger to the host. As Ibn Battuta notes, the *mustajir* is compelled to go to the house of the host. At this point the host is not only the protector of the guest, but also a supplier, broker, and, importantly, guarantor, highlighting the transactional and commercial structure of this relationship. There is an aspect of coercion to this encounter: to buy and sell without the presence of the host, as reported by Ibn Battuta and other medieval travelers, not only renders the sale invalid, but has consequences for the unfortunate *mustajir*. Ibn Battuta's writings, as well as the work of other medieval travelers, are filled with this mix of protection and coercion. To be a *marti* on a dhow, as many pirates described their time aboard motherships, was to engage within the forms of relationality outlined by Ibn Battuta and his fellow fourteenth-century travelers. There were stories of sharing food, of locating each other within economies on land, and finally coercion, but also protection.

After Jafaan told me of his time at sea, he decided to accompany me during my fieldwork at the port of Bosaso. His linguistic proficiency in Urdu and his seemingly endless network of friends in the customs office made him an ideal companion for navigating the port. In the brief lulls of our day when we would find ourselves alone, I would try to ask him more questions about his time aboard a dhow. For Jafaan, being a "guest" on the dhow meant being in a space where he could claim protection. This form of protection meant an escape from seasickness and a modicum of stability in the unstable maritime realm. Like other pirates, he arrived on board armed and slowly settled into the rhythms of life on the dhow. These rhythms included debates over cooking. When I asked him about life on board, he repeatedly emphasized the exceedingly spicy nature of the food cooked by the dhow crew and the notable absence of spaghetti (an Italian legacy from colonial times). Additionally, he remembered the DVD collections and how he enjoyed watching Bollywood movies. These material objects and the proximity of captor and captive are central to negotiating the hospitality of the mothership and transforming the mothership into a space of protection.

In opposition to Jafaan's sensorial experience of the dhow built around an absence of seasickness, regular albeit spicy food, and DVDs and forms of onboard entertainment (a recollection shared by a number of other pirates), Cawil, an ex-pirate, recalled his time on the dhow in a distinct register, one that made him reconsider his decision to become a pirate. On what turned out to be an unsuccessful attempt at a hijacking, Cawil and his crew got lost at sea. "We were floating without food and water. I could only taste the salt on my lips. One of the crew members had tried to drink water from the sea and was in a miserable condition." As day turned into night, Cawil and his crew thought this would be their last night when suddenly a light was visible at sea. "When we first saw the dhow, I was worried it was a *djinn*. But we decided that if the djinn was a deceptive djinn, there was nothing we could do to resist it." As they set out in pursuit of the lights, a heavily loaded Indian dhow came into view. "We were so happy when we got onboard. I was pleased the crew was Muslim. I could perform *salat,* instead of just offering *dua* from the skiff. It was a sign from God, and when we returned I gave up piracy." Cawil's recollections reframed the hijacking of the dhow into an act of rescue and redemption. His recognition of djinns is one familiar to many dhow captains and part of a shared idiom of understanding encounters at sea. Beyond the sensorial stability that Jafaan experienced, for Cawil the dhow transformed into a shrine, a place to perform ablutions and thus properly engage in prayer (Parkin and Headley 2000). As for seafarers who engage in visitation of shrines along coastal regions, the sanctuary of the dhow is oriented within a shared Islamic project of pilgrimage. The protection afforded through capture is embodied here as well, but oriented towards a different scale, and serves as a reminder of the human and nonhuman energies that animate mobility in this oceanic realm.

As Andrew Shryock (2012) has noted, the subtle interplay of welcome and trespass that characterizes the dynamics of hospitality is one located in particular name-spaces and often premised on the pervasiveness of hierarchy, but also on its deferral through the idea that the host today can reappear as a guest another day. In the hospitality of the mothership, in addition to the incorporation into everyday life on board, it is previous social relationships as well as ones on land that are essential in defusing tensions and transforming pirates into guests. By 2010, the "Somali route" (as dhow captains called it) had become one of the most important sources of revenue for the dhow economy, as well as being the primary shipping connection for Somalia with the outside world. Big cargo ships had started to avoid Somali waters altogether. Rahimullah had told me earlier how dhow owners started building bigger and wider ships to accommodate Somalia's shipping needs. "With the big container ships, they make them big enough to go through [the] Suez Canal. They call them 'Suezmax.' For us [dhows], the average size now is that which can transport things to Somalia, so we jokingly call them 'Somali-max dhows.' Somalia is very important to us": so much so, he continued, that by 2011 "we had Somali businessmen who would buy dhows. So many of the boats in Mandvi [Gujarat] are actually all owned by Somalis." This close intimacy of the dhow and Somalia meant that encounters between pirates and dhows occurred within frameworks of familiarity, and both dhow crews and pirates were able to draw on these other scales and histories in order to transform dhows into motherships and pirates into (armed) guests. As a dhow owner in Bosaso noted, "If my dhow gets captured, I can immediately find out who the pirates are and make sure that either they leave as soon as possible, or nothing is interrupted too much."

Encounters contain within them moments that seemingly escape narration. Moments of cohabitation between dhow crews and pirates also offer their own aporias and awkward silences. Crew members would retell in vivid detail the moment of arrival. The fear and anxiety of being hijacked or for pirates the respite and relief of finding a boat that could lead one to larger ships at sea and potential riches featured prominently in these stories. In addition, the time of captivity, including the repurposing of the dhow into the mothership and the modes of living together in the hold, were seen as unremarkable, but nonetheless shared freely with audiences in Gujarat,

Sharjah, and Somalia. Crew members would often snatch my notebook when I asked them questions about cooking and eating together with pirates. At first, I worried about the ethics of my transcription. In those moments I would reiterate my university Institutional Research Board protocol and inform them of their right to refuse to participate or divulge any further information. The crew would usually shrug and after a distracted perusal return my notebook. One day, as he returned the notebook, a crew member remarked that he wanted to see the notebook because it seemed strange that I would want to know about such a "basic thing":

> It's a surprise when you ask questions like "what did you cook with the pirates" or "where did they sleep." It's basic information. Of course, they slept like crew and ate what we were eating. Sometimes they would complain about this or that, and smoke all our cigarettes. Then we would secretly curse them using Urdu! But it's such basic life, so that's why I looked at your notebook. (Ameem, interview with author, June 2013)

But what was studiously avoided was a discussion of departures (more on that below), as well as questions about collusion and payment. When I asked the dhow captains if they actively helped pirates get on board ships or if they received any payment for acting as motherships, captains would reiterate that they are simply merchants who were held hostage. Similarly, when I asked pirates if they preselected which dhows to use as motherships, I would be met with a deafening silence. These silences suggest a distance, a mode of plausible deniability at the heart of these encounters. It is important to understand that I'm not suggesting a collusion between pirates and dhow captains (a question that animates the NATO Dhow project), but rather that these silences and aporias point to what is happening in the space of captivity. These are spaces of temporary coming together, where identities blur (through cooking and cohabitation), but never dissolve (through the denial of collaboration, or through the absence of stories of dhow captains turning pirate).

Captivity, then, is not time out of time, but rather a productive space that both is built on prior histories and also builds social relationships that exceed the time of capture and the space of the hold. These social relations are what transform the violence of capture into a temporary form of cohabitation. But this is not to assume a structural-functional "law of hospitality" or a form of captivity without captives. Things break down, and itineraries get permanently disrupted. It is to those moments that we now turn to see the limits of this space of protection.

FIGURE 11: Mothership.

BREAKDOWN AND DEPARTURE

The process of transforming the dhow into a mothership entails transforming armed pirates who arrive at the dhow into guests. This is a process mediated through everyday objects and encounters, such as the DVDs watched together and sharing food in the hold of the ship, where pirates and crew draw on different scales of relatedness (Ben-Yehoyada 2016) and sensoria in order to create a temporary form of protection (one nonetheless framed within limits) during the time of captivity. But this seeming symbiosis is constantly threatened by the possibility of breakdown, specifically the danger of pirates becoming bad guests and dhow captains becoming bad hosts.

When do pirates become bad guests, and when do captains become bad hosts? The claim of protection is built on the idea that once the pirate comes on board, capture must then be supplemented by cohabitation. The gun is put away; violence is relegated only to the beginning. A working understanding emerges. The mothership is a space of captivity but of a form of captivity shared by pirate and crew alike. These tensions echo the wider ways in which hospitality encounters are haunted by the specter of bad hosts and bad guests, moments where exchange and obligation are refused or denied (Candea 2012; Derrida 2005; Shryock 2012). In the case of the dhow as mothership, moments of breakdown occur when the violence of arrival is unable to transform into a mode of living together in the hold. When the dhow is no longer a means to an end—a mothership for the capture of cargo ships—it becomes simply a hijacked vessel. The following two narratives highlight these moments of breakdown.

A relatively young dhow captain, Ramu had "retired" when I met him in Sharjah. "I have seen many bad things at sea and never want to go back to it," he explained, accounting for his initial reticence to speak with me. Ramu's name had come up when one of the dhow captains complained that no one cared for seafarers in India. "In America, they make movies about the captain who got hijacked [*Captain Phillips*], but Bollywood movies have no time for us, even though we have had so many experiences and seen so many things." The captain suggested I meet with Ramu, whose ordeal he noted was worthy of a movie at the very least.

Unassuming in his shirt and trousers, sitting behind a desk in a small Sharjah building near the corniche, it was hard to imagine Ramu taking the helm of a dhow at sea. "I don't really talk about piracy these days," he said almost apologetically, as he started telling his tale of capture. "We were coming back from Mombasa when it happened. We were close to Kenya so I didn't really pay much attention, but, all of a sudden, a boat chased us down and one of them pointed a rocket launcher in our direction. We stopped, they got on board, and immediately they started hitting us." At this point he unrolled his sleeves, pointing to a deep gash on his right arm. "I still have a souvenir from them," he smiled with a somewhat pained expression. "They tied us up and would beat us if we asked for anything." His ordeal continued for a little over a day until, in the aftermath of an argument among the pirates and what Ramu found out later was an approaching naval vessel, they departed and escaped from the dhow. A few hours later a naval boarding party approached their dhow and helped untie them, and they continued their journey to Oman.

Whereas Ramu's experience was about violence without incorporation, and there was no form of relationality with the crew members,[8] other dhow captains would recount similar violent breakdowns that began in the more familiar idiom of capture and cohabitation. When Nadeem's dhow was hijacked, he was surprised when guns were put away, and by the seeming normality of time together in the hold. "It was almost like nothing changed," he noted—that is, until things did. "After a week they had no luck finding ships and I could tell things were getting tense. One of the guys, who seemed like the leader, was a guy I jokingly started calling 'Sheikh' because he had a little beard. After a week, one day, out of nowhere he grabbed his gun and said, 'Give us all your money.' I informed him that the boat was carrying things belonging to a Somali, but Sheikh refused to hear anything. After taking money, he was not happy and wanted us to call our families and *hawala* [money transfer] him a million dollars."

In both cases, the point when the relationship of protection aboard the dhow turns into simple extraction, when the dhow becomes an end in itself, is when the possibility of transforming dhows into motherships falls apart. In these moments of breakdown, we see the social relationships that had been central to sustaining captivity all along. But most attempts at dhow capture did not entail these forms of breakdown. Hijackings in the Indian Ocean, as opposed to the Red Sea, required the successful transformation into motherships. Even at the best of times these are temporary relationships, and mothershipping ends with departures.

If stories of arrival and cohabitation on board featured prominently in interviews I had with dhow captains, narratives of departures were less pronounced. Recall Shafiq's story of capture. I first met Shafiq in Sharjah, and we stayed in touch and met each other in Somalia as well as his village in Gujarat. Every time we met, Shafiq would retell his story of capture as a way of incorporating me into the conversation or social space. In all these retellings, the end would be the same: "They [the pirates] tried for a while [to hijack a ship], but then gave up and slipped out at night right before we arrived in Mogadishu." In private conversations, I would sometimes push Shafiq to give more details on what happened when pirates tried to board cargo ships or why they decided to leave the dhow. He studiously ignored those questions or would just dismiss them with a simple shrug. This erasure of departure was one repeated by most dhow crews. The time of capture ends with no narrative flourish; there are no dramatic spectacles to mark departures, simply the quiet exit, always under the cover of night.

In addition, no dhow crew ever admitted to their boat being used successfully for a hijacking (perhaps understandable given the surveillance of NATO), even though it is unlikely I never met anyone whose mothership was involved in a hijacking. As noted earlier, forms of cohabitation on board motherships had their limits. Detachment and distance are equally productive to relations (Candea et al. 2015) and through these narrative aporias and refusals, a distance between crew and pirate and between captor and captive was maintained in order to emphasize the temporary nature of this encounter and the transformation of the dhow back from mothership to mere trading vessel.

In 2014, this transformation was underscored to me when I returned to Sharjah for follow-up research. With Somali piracy seemingly on the wane, once again the dhow had shape-shifted. "We're going to Iran a lot these days. The sanctions mean we have more work on that side now." Shafiq was explaining on the phone why he was spending more time in Dubai and wouldn't have time to meet with me. "Sharjah is for the Somalia market. Come to Dubai, it's nicer here and we can go to a mall together."

RESONANCE OF CAPTURE

I was never captured, at least not in the Indian Ocean. I know about captivity at sea through narratives: stories told in holds, at ports, in offices and homes, or written in newspapers and magazines. These captivity tales sit alongside captivity narratives from other times and places (Blum 2003; Strong 1999). From the Barbary coast to colonial North America, the captivity narrative is premised on returns and a sense that captivity is a marked period of time with a beginning, middle, and end. Unlike the structure of captivity narratives built on a telos of return, the captivity of the mothership emphasizes the ways that captivity is about being tethered, about being bound together. There is no end or any necessary deliverance from captivity (except perhaps in the case of Cawil's rejection of piracy). For both dhow captains and pirates, there is just a continuation of life at sea. This is a world of awkward collaborations, of reversals and ways of being afloat together in an unpredictable and dangerous ocean. Finally, captivity calls our attention to its multiple scales and histories: in the case of piracy in Somalia, this is the scale of empire. As the anthropologist Bruce Grant (2009) has reminded us, capture is always central to the forms of violence that shape imperial encounters. Captivity, from Somalia to the Caucasus and from the Barbary Coast to North America, frames these "tensions of empire" (Cooper and Stoler 1997).

In 2011, spurred by the sudden popularity of all things camel in the Arabian Gulf and Kenya, from camel milk chocolate to camel burgers, the price of camels reached an all-time high in the livestock markets of northern Somalia. At the same time, a rumor started circulating in the port cities and the "pirate towns" of northern Somalia: a tale about captivity. One evening, as I walked near the *geelher* (camel camp) located on the outskirts of one of these towns after a session of tea and watching soccer, my companion, a local merchant, urged caution. "On nights like these we must be very careful." It was pitch black outside, the moon hidden by rare cloud cover. The darkness was only broken by the occasional headlights of a passing vehicle and our flashlights as we made our way back to my guesthouse. He continued, "My cousin's son, Dahir, disappeared from a *geelher* about a week ago."

He described how Dahir had been guarding the camels when he heard a loud noise in the sky. "It was a helicopter that had come from the navy ships out in the ocean. All of a sudden, some marines jumped from the helicopter and quickly tied camels with ropes. Then they climbed back into the helicopter, and Dahir could only watch as helicopters came one after another and stole four camels." "Did they take Dahir as well?" I inquired, somewhat perplexed at this tale of camel capture. "Yes, when the fifth helicopter came, Dahir tried to fight the marines, and I think that's when they captured him as well." For my companion, and others who recounted versions of this tale, marines from navy ships stealing camels confirmed their hunch that ulterior motives existed for the naval presence that was amassing offshore. "Piracy is an excuse," the merchant opined. "They [the international naval coalition] are here to steal our wealth."

Marines in Blackhawk helicopters, livestock raids, the disappearances of young men—these are not strange images in Somalia. They recount recent and not-so-recent histories—of violence, of dispossession, of intervention— and frame the ways in which maritime piracy is understood within Somalia. In a provocative rereading of American Indian captivity and UFO abduction narratives, Susan Lepselter highlights the resonances of capture and the ways in which images and stories of captivity index anxieties about power and containment within specific histories. Since the recent upsurge in incidents of maritime piracy, numerous young Somali men have been detained and killed, and many others have disappeared or drowned. By openly describing the violence of the world of piracy, these narratives are at one level a way of working through personal distress. As Ayan, the mother of one disappeared pirate, reminded me, "We don't know whether to laugh or cry. My son could be in Kenya buying a big house, he could be in jail in Denmark where he will get asylum and bring me to Europe, or he could be at the bottom of the ocean."

But there is also a wider logic at stake. The histories of intervention from the colonial era onwards that have shaped Somali engagements with empires are the "half-forgotten" (Lepselter 2012, 86) that refuse to stay down.[9] These are histories of extraction and exploitation. These are histories that remind

Somalis that beyond humanitarian concern, Somalia's "strategic location" has been crucial in shaping various international projects. By locating piracy within this history, these stories highlight the resonance of piracy as a frame for thinking through global credits and debts, and the role of Somalia within this global order.

Epilogue

THE GIFTS OF THE SEA

Who would think, then, that such fine ladies and gentlemen should regale themselves with an essence found in the inglorious bowels of a sick whale! Yet so it is. By some, ambergris is supposed to be the cause, and by others the effect, of the dyspepsia in the whale. How to cure such a dyspepsia it were hard to say, unless by administering three or four boat loads of Brandreth's pills, and then running out of harm's way, as laborers do in blasting rocks.

HERMAN MELVILLE, *MOBY DICK*

IN THE WEEK BEFORE I LEFT SOMALIA in 2011, Sheikh Usman suggested trying again to go to the lighthouse of Cape Guardafui, which marks the spot where the Red Sea meets the Indian Ocean. Our first trip had failed due to bad roads and security concerns, and this trip began the same way. From encountering a less-than-accommodating checkpoint right after leaving town to the car breaking down repeatedly, the two-day trip was in its fourth day and we were a least a hundred kilometers from our destination. "The water in Ras Asir [Cape Guardafui] is the bluest water you will ever see, but it looks like we are not fated to see the place together," the Sheikh remarked, declaring that the trip was cursed and it was time for us to return. There was nothing I could do to convince the Sheikh otherwise. Disappointed, I agreed to turn back. "We'll take a little detour," the Sheikh said, and proposed a brief visit to one of the fabled ambergris villages on the northern Somali coast. This too was far from straightforward. It turned out the village we planned to visit was now a pirate hideout. A ship was anchored offshore and the guards shooed us away. Determined to redeem some aspect of the trip, Sheikh Usman mustered all his connections and finally got us permission to visit with the *Oday* (elder) of the village.

Shirmayo, the *Oday,* a frail older man with a bright orange henna beard, apologized for the unfriendly welcome in perfect English punctuated with a slight Australian drawl and expressed concerns about my safety. "These pirates are very dangerous, you shouldn't stay too long," he explained, apologizing again. When I described my interest in ambergris, Shirmayo jumped to his feet with an energy that was startling given his slight frame. Disappearing to the back of the house, he reemerged a minute later holding a copy of *Moby Dick.* "Look here . . . there is a whole chapter about ambergris." Shirmayo leafed through the Dover Thrift edition, stopping at chapter 92, and began reading Melville's description of ambergris. After this impromptu book reading, the *Oday* accompanied Usman and me to the beach for a brief stroll before the two of them went for *maghrib* (sunset prayers).

Sitting in the courtyard of the shoreline mosque before prayers began, Shirmayo told me of growing up and waiting daily by the shore in the hope of collecting ambergris. "We used to sit patiently, hoping and praying to get a gift from the sea." Our conversation was interrupted by the call to prayer, and I remained in the courtyard watching the light fade over the Red Sea, waiting for Usman and Shirmayo to return. Close to the equator day turns into night quite rapidly, and soon the sea was pitch black, with only a few lights twinkling along the coast. When my hosts returned from prayer, the conversation turned again to ambergris. Shirmayo sighed, noting the changing times: "There is no ambergris here anymore. The whales have all gone away, and also they can just make the chemical in a factory."

As we chatted about the economic prospects of the coast, Shirmayo noted that piracy had at least made the Somali coast famous. "People know we exist. Do you know the tsunami wave [in 2004] came all the way to Somalia? I was fishing that day. All of a sudden, the water started going out. It was totally quiet for a few hours before the wave came back." He recounted that his village was lucky, but down the coast in Haafun many died, and many houses and boats were destroyed. "Nobody at that time knew anything about the damage to the Somali coast."

Shirmayo described how the tsunami, in addition to destroying a number of villages and fishing boats, deposited more misery on the shore in the form of containers full of toxic waste. The aftermath of the Indian Ocean tsunami washed ashore wreckage in northern Somalia from as far as coastal Sri Lanka, including mysterious containers. Rumors of toxic waste dumping had circulated in this region for many years, but were seldom investigated. "From the Bari down to Mudug you can see many containers that have nuclear waste in them. Many people, especially children, got sick from these containers." When I told Shirmayo that a UN commission on the Indian Ocean tsunami had confirmed exposure to radioactive substances in some of those villages in northern Somalia, both he and Usman shook their heads. "Nothing will change." We sat quietly, listening to the howling wind and the waves in the dark. Pointing in the direction of the sea, Shirmayo concluded philosophically, "Today you cannot just wait for a gift from the sea like we used to in the past—gifts of ambergris or gifts from the UN. You have to be like these pirates, you have to go out to sea and bring the gift of the sea home."

The sea has many gifts. At times these gifts wash ashore, often unexpectedly and without asking. From ambergris to toxic containers, these unexpected surfacings contain possibilities as well as perils. Their sudden arrivals make visible entanglements and obligations, including toxic obligations. At other times, one leaves land to possess the bounty of the ocean. For millennia those who inhabit the port cities and villages of the Red Sea and the Indian Ocean have sought to cross the threshold of land and sea and transform their world by bringing back gifts from the sea. In Somalia, to go to sea is to become a *badmaax* (seafarer)—a term used to refer both to those who work at sea and to those who travel to foreign lands in search of wealth and prestige. To go to sea is to leave with the anticipation of a heroic return amongst those left behind. The sea and its gifts in this way make people and places bigger—as Shirmayo reminded me: thanks to the pirates, people know Somalia. "Now they see that a small fishing boat can take over a big container ship." To be feared, as he explained, is also a form of status in the world. Somali pirates, like many other itinerant sojourners throughout the world's oceans, know that violence, too, marks a possibility, a way to enter the world and make a claim on circulation and on profits and power.

Until my visit to Shirmayo's village, I had felt relatively immune to the violence of piracy. While weapons and armed men were a visible part of the landscape, I also recognized the ways in which I was a protected visitor. I arrived either in the company of figures like Sheikh Usman or armed with introductions and phone numbers that made me confident that the gun wasn't going to be pointed at me. Beneath the visible threat of violence, protection after all is about the invisible forms of care and management that contain this threat. However, on this night as we talked about gifts of the ocean, Sheikh Usman was visibly nervous—with good reason, as it turned out. The US Navy had shot pirates who hailed from this village at sea. Suddenly, we were confronted by angry voices. Shirmayo leapt to his feet again and ran towards those voices before they could make their way to us. A few minutes later he returned and got into a heated discussion with Sheikh Usman. "It's very dangerous for you right now," he explained. The pirates were convinced a spy was in their midst and no negotiations seemed possible. I was no longer a protected guest, but an American. "It's time for you to go." He kept repeating those words, as if for emphasis, as we ran towards the car. The fragility of protection was revealed in that moment as we hurriedly departed.

Long rendered a mythical figure, a character from children's fables brought to life in Disney cartoons and Hollywood films or in the dusty archives of company states like the VOC, pirates had seemingly returned to reality when ships like the *Nori* were hijacked off the coast of Somalia. From 2007 to 2012, the world was fixated on coastal Somalia and these dramas of multi-million-dollar hijackings at sea. In this book, I have shown that these moments of hijacking were not only localized encounters between small boats and big ships, but also encounters between parallel and competing systems of protection. Forged in the interruption of the hijacking, piracy makes visible the centrality of protection to communities in coastal Somalia as well as insurance offices in London. It is protection that makes possible the journeys of oil tankers through the Suez Canal and the post-deployment career pathways of American soldiers globally. It is protection that makes possible the monsoonal journey of dhows in the Indian Ocean. The hijacking of container ships forced these different forms and scales of protection to cooperate—however unwillingly, and constantly in the shadow of violence—in order to create a hijack-and-ransom economy in the Red Sea and the Indian Ocean. Piracy thus reveals an alternative form of connectivity forged in interruptions: interruptions that make visible not only the fragility and violence of certain connectivities, but also other possibilities forged through claims of protection.

Whether criminalized as sea robbers who take without giving, or expelled from the commonwealth of humanity as enemies of mankind, or even valorized as subaltern resistors, pirates have long been understood via stories of sovereignty in crisis and questions of state failure and criminality. An analysis of piracy specifically in terms of protection (rather than criminality and state collapse) offers a way of getting at larger questions having to do with interruption and circulation. The hijacking of a ship reveals the multiple histories and scales of protection—where colonial officials, clan chiefs, khat dealers, fishermen, naval sea vessels, insurance agencies, private security contractors, and others encounter each other with often surprising results and afterlives. Piracy makes visible parallel systems of risk-pooling essential to projects of global mobility, from the meanderings of small fishing skiffs in coastal waters to the voyages of Suezmax container ships as they ply along global shipping lanes. These distinct scales, and often incommensurable histories of protection, encounter each other in the aftermath of the hijacking, in an attempt to transform capture into profit and possibility. This is a story of these transient engagements with their supple interplay of violence and intimacy, of possibilities and reversals, that occur within frameworks of enduring inequalities. These encounters that constitute piracy (and counterpiracy) in the western Indian Ocean are central to the making and unmaking of relationships tied to property, profit, and power at sea and on land.

Beyond piracy, this book has proposed an anthropology of protection as a way to rethink enduring questions from the nature of law and economy to the nature of encounters between strangers. Social theory continues to remain trapped either in the parochial gaze of the nation-state or the boundless imaginary of deterritorialization that often replicates the spatial fantasies of global capital and its neoliberal proponents. Correctives on either side miss the flexible and precise ways within which mobility is channeled and regulated, and the historical antecedents of these practices. The worlds of protection introduced in this work show how order without law is constructed without emphasizing either the enduring importance of the state or its contemporary weakness under globalization. Protection thus exceeds the national and territorial frame without losing sight of the ways in which authority and political community are constructed, from the norms of insurance adjustors to the protection of *diya* groups in coastal Somalia as well as encounters on board a variety of ships at sea.

Global connectivity is deeply tied to the ocean. Capitalism was forged at sea in the voyages of the multitude of East and West India Companies and their cargo of silver, spices, and slaves. Contemporary trade too relies heavily on the sea, with millions of ships crisscrossing the world's oceans daily. This global sea of trade is also dependent on a variety of risk-pooling techniques. From their earliest days, maritime voyages have been journeys of chance and gamble. Techniques such as bottomry, risk-sharing agreements of *mudarabah,* and the surety of insurance were important strategies of transforming uncertainty into governable risk, as were mercenaries, privateers, and navies. These forms of protection emphasize the intimacy of trade and cannon, an intimacy as central to the world of contemporary supply-chain capitalism as it was to the city-centered economies of antiquity. A focus on protection reveals how the management of violence is crucial to the extraction of profits and the longer histories of contemporary neoliberal capitalism. Global orders are built on temporal and spatial divides—between trade and finance, between land and sea, between piracy and counter-piracy. By removing these temporal and spatial divides—by emphasizing how Aisha's quest for super-profits from selling khat to pirates is tied to calculations of war-risk cover at Lloyd's—protection reveals an alternative form of connectivity and a mode of understanding market-making and capitalism that is both transregional and not (solely) forged through imaginaries of center and periphery. The economies of protection formed through the alternative form of connectivity of piracy are both enduring and transient. Protection, like the sea, is a reminder that everything we undertake is an attempt, a gamble, though one felt unevenly for those who attempt to make their way across this sea of protection.

This final point was brought into sharp focus when I returned to Somalia to follow up on the lives of self-proclaimed pirates in the aftermath of the "piracy boom." By the end of 2012, the golden age of Somali piracy had ended and incidents of maritime piracy, successful or otherwise, had plummeted by over 80 percent (IMB 2012). Just as suddenly as piracy had appeared on the global stage, it receded from view. The increasing use of private security on ships transiting through the region had greatly increased the dangers involved in hijackings. In addition to showing little hesitation in attacking pirate skiffs at sea, private security also significantly decreased the success ratio for pirates. Given the debts involved in becoming a pirate, this decline in success-ful hijacking had reverberations throughout the economy of Somali piracy, with fewer deciding to invest in piracy or travel to sea. In Puntland, many also pointed to government interventions, including the establishment of the Puntland Maritime Police Force, as well as the promise of an oil-rich future, as partly responsible for the decline in piracy. When I returned to Puntland in 2013, it was abuzz with rumors of offshore oil. Since 1992, many had specu-lated about the possibility of untapped oil reserves off the coast of Somalia. In 2012, the Puntland government gave the green light to the first official oil exploration project in Puntland and Somalia at large. Led by the Canadian oil company Africa Oil (the former Canmex Minerals) and its partner Range

Resources, initial drilling in the Shabeel-1 well on Puntland's Dharoor Block in March of that year successfully yielded oil. Sensing these shifting currents, a number of self-proclaimed pirates sought to create itineraries beyond piracy.

In January 2013, the notorious pirate boss Mohamed Abdi Hassan "Afweyne" (Big Mouth) announced his retirement at a press conference in Hardadhare, a once notorious pirate base in the Mudug region of central Somalia. Afweyne's group, the Central Somalia Piracy Network, had allegedly been responsible for a number of high-profile hijackings, including the 2008 capture of the Saudi oil tanker the *Sirius Star,* the largest ship ever to be hijacked. Surrounded by members of the local government and a number of business and religious elites, Afweyne delivered a minute-long statement in which he announced:

> We've been in this dirty business for a long time, but we tasted the bitterness and bad consequences. I have chosen to retire from this business and want to make my intentions clear to everyone, including people in the government, about wanting to end this dirty business. I also believe the new [Hassan Sheikh Mohamud's] government will eradicate this work. I would like to encourage my colleagues to retire from piracy as well and hand over their weapons, boats, etc. Some have already announced their retirement, and I hope the rest who are still in the business follow in their footsteps as well.[1]

Within a few months of his retirement, the UN-funded Somali radio station Bar-Kulan reported that Afweyne was traveling around Central Somalia with a letter from the Galmudug government stating his new position as "antipiracy officer." In an interview with the radio station, Afweyne explained he was traveling around demobilizing pirates and wanted to protect Somalis from the scourge of piracy. In a surprising, Hollywood-style twist to Afweyne's story, in October 2013 Belgian government officials announced that they had arrested Afweyne as he landed in Brussels, having been lured there by the fake promise of being a consultant for a documentary on Somali piracy. In 2016, after a somewhat controversial trial, he was sentenced to twenty years' imprisonment for his leadership role in the 2009 hijacking of the Belgian-flagged vessel the *Pompei,* joining the more than one thousand pirates currently in prison in over twenty countries.

If Afweyne was the classic pirate boss with the right kinship and political connections, Arale could hardly be more different. An Abgaal from the Hawiye clan, who consider southern Somalia and the fertile Jubba valley their homeland, Arale seemed quite at home on the desolate northern Somali coast working with groups far removed from his patrilineal network. When I first encountered him in 2010, he openly talked about his distinct ancestry as proof that pirates were a motley crew of local fishermen rising up to protect their livelihoods, regardless of clan and regional affiliation. "We are now our own clan—those who are trying to defend from illegal fishing and dumping," he insisted when I asked whether he encountered any tensions or hostility as an outsider. A year later, as the tide of public opinion and official patronage began to turn against maritime and land-bound crews like Arale's, the romance of piracy and the narrative of illegal fishing were long gone, and Arale was eager to know if I had any connections with the Puntland Maritime Police Force (PMPF). When I responded that not only did I not know anyone in the PMPF but I had in fact been physically chased from their compound by a gruff-looking South African mercenary, Arale reassured me that he would get a job with PMPF and eventually get me access to their compound in Bandar Siyada, a few miles west of Bosaso. Unfortunately, Arale never got the job with PMPF, and the closest I got to the compound was from the air, when flying out of Bosaso. Yet Arale remained unfazed and by 2012, like many in Puntland, he was seeking to tie his destiny to oil. "We have oil in Puntland now. The country is going to be like UAE very soon. *Inshallah* I will get a job for the oil company. I have retired from piracy and am waiting for oil to make my life better." I asked Arale what he would do if oil wealth never materialized. "In that case, I'll take to the sea again, but this time maybe for *tahrib*," he explained, referring to the many thousands who are smuggled annually on boats across the Bab-el-Mandeb, en route to better futures in Dubai or Europe.

Arale and Afweyne follow in a long tradition of pirates as slippery shape-shifters who move between the worlds of licit and illicit, trade and raid, violence and intimacy, confusing and confounding these categories (Dua 2015). Within this shape-shifting world, social worlds are constituted and transformed through the giving and receiving and the selling and buying of protection, remaining acutely aware of the wider frames of geopolitics, empire, terrorism, and free trade that shape the possibilities and impossibilities of specific itineraries.

Amidst tales of piracy's decline and the aspirations of oil, there was a sense among those I met in Puntland that, like the ocean, the story of piracy is one of constant returns. The first year without a single successful hijacking was marked in 2013, and by 2014 international attention had shifted to West Africa and Southeast Asia. The era of Somali piracy was seemingly over. Yet something important and initially unnoticed started happening in Somalia in those years. In its annual report, the UN monitoring group on Somalia and Eritrea reported that the PMPF had transformed from an anti-piracy group to a militia fighting the Puntland government's political rivals, including Al-Shabaab, on land (UNSC-SEMG 2012). And at sea, 2013 also marked the first year when foreign fishing vessels appeared again off the Somali coast. A mix of licensed and unlicensed trawlers, these vessels had stayed away from Somalia during the peak years of piracy. With pirates gone, illegal fishing was back. Rumors surfaced of the reemergence of both local protection groups and coastguards that were seeking to curb or profit from these old familiar foes.

Away from the Somali coast, in the offices of shipping lines, other rumblings were afoot. By 2012, almost all cargo ships transiting through the western Indian Ocean were hiring armed guards. Armed guards were essential, due both to the fact that no ship carrying armed guards had been hijacked and, importantly, that insurance companies required these guards as part of the war-risk cover negotiations. But, at $30,000–40,000 per voyage, the cost of guards was turning out to be prohibitive. Samir, a Singapore-based broker for oil tanker chartering companies, complained that ships were still being held hostage, but this time through the collusion of private security companies and insurance firms. "With pirates, there is at least a small probability of getting hijacked. With these private security firms, you're paying a small ransom every voyage," he joked as he explained how shipping companies had recently started campaigning to change what he termed the "protection model" for the Indian Ocean. "We've started hiring mixed groups to keep costs down." Samir was referring to the racialized systems of compensation in private security not dissimilar to the larger racialized forms of compensation within the shipping economy. "At the top you have Americans, Israelis, British, and Europeans—these are the guys who command top dollar. Then you have white South Africans, who are a little cheaper, but not by much. Finally, you can hire Sri Lankan, Filipino, and Indian soldiers; they are the cheapest, but often insurance companies won't certify them." Samir laid out the hierarchy of global private security and explained how in recent months his company had negotiated for a mixed Sri Lankan and British team that would cost $25,000 per transit. "We have ten tankers, so this makes a big difference for us." Other companies were sometimes eschewing the hiring of private guards or cutting back on other onboard security measures. As the longer historical framework of this book has shown, costs of protection continue to remain key in calculations of profit and loss, risk and reward for maritime adventures.

In 2017, the restive calm at sea was broken. On March 13, a Comoros-flagged oil tanker, en route from Mogadishu to Djibouti with a crew of eight Sri Lankan seafarers, was hijacked eighteen nautical miles off the coast of Somalia. The first successful hijacking of a cargo carrier, the *Aris 13* incident came at the heels of a number of attempted hijackings of dhows and other smaller vessels. However, unlike the *Nori,* whose hijacking began this tale of capture at sea, the hijackers of the *Aris* did not win. The ship was released without the payment of a ransom four days after the hijacking, as the pirates were unable to find investors or others who would offer protection to the hijacked ship on land. Since the hijacking of the *Aris 13*, many have wondered if pirates are back (Gettleman 2017; Macguire 2016), but, as I have shown in this book, the systems of protection that make it possible to become a pirate in fact never disappeared. As long as things move, the need for protection—and thus also the possibility of piracy—will remain.

· · ·

Sheikh Usman and I never made it to Cape Guardafui by road. But on a container ship transiting through the Red Sea on its way to Dubai, I finally saw the blue waters of that cape. "We'll be entering the Indian Ocean tomorrow," Nicholas, a Filipino seafarer, had mentioned the previous night over dinner at the staff table. I was transiting to Dubai on a cargo ship owned by the French shipping conglomerate. The next morning Nicholas and I went for a walk on the deck, and I asked him if there were shipboard rituals to mark the entry into the Indian Ocean. "No, we'll just keep our anti-piracy watch for a few days more." We were walking amidst the containers. "Don't be too close to them, for safety reasons," he warned, suggesting a walk instead to the bow of the ship. "Too bad you're not going on to Pusan [South Korea], we would initiate you into the cult of Neptune then." He smiled as he explained the line-crossing ceremony for "pollywogs" who had never crossed the Equator. "Someone suggested dressing like a pirate when we enter the Indian Ocean. But we've all had our brush with piracy, so it's hard to make a joke about it."

Handing me the binoculars, he said, "See if you can spot land—this is the closest we're going to Somalia." As I stood amidst the jumble of mooring lines and anchor of this 360-meter-long leviathan and stared out at the ocean, all I could see was a deep blue interrupted by a few whitecaps indicating choppy seas or coral reefs. "On my old ship, we were hijacked around this spot," Nicholas mentioned as we both fell silent. Suddenly distracted, he snatched the binoculars that were dangling around my neck, looking out towards the water, panic visible on his face.

"What do you see?" I asked. He ignored me, agitatedly, scanning the horizon. "It's dolphins," he then sighed, as his face relaxed. Handing me the binoculars again, he suggested I take a look as well. "It's just a school of dolphins, you can see them playing in the water. I thought for a minute it was pirates."

NOTES

INTRODUCTION

1. The term *dhow* describes a range of sailing ships in the Indian Ocean that utilize a lateen sail.

2. A green leafy plant with narcotic properties.

3. According to the photographer and theorist Allan Sekula, the contemporary maritime imaginary only focuses on the sea as "the site of intermittent horrors and extraordinary, but brief, expenditures of energy, quite distinct from the dramas of everyday life" (Sekula 1995, 32).

4. These histories have been evocatively rendered in the works of scholars such as Lapidoth (1982), Reese (2008), Alpers (2009), Cassanelli (1982), Dudd (1989), Miran (2009), and Wick (2016).

5. Scholars such as Chaudhuri (1983), Ho (2006), Pearson (2003), Abu-Lughod (1989), and Bose (2009) have sought to emphasize the ocean as a means of not only connecting regions divided by water but, through repeated exchange, creating an Indian Ocean society centered around port cities stretching from Europe to Asia—from Venice to Pasai in northern Sumatra.

6. See for example the work of authors like Blum (2010), Desai (2013), Steinberg (2013), and Mawani (2018). These authors productively bring in questions of racial power and difference as well as emphasizing connections across the Pacific, Atlantic, and Indian Oceans. Emerging primarily in the humanities, but also in conversation with science and technology studies (Helmreich 2009; Moore 2012), this recent oceanic turn in scholarship has emphasized the materiality of maritime spaces, focusing on waves, currents, and nonhuman life forms under the surface of the water in order to move beyond a story of connectivity. An important contribution of this literature has been charting a way beyond the geographic silos that divide the world's oceans as legacies of a Eurocentric geography.

7. The work of scholars such as Catherine Besteman, Peter Little, Ahmad Samatar, Said Samatar, Markus Hoehne, Tobias Hagmann, Lee Cassanelli, and Abdi

Kusow, among others, has been an important corrective to popular conceptualizations of Somalia that emphasize narratives of state failure and anarchy.

8. A more nuanced set of literatures has sought to critique simplistic narratives of state failure and instead has focused on the development of plural forms of regulatory authority and the creation of governance without government in Somalia since the collapse of the state in 1991 (Menkhaus 2006; Hagmann and Hoehne 2008). These works resonate with other forms of local governance in Somalia and wider examples throughout sub-Saharan Africa that note the ways in which state-like formations appear in the absence (or in the aftermath) of a strong centralized state (Bayart 2009; Ferguson 1999; Piot 2010; Raeymaekers 2010; Roitman 2005; Comaroff and Comaroff 2012; de Sardan 1999). The recent rethinking of the state in Africa has significantly enhanced our understanding of governance and sovereignty, and has sought to move beyond the idealized narratives of state formation that continue to inform academic scholarship and policy-making in this part of the world and beyond.

9. See Bueger (2013) and Singh and Bedi (2012) for, inter alia, a discussion of this literature and its consequences in constructing what Bueger (2013) refers to as the grand narrative of Somali piracy.

10. Writing from a variety of disciplinary backgrounds, including anthropology, international relations, criminology, and public policy, these works note a necessary though not sufficient correlation between governance and piracy. See for example Percy (2009), Coggins (2016), Daxecker and Prins (2017), Weldemichael (2012), and World Bank Group (2015).

11. See Aitchison (1929) for a copy of this treaty. For a detailed discussion on the protectorate system, see Johnston (1973) and Benton, Clulow, and Attwood (2018).

12. In its earliest meaning, diaspora signified a form of scattering and dispersal from the *polis* to expand the reaches of the empire. As Rubin (1986) and Gabrielsen (2001) note, these dispersed populations sustained themselves and the city-states they were attached to through inter alia practices of raiding. Piracy then was not antagonistic to trade, but part of a larger raiding system where "merchants, pirates and naval *prostates* were tangled into an intricate relationship of mutual dependence" (Gabrielsen 2001, 220).

13. As Cicero (1833, 107) notes, "There is no perjury if the ransom for life, which had been agreed upon even under oath, is not paid to pirates, for the reason that the pirate is not entitled to the rights of war, but is the common enemy of all, with whom neither good faith nor a common oath should be kept." Although seen as foundational for establishing the crime of piracy as universal crime, a number of scholars, including the Dutch legal scholar Hugo Grotius, have cautioned against such a reading of Cicero. While writing his highly influential natural law treatise *The Rights of War and Peace,* Grotius criticized this passage as a non sequitur and noted, "It seems there is no reason why an oath to God should not be kept even with brigands; it is hardly logical or moral to construe a violation of law to lead to the conclusion that the violator is no longer protected by law. Observance of an oath is owed to God, not to the person receiving the benefit of the oath" (Grotius [1625] 2005, 17). Others such as Alfred Rubin have noted that the passage from Cicero appears in a "work of

moral duties and not law; as Cicero himself noted the two do not always coincide" (Rubin 2006, 10). While it is debatable whether Cicero's conception of the pirate as the common enemy of all was intended as legal argument or moral critique, there is nonetheless a move within the rest of his juridical corpus to treat piracy and pirates as distinct from bandits and criminals and squarely in the distinction between friend and enemy.

14. In his work on the Mafia in nineteenth- and twentieth-century rural Sicily, Anton Blok (1974) invoked the figure of violent peasant entrepreneurs to understand the Mafiosi as middlemen between the peasantry and absentee landlords. Similarly, Vadim Volkov (2002) focuses on violent entrepreneurs as essential to the transition to a market economy in contemporary Russia. However, here I want to emphasize that violent entrepreneurship can be usefully transposed to the making of the Atlantic world. Privateers as well as those who worked for the VOC and the BEIC were crucial middle figures in the transition to Dutch and British maritime empires.

15. A similar story unfolded in the Persian Gulf. The British accused the Qawasim of piracy, blockading ports in what is now the United Arab Emirates until the Qawasim signed treaties in which they agreed to give up piracy in return for British protection. See Onley (2004) for a discussion of the Qawasim affair.

16. The most famous example of this is Kanhoji Angrey, the eighteenth-century chief of the Maratha Navy in Western India. Accused of piracy, Angrey is celebrated as an anticolonial hero in contemporary Maharashtra (Malgaonkar, 1981, Layton 2012).

17. There is a significant literature that seeks to understand maritime piracy as a fundamentally economic activity, practiced often by communities seeking economic enrichment at the margins and peripheries of maritime trade networks (Anderson 1995). Piracy in this narrative is seen as cyclical in ways that mirror wider economic cycles (Gosse 1932). Piracy begins as an opportunistic form of plunder taken by small, loosely organized coastal communities. With success, this form of raiding transforms into an organized structure for more effective predation. Finally, piracy morphs into a virtually independent state that is "in a position to make a mutually useful alliance with another state against its enemies" (Gosse 1932, 1). In this emphasis on pirates as economic actors, the question of the kind of economic actor is often paramount. As Shannon Dawdy and Joe Bonni have noted, "pirates fuel not only competing, but contradictory economic fantasies—as the ideal rational-choice individualist (a consumer of monstrous proportions) or as a profit-sharing, utopian socialist" (2012, 675).

18. This is, of course, one legal genealogy of piracy. Islamic law provides an interesting counterpoint to this question, where piracy is located between a world of banditry on one hand and just war on the other. "Piracy" does not appear as a distinct crime, but rather is a seaborne extension of land-based debates on distinctions between just and unjust takings. See Khalilieh (1998) for a discussion on piracy and maritime crimes in Islamic law.

19. Beginning in the late seventeenth century, there was also a move to pluralize and territorialize the realm of piracy in the world of printing and patents. The current proliferation of digital piracy, media piracy, and intellectual property rights is a legacy

of this attempt (on land) to label as piratical forms of circulation and innovation that eluded or circumvented the reach of the state or private monopoly. This introduction does not engage with this (now burgeoning) literature on piracy in other guises, but is nonetheless informed by these approaches—specifically on questions of circulation and the boundaries between legitimate and illegitimate. For a good overview on the history of piracy outside the maritime realm, see Johns (2009). For exemplary recent ethnographic engagements with intellectual property and media piracy, see Coombe (1998), Larkin (2008), Dent (2012), Coleman (2013), and Thomas (2016).

20. The IMB is a commercially funded organization that maintains piracy statistics for the global shipping and insurance industries. The IMB's definition of piracy is more expansive than the international legal definition, and includes armed robbery in territorial waters as well as attacks on ships at port.

21. Exceptions to this generalization included the November 2005 attack on the luxury cruise ship the *MV Seabourn Spirit,* an attack that was repelled by the crew using water hoses, and the successful capture of the *MV Danica White,* a few months prior to the attack on the *Nori* in 2007. However, the *Nori* was the first ship to fetch a million dollars in ransom. This successful negotiation, under the watchful eyes of international navies, emboldened the hijack-and-ransom economy.

22. The question of trust has been salient in discussions on long-distance trade networks. Scholars such as Cohen (1969) and Curtin (1984) emphasized the centrality of trust in the rise and endurance of ethnic trading communities such as the Armenians of Jaffa and the Hausa of West Africa. Recent work has sought to challenge the primacy of trust, emphasizing the role of law and contracts in structuring long-distance trade networks (Trivellato 2012; Bishara 2017). As an infrastructure of sociality, central both to kinship and to law, protection bridges the worlds of trust and law, creating a shared conceptual space in which to theorize commercial and social engagement across space and time.

23. See Shryock (2004) for a related discussion in the context of Jordanian hospitality.

24. Rooble Afdeed appeared prominently in oral recollections of the history of northern Somalia during fieldwork partly due to his presence in Richard Burton's (1856) memoir, *First Footsteps in East Africa,* where he escorted Burton from Zeila to Berbera. References to *abaan* also figure in Captain Mile's reports on the Mijjerteyn (Majeerteen) (IOR R/20/E/86) and the Italian administrator Giulio Baldacci's (1909) chronicle of the Northern Somali coast.

25. The household, or *oikos,* was central to Aristotle's understanding of what we term the economy. See chapter 2 for a discussion on oikos and piracy.

CHAPTER I

1. For a discussion on the contentious issue of state recognition in Somaliland as well as the border conflicts between Somaliland and Puntland, see Gandrup (2016) and Hoehne (2016).

2. In opposition to what he terms the singularity of ruins, Gastón Gordillo (2014) puts forth the idea of rubble as a way to understand how histories of violence and destruction have shaped the Chaco province of northern Argentina. In contrast to the concept of the ruin, which Gordillo associates with a modern and elitist sensibility, the concept of rubble deglamorizes ruins by focusing on the processes of destruction, even as these remains help constitute new social spaces and figure in collective mentalities.

3. For an example of this narrative in popular media accounts, see Johann Hari (2009). Academic and policy discussion has generally simultaneously acknowledged and minimized the role of overfishing and toxic dumping in Somali piracy. A notable exception is the work of Samatar, Lindberg, and Mahayni (2010). They argue for moving beyond the legal definition of piracy as the illegal capture of ships in international waters, instead describing the different forms of piracy operating off the coast of Somalia. Illegal fishing in this narrative is a form of "resource piracy" that emerged in 1991 and led to a response from Somali fishing communities, a response they label "defensive piracy."

4. Bulk carriers are merchant ships designed to carry goods directly in the hold of the ship, as opposed to within containers. While used primarily to transport goods such as coal and grains, they are also used to transport cargo to smaller, noncontainerized ports such as Bosaso.

5. This concept is found in the Qur'an, Surah ar-Rahman 19–21. The idea of the edge is a useful frame through which to understand the relationship between land and sea along coastal Somalia.

6. For an analysis of the shifting nature of this incorporation of northern Somalia within global capitalism in the immediate aftermath of the opening of the Suez Canal, see Kapteijns (1995), Laitin and Samatar (1984), and Reese (2008). For a broader discussion of the role of the British in the Red Sea, see Marston (1961).

7. Twentieth-century American jurisprudence on capture and rights in fugitive resources was heavily influenced by concepts of fugitive property in Roman law and continental European legal traditions. See Donahue (1986) for an exploration of this history, specifically a discussion of *Pierson v. Post,* an iconic case in US property law and legal pedagogy.

8. *Hammonds v. Central Kentucky Natural Gas Co.,* 75 S.W.2d 204, 255 Ky. 685 (1934), 1314.

9. *Hammonds v. Central Kentucky Natural Gas Co.,* 75 S.W.2d 204, 255 Ky. 685 (1934), 1314.

10. This focus on imaginaries draws from Carol M. Rose's scholarship on property, narrative, and vision. In *Property and Persuasion* (1994), Rose highlights the centrality of storytelling in naturalizing concepts of property. While Rose's emphasis is on the power of stories about private property and propriety, this idea is equally relevant to the manner in which imagining the commons as always constituted by scarcity and the idea of inevitable overexploitation continues to frame discussions on the commons. See also Raffles (2010) for an imagining of air outside the notion of the commons by exploring the vantage point of insects.

11. As Ian Angus (2008) has noted, "Since appearing in *Science* in December 1968, 'The Tragedy of the Commons' has been anthologized in at least 111 books, making it one of the most-reprinted articles ever to appear in any scientific journal."

12. See for example the work of Elinor Ostrom, whose scholarship on polycentric governance (2010) has been influential in understanding the role of communities and entities beyond Hardin's exclusive focus on market and state in regulating the commons.

13. According to Pirie and Scheele (2014), legalism refers to the use of explicit rules and generalizing categories.

14. For an insightful discussion on the changing geographies of developmentalism in the context of fishers in postcolonial India, see Subramanian (2009).

15. Neil Brenner's rethinking of scale-making as inherent to the "continual deterritorialization and reterritorialization that has underpinned the production of capitalist spatiality since the industrial revolution of the early nineteenth century" (1999, 42) is a useful frame for thinking through the transformations that occurred in the Scientific Socialism moment. At the same time, as this chapter emphasizes, scale-making needs to be historicized beyond the nineteenth century.

16. While Ferguson (2005) and Mbembe (2008) locate licensing—namely the transformation of sovereignty in sub-Saharan Africa into a rubber stamp for resource extraction—as a central feature of the neoliberal post–Cold War state, the Somali experience shines light on the centrality of licensing during the heyday of the socialist moment, with wider consequences for thinking about state and sovereignty in Cold War Africa.

17. For an influential critique of the idea of maximum sustainable yield (MSY), see Larkin (1977). Even as MSY has been critiqued for its failure to take into consideration a holistic view of fish stocks, including mobility and ecological transformation, this principle continues to shape regulatory policy at regional and international levels.

18. For detailed studies on the collapse of the Somali state, see Simons (1995) and Besteman (1999).

19. Somcan was one of the numerous private maritime security companies involved with the Puntland government in providing licensing to foreign fishing vessels and "antipiracy activities." Unlike its predecessor, Hart Security, Somcan was locally owned, although registered in the UAE. The company was run by the Taar family, which had close personal relationships with former president Abdullahi Yussuf. It is this personal connection that has been seen by many as resulting in rapid deterioration in relations between the company and the administration following the election of Mohamud Muse Hersi. For exclusive focus on political connections or lack thereof as determinants of efficacy, see Kinsey, Hansen, and Franklin (2009). My focus on private companies concerns specific claims to the ocean and rent-seeking. The coastguard projects of Puntland in my account are tied to a longer history of protection, as this chapter elaborates. Protection, in this sense, is a source of resource extraction and also a modality of governance, as opposed to reflecting just corruption or nepotism.

CHAPTER 2

1. The idea of normality is not to suggest that piracy is seen as acceptable or to deny the violence and exploitation inherent in this practice. As the previous chapter suggested, far from a blank space, maritime worlds are deeply inflected with meaning and histories that make legible new forms of encounter. Here I want to highlight how these maritime worlds are anchored within practices of debt, work, and accumulation and the economies generated through these encounters.

2. In a *mudarabah* partnership, the *rabb al-mal* (investor) provides money to a *mudarib* (manager) for investment in a commercial enterprise. The mudarib then returns to the *rabb al-mal* the principal and a pre-agreed percentage of profits. Bill Maurer (2002) highlights the ways that "scaled up" *mudarabah* contracts are essential in generating liquidity for Islamic banks and these contracts foreground the "close relationship, indeed, an identity, between the morality of the business ventures and that of the depositor-investors." (654). At the same time, the *rabb al-mal* is insulated from the business venture and the judgment of the *mudarib* in investment decisions. In the case of piracy, *mudarabah* is both a technical term of art for the risk-pooling essential to the making of piracy and a general logic of risk-pooling that brackets the ethics of investing in the ransom economy.

3. Eric J. Hobsbawm's (1959) influential idea of social banditry fails to account fully for what is happening here, namely the transformation of piracy into a story of obligation. Pirates *qua pirates* are not supported or seen as honorable. Rather, piracy is transposed from taking at sea into the everyday world of exchange, debt, and credit.

4. The relationship between piracy and the wider economy has a long history. One surprising moment comes from ancient Greece and Aristotle's discussion on piracy within his discussion of *oikonomia* (the art of household management). For Aristotle, the provision of the household is the central end towards which all productive activity is directed, and he emphasized the connection between the need for household acquisition and one's way of life (for a discussion on Aristotle's understanding of economy see Roll 1954, Finley 1970, and Polanyi 1957). These needs for the household could be procured through natural or unnatural modes of acquisition, with nomadism, hunting, and farming considered three natural modes. As Aristotle notes, "If then we are right in believing that nature makes nothing to no purpose, it must be that nature has made all things for the sake of man. This means that it is part of nature's plan that the art of war, *of which hunting is a part*, should be a way of acquiring property" (1962, 39–40; emphasis added). Within the framework of hunting, Aristotle surprisingly includes piracy as a natural mode of acquisition. For Aristotle, taking and piracy acquire a form of naturalness so long as the ends of war and piracy are not limitless expansion, but rather the provision of that household. Anchoring through kinship and through principles of *mudarabah* similarly transforms piracy into a natural form of accumulation, though as I highlight in this chapter, this coexists with other temporalities of accumulation that defy this form of embeddedness.

5. Scholars like Chaudhuri (1983) and Pearson (2003) have conceptualized the Indian Ocean by emphasizing the centrality of the monsoon in shaping the regions that border the Indian Ocean. For a recent theorization of the centrality of the monsoon for the Indian Ocean via Latour, see Gupta (2012). The question of unity/disunity in understanding the Indian Ocean has a long history. See also Vink (2007) and Bishara (2017) for valuable discussions of this literature.

6. Kavalam Madhava Panikkar's (1953) framing of the Vasco da Gama epoch seeks to create a before-and-after for many scholars of the Indian Ocean. Vasco da Gama's entry marks both the connection to the Atlantic, thereby creating a global economy, and also, in Panikkar's view, the introduction of violence to an erstwhile peaceful trading world. Numerous scholars have critiqued this temporal framing and highlighted the centrality of violence in shaping pre-European Indian Ocean trade networks.

7. For Ahmed Samatar (2003), clan was transformed during colonial and post-colonial times in the context of political and economic change, and disembedded from its local and customary contexts in ways not accounted for by Lewis. Catherine Besteman (1996) highlights the limits of thinking through clan as an object of analysis to understand Somali society. As Besteman notes, this mode naturalizes the post-1991 dissolution of Somalia as inevitable while glossing over other kinds of segmentations, which are historically embedded within Somali society—especially class, race, and regional divisions—that have added fuel to sectarian violence.

8. Collateral, within lending agreements, is defined as the pledge of a specific property in order to secure repayment for a loan. Collateral is a form of protection for the lender from the borrower's default. Within the credit economy of diya, a kinship connection made visible through the diya group is collateralized, essentially making kinship a form of property that can be securitized in this system.

9. On the relationship between media piracy and the discourse of terrorism, see Sarkar (2016).

10. Pamphlet on file with author.

11. Thomas Gieryn's (1983) idea of the literary foil is what I use here to talk about the economy of piracy. For Gieryn the foil is a contrasting character that can serve to highlight three kinds of qualities of the other character: namely, heightened contrast, exclusion, and responsibility. In this chapter khat becomes a foil for piracy. This foil counters both an ethnographic refusal and the ways in which intelligence reports have told this story. This methodological and analytic intervention follows Appadurai (1986) and Tsing (2015) in telling object-centered stories.

12. It is critical to note the poetics of the *mafresh* through which the pirate is constructed ex post facto. In Somali oral traditions (see Samatar 1989), spaces of male sociality are central to constructing heroic narratives (for a related discussion in the context of Afghanistan, see Edwards 1996). In the Yemeni context Wedeen (2008) notes the centrality of *qat* (khat) in creating publics. This resonates throughout Somalia, especially in northern Somalia and Somaliland. Within the context of piracy, the khat session is also performance, a poetics that after the fact narrates the story of piracy. It is thus a central space to construct the pirate as much as the high seas.

13. For discussions on affective labor, see Hardt and Negri (2005); Virno (1996); and Weeks (2011).

14. Braudel (1992) and Marx ([1893] 1993a) in different ways emphasize the centrality of circulation in shaping capitalism and profits. For Braudel, capitalism emerges precisely through perfect circulation, and hence he locates the birth of capitalism in the city-centered economies of the Mediterranean as well as Amsterdam and London. For Marx, circulation is key to transforming money into capital. In *Capital Vol. 2* Marx discusses more explicitly the centrality of circulation in his discussion of merchant capital, even if in his overall labor theory of value merchant capital is subsumed to industrial capital.

15. For a recent example see Anna Tsing's (2013, 2015) work on Matsutake mushrooms and the ways that "matsutake worlds" defy the gift/commodity binary with gift relationships often being central to the production of capitalist value. Similarly, Appadurai (1986), and scholarship influenced by the "social life of things," focuses primarily on the "commodity potential" of all goods. See Graeber (2011) and Gregory (2015) for an insightful critique of Appadurai's focus on the social life of things.

16. For an enlightening ethnography of illegality, see Janet Roitman's (2006) "Ethics of Illegality in the Chad Basin." Roitman's work is exemplary of a wider literature on legality and illegality within anthropology that highlights the processual and ethnographically nuanced nature of illegality, including a focus on criminalization and illegalization and the slippage, indeed co-constitution, of the legal and illegal (Andersson 2014; Comaroff and Comaroff 2006, 2016; De Genova 2005; Galemba 2018; Galemba and Thomas 2013; Heyman 1999; van Schendel and Abraham 2005). My work is indebted to this archive, though this chapter emphasizes how the question of illegality (and, indeed, ethics) is often bracketed and transformed into a question of obligation.

CHAPTER 3

1. Luis Lobo-Guerrero's work is an important exception in the burgeoning literature on counter-piracy. In his works he highlights the importance of insurance companies as proactively "rendering marine war risks such as piracy, insurable, and in the process, governable" (2012, 79).

2. On the broader history of piracy in the Atlantic and the movement of European pirates between the Atlantic and the Indian Ocean, see Stern (2006), Games (2006), and Ritchie (1989).

3. For a detailed and evocative description of this world, see Rediker and Linebaugh (2013), for whom hydrarchy designates "two related developments of the late seventeenth century: the organisation of the maritime state from above, and the self-organisation of sailors from below" (145).

4. On drone warfare, see Gusterson (2016).

5. The aftermath of the attack on the *USS Cole* in October 2000 in the port of Aden, Yemen, created a spatial imaginary of the western Indian Ocean as a space of

terror and threat. A number of practices that developed in the aftermath of these attacks, including extra-judicial killings, became central to the post-9/11 Global War on Terror. The naval response to piracy is thus always haunted by the specter of "terrorism." See Prestholdt (2013) for an insightful discussion on US engagements in East Africa through a focus on the specters of the "terrorist."

6. UN Resolution 1816, on file with author.

7. The problematics of legibility, of rendering piracy onto satellite maps (or insurance profiles), were never contested; as Pierre's comments show, they were in fact often anticipated by my informants. This anticipation of the anthropological critique is one that Strathern (2005), Riles (2006), and Maurer (2007a), among others, have drawn attention to in their work, and was clearly evident in my encounters at Northwood (and indeed throughout my encounters with institutions and actors involved in counter-piracy). Management as a "good enough" practice allowed for the folding of critique onto itself and is a feature shared across the economy of counter-piracy.

8. This is shared by an EU official. The location and weather conditions were redacted to preserve anonymity.

9. In finance, locational arbitrage refers to the arbitrage strategy where one seeks to profit from differences in exchange rates for the same currency at different banks. Here, following Miyazaki (2007), where he expands arbitrage into both practice and metaphor for the "daily comparative work of Japanese financial professionals" (13), I emphasize that locational arbitrage can be extended beyond a financial practice to understand how Djibouti transforms its location into a site of profit and power.

10. It is important to note the longer history of this project in Djibouti, and the ways in which protection and economy come together through the simultaneous presence of military bases and the port in ways not anticipated by Ferguson's work. The enclave is sustained not only through the invisible powers of the sovereign contract, but also through the very visible presence of military bases and other infrastructures of security.

11. This distinction maps onto Foucault's (2004) discussions on security and discipline. Beyond piracy, as Gregory Feldman (2011) has shown, this mode of policing in central in regulating mobility across the Mediterranean within Frontex and other European Union agencies policing migration to Europe.

12. The South Sea bubble was also an impetus to regulate commercial speculation from gambling. See A. Murphy (2009) for a discussion on the South Sea bubble and the emergence of financial markets in England.

13. Ian Baucom (2005, 154) notes the centrality of insurance as a form of capital accumulation crucial to the development of the system of finance capitalism we inhabit today: "Absent the principle of insurance, finance capitalism could not exist. The world of things would stage its revenge on value each time some object or another was destroyed, would refasten value to embodied things and make one as mortal as another. Licensed by insurance to utterly detach value from the material existence of objects, however, finance capital is free to speculate in and profit from its imaginary markets."

14. Marine Insurance Act, 1906, 6 Edw. 7 c. 41.

15. The work of insurance in this way resonates with the institutional practices of "soft law" organizations that participate in rule-making at an international level outside the judicial realm. Insurance thus adds to the anthropology of global governance in ways that move beyond questions of translation or vernacularization (Merry 2006), or a focus on the aesthetics of norm production (Riles 2000, 2011).

16. This is not to deny the importance of asking these questions. As Laura Bear and others have argued, it is essential, especially in ever-increasing times of austerity, to make claims on the public (Bear and Nayanika 2015). But here I'm drawing from the tradition of legal anthropology, namely the debate over rules and processes (Comaroff and Roberts 1981). In response to the question of whether law (namely state law) was a universal category and the appropriate methodology to study law, anthropologists ranging from Bronislaw Malinowski (1926) to Max Gluckman (1963) highlighted instead a processual method that did not focus on absence or presence of state law, but on processes through which disputes and disagreements were managed. Counter-piracy should be understood as a scaling up of this processual mode of dispute resolution onto a global scale. This form of global scale-making, however, as the Puntland minister's complaints about being excluded from counter-piracy emphasize, is only one mode of defining and fighting piracy.

CHAPTER 4

1. There is a diverse set of literatures that focus on the centrality of intermediaries. This subfield can be productively divided into works that emphasize the role of intermediaries in the creation of markets, colonial orders, legal regimes, trading networks, and other large-scale systems (see Benton [2002] on legal intermediaries; Rothman [2012] on imperial governmentality; Mintz [1957] on market-making; Markovits, Pouchepadass, and Subrahmanyam [2006] on trade networks) and literature that emphasizes the ways intermediaries are essential to projects of translation, vernacularization, and localization (Merry 2000; Clarke 2009).

2. Many of these rumors stem from a history of contentious and tenuous relations between Somalia and Kenya, a history that has often caused a great degree of suffering for Kenyan Somalis and more recent arrivals from Somalia. For a good overview on this relationship between Somalia and Kenya, see Mburu (2005) and Weitzberg (2017). Mburu highlights the history of the ethnically Somali Northern Frontier Districts and the various ways in which the Somali question was central to defining the relationship between Kenya and Somalia, from the Imperial Partition in the late nineteenth century until the post–Cold War context, especially in the aftermath of state collapse in Somalia. Weitzberg's work seeks to describe the ways in which Kenyan Somalis have understood the predicament of borders in shaping ideas of belonging in northern Kenya.

3. In his account of Somali piracy, the journalist Jay Bahadur (2011) mentions Computer as a particularly famous pirate boss who drew on divination techniques

to predict both the possibility of hijacking ships and the ransom amounts that could be secured. His uncanny accuracy, according to Bahadur, gave him the nickname Computer.

4. The Gosha are Somali Bantu known for their magical powers and abilities of divination. For a discussion on Gosha and their role as diviners in Somali life, see Menkhaus (2007), Besteman (2017), Cassanelli (1982), and Blaha (2011).

5. See Maurer (2007b) on payment and its distinctions from systems of exchange or the more traditional anthropological focus on gift-exchange, which emphasizes reciprocity. The focus on reciprocity can be traced back to Mauss ([1954] 2002) and a resulting distinction between gifts and commodities in the larger anthropological literature. However, Parry (1986) critiques Mauss for imagining reciprocity as central to gift-exchange. For a recent appraisal of Parry, see Sanchez et al. (2017).

6. Gosha traditionally are also rewarded for their soothsaying through protection and gift-giving from clans that seek out their services. Divination in a larger context is squarely located in a world of payment.

7. Clifford Geertz's "The Bazaar Economy" (1978) is a classic attempt to bridge anthropology and economics, specifically to use ethnographic insights to answer questions about information asymmetry. In an earlier book Geertz (1963) describes the logic of the bazaar: "The sliding price system, accompanied by the colorful and often aggressive bargaining which seems to mark such systems everywhere, is in part simply a means of communicating economic information in an indeterminate pricing situation … Pricing is much more a matter of estimates in a situation where highly specific comparative and historical data are simply not available; instead of exactly calculated prices, one finds the setting of broad limits within which buyer and seller explore together the finer details of the matter through a system of offer and counteroffer. The ability to operate effectively in the gap of ignorance between a price obviously too high and one obviously too low is what makes a good market-trader: skill in bargaining—which includes as its elements a quick wit, a tireless persistence, and an instinctive shrewdness in evaluating men and material on the basis of very little evidence—is his primary professional qualification" (32–33). While the ransom negotiation lacks the physical space of the marketplace, the bargaining itself—offer and counteroffer—does initially resemble the negotiation tactics described by Geertz. However, here I emphasize the dynamic nature of the transaction as it unfolds in time and the gendered and racialized forms of value that constitute the world of ransom negotiation.

8. In contrast to an ethic of apatheia in Stoicism or the renunciative watchfulness that animates Buddhist, Jain, and early Christian monasticism, the claim to detachment here echoes what David Valentine notes as "authorizing detachment" (2016, 516). In an exploration of context and detachment within practices of "space-faring humans," Valentine highlights that detachment is "a foundational moment in establishing anthropological context" (516). For both Malinowski and Boasian anthropology it was the anthropologist's ability to detach "objective scientific facts from native contextualizations by reducing the latter to 'secondary explanations'" (516) that gave authority to an emerging discipline. In a different context, Peter

Redfield (2012) emphasizes the role played by detachment in humanitarianism, by showing the "lightness" and mobility of expat staff in the everyday operations of *Médecins Sans Frontières*.

9. For Arjun Appadurai, "tournaments of value" are complex periodic events removed from everyday economic life. As he notes, "participation in these events is both a privilege and a status contest between them" (1986, 21). For Appadurai, the *kula* exchange is the paradigmatic form of the tournament of value. Moeran (2010) uses this concept to study the ways book fairs are related to global publishing industries. Ransom negotiation, like tournaments of value, are at once both removed from the work of piracy and essential to its making.

10. A TEU (twenty-foot equivalent unit) is a measure of cargo capacity used to describe the space by volume on container ships as well as container terminals. It is based on the volume of a standard (20-foot-long) cargo container where one TEU equals one 20-foot container. As of 2019, the largest container ships operating at sea, such as the *OOCL Hong Kong*, have a carrying capacity of over 21,000 TEU.

11. On sovereignty and legitimacy, see Schmitt (2006), Weber (1958), and Benton (2002). See the preceding chapter for an example of how the global war against piracy drew on longer histories of manhunting and waging public wars by private means in ways that don't easily fit divisions between public and private.

12. On the shifting norms regarding the use of mercenaries in US conflicts from Vietnam to Iraq, see Dickinson (2011). Singer (2003) provides a more global perspective on the rise of private militaries in the aftermath of the Cold War. Finally, Percy (2007) provides a *longue durée* discussion on the norms regarding mercenaries in conflict ranging from Machiavelli to the present.

13. For discussion of legal issues regarding private military contractors in Iraq and Afghanistan, including questions around immunity, see Elsea (2011).

14. On recommendations for resolving Somali piracy through a return to privateering, see Hutchins (2011) and Kraska and Wilson (2008).

15. The Montreux Document on Pertinent International Legal Obligations and Good Practices for States related to Operations of Private Military and Security Companies during Armed Conflict (Montreux Document) is an international agreement outlining obligations regarding private military and security companies in war zones. The Document was ratified in September 2008 and as of April 2019, fifty-four states have signed on to it. The Montreux Document is non–legally binding and lists over some seventy recommendations for good state practices in the use of private military and security companies.

CHAPTER 5

1. The best authorities on the history of dhow architecture and design, including the naming practices of vessels in the Indian Ocean, are Sheriff (2010), Al-Hijji (2006), and Agius (2017).

2. Two recent works thoroughly render the transformation of the dhow economy and the western Indian Ocean economy more broadly during the nineteenth century. For a view that focuses primarily on colonial debates and attempts at regulation, see Mathew (2016); for a more trader-centric view of the dhow economy, see Bishara (2017).

3. These attempts at surveillance produced a rich array of documentation from case records scattered throughout western Indian Ocean port cities involving *nakhodas* (captains) accused of a variety of offenses, from gunrunning to slavery, as well as the travelogues of European captains involved in the surveillance of maritime traffic. See, for example, George Lydiard Sullivan's (1873) narrative of his time in the Indian Ocean. For broader works on the ways that slavery and piracy were central to reshaping the world of the dhow, see Alpers (2014), Beachey (1962), and Onley (2007).

4. On the rise of containerization, see Levinson (2016).

5. Delays continue to be a significant part of the container economy due to conditions ranging from unsafe wind speeds, which make loading and unloading difficult, to port congestion and other labor and capacity issues. These forms of slowdown are as crucial to the story of containerization as is the emphasis on speed and frictionless transit.

6. Arbitrage is central to the larger maritime economy. As Adrienne Mannov (2015) has highlighted, drawing from Miyazaki (2007), seafarers onboard cargo ships use a logic of arbitrage to quantify the risk of maritime labor.

7. Transshipment is the shipment of goods or containers to an intermediate destination, then to yet another destination. One possible reason for transshipment is to change the means of transport during the journey (e.g., from ship transport to road transport), known as transloading. Another reason is to combine small shipments into a large shipment (consolidation), dividing the large shipment at the other end (deconsolidation). Transshipment usually takes place in transport hubs. Much international transshipment also takes place in designated customs areas, thus avoiding the need for customs checks or duties, otherwise a major hindrance for efficient transport. The dhow trade to Somalia often loads its cargo from container ships in ports like Sharjah and Salalah and transports them to places where container ships are unable to travel due to size or insurance restrictions.

8. On relationality and violence in a different context, see Bolt (2016).

9. For a discussion of the histories of intervention that have shaped the Somali region from the colonial era onwards, see Besteman (2017).

EPILOGUE

1. Radio Mudug, broadcast January 12, 2013, translation by the author.

REFERENCES

Abu-Lughod, Janet. 1989. *Before European Hegemony: The World System AD 1250–1350*. Oxford: Oxford University Press.

Adam, Hussein M., and Charles L. Geshekter, and the Somali Studies International Association. 1992. *Proceedings of the First International Congress of Somali Studies*. Atlanta, GA: Scholars Press.

Agius, Dionisius A. 2017. "Red Sea Folk Beliefs: A Maritime Spirit Landscape." *Northeast African Studies* 17, no. 1: 131–62.

Aitchinson, Charles. 1929. *A Collection of Treaties, Engagements and Sanads Relating to India and Neighbouring Countries*. Calcutta: Government of India Central Publication Branch.

Al-Hijji, Ya'qub Yusuf. 2006. *The Art of Dhow-Building in Kuwait*. Al-Mansuriyyah, Kuwait: Center for Research and Studies on Kuwait in association with London Centre of Arab Studies.

Allianz Global Corporate and Specialty. 2011. *Piracy: An Ancient Risk with Modern Faces, An Insurer's Perspective from Allianz Global Corporate, and Specialty*. Munich: Allianz Global Corporate and Specialty.

Al-Muqaddasī. 2014. *Aḥsan al-taqāsīm fī maʿrifat al-aqālīm*. Leiden: Brill.

Al-Qarafi, Shihāb. 2001. *Al-furuq*. Cairo: Dar al-Salaam.

Allison, Anne. 2013. *Precarious Japan*. Durham, NC: Duke University Press.

Alpers, Edward. 2009. *East Africa and the Indian Ocean*. Princeton, NJ: Markus Wiener.

———. 2014. *The Indian Ocean in World History*. Oxford: Oxford University Press.

Andersson, Ruben. 2014. *Illegality, Inc.: Clandestine Migration and the Business of Bordering Europe*. Oakland: University of California Press.

Anderson, John L. 1995. "Piracy and World History: An Economic Perspective on Maritime Predation." *Journal of World History* 6, no. 2: 175–99.

Anderson, David M, Hannah Elliot, Hassan H. Kochore, and Emma Lochery. 2012. "Camel Herders, Middlewomen, and Urban Milk Bars: The Commodification of Camel Milk in Kenya." *Journal of Eastern African Studies* 6, no. 3: 383–404.

Anghie, Antony. 2005. *Imperialism, Sovereignty, and the Making of International Law*. Cambridge: Cambridge University Press.

Angus, Ian. 2008. "The Myth of the Tragedy of the Commons." *The Bullet: A Socialist Project E-Bulletin* 133. www.socialistproject.ca/bullet/bullet133.html

Appadurai, Arjun, ed. 1986. *Social Life of Things: Commodities in Cultural Perspective*. Philadelphia: University of Pennsylvania Press.

Appel, Hannah. 2012. "Offshore Work: Oil, Modularity and the How of Capitalism in Equatorial Guinea." *American Ethnologist* 39, no. 4: 692–709.

Aristotle. 1962. *Politics of Aristotle*. Edited and translated by Sir Ernest Barker. Oxford: Oxford University Press.

———. 1999 (reprint). *Nicomachean Ethics*. Cambridge, MA: Hackett.

Armitage, David. 2000. *The Ideological Origins of the British Empire*. Cambridge: Cambridge University Press.

Babül, Elif M. 2015. "The Paradox of Protection: Human Rights, the Masculinist State, and the Moral Economy of Gratitude in Turkey. *American Ethnologist* 42, no. 1: 116–30.

Bahadur, Jay. 2011. *Deadly Waters: Inside the Hidden World of Somalia's Pirates*. London: Profile Books.

Baldacci, Giulio. 1909. "The Promontory of Cape Guardafui." *African Affairs* 9, no. 33: 59–72.

Baker, Tom, and Jonathan Simon. 2010. *Embracing Risk: The Changing Culture of Insurance and Responsibility*. Chicago: University of Chicago Press.

Barnes, Cedric. 2006. "U dhashay—Ku dhashay: Genealogical and Territorial Discourse in Somali History." *Social Identities* 12, no. 4: 487–98.

Barnes, Robert H. 1999. "Marriage by Capture." *Journal of the Royal Anthropological Institute* 5, no. 1: 56–73.

Barre, Siyad M. 1974. *My Country and My People*. Mogadishu: Ministry of Information and National Guidance.

Baucom, Ian. 2005. *Specters of the Atlantic: Finance Capital, Slavery, and the Philosophy of History*. Durham, NC: Duke University Press.

Bayart, Jean-Francois. 2009. *The State in Africa: The Politics of the Belly*, 2nd ed. Cambridge, MA: Polity.

Beachey, Raymond W. 1962. "The Arms Trade in East Africa in the Late Nineteenth Century." *Journal of African History* 3, no. 3: 451–67.

Bear, Laura. 2015. "Capitalist Divination: Popularist Speculators and Technologies of Imagination on the Hooghly River." *Comparative Studies of South Asia, Africa and the Middle East* 35, no. 3: 408–23.

———. 2016. *Navigating Austerity: Currents of Debt along a South Asian River*. Stanford, CA: Stanford University Press.

Bear, Laura, and Mathur Nayanika. 2015. "Introduction: Remaking the Public Good: A New Anthropology of Bureaucracy." *Cambridge Journal of Anthropology* 33, no. 1: 18–34.

Beck, Ulrich. 1992. *Risk Society; Towards a New Modernity*. Newbury Park, CA: Sage Publications.

Beito, David T. 2000. *From Mutual Aid to the Welfare State: Fraternal Societies and Social Services, 1890–1967*. Chapel Hill: University of North Carolina Press.

Benton, Lauren. 2002. *Law and Colonial Cultures: Legal Regimes in World History, 1400–1900*. Cambridge: Cambridge University Press.

———. 2005. "Legal Spaces of Empire: Piracy and the Origins of Ocean Regionalism." *Comparative Studies in Society and History* 47, no. 4: 700–24.

Benton, Laura, Adam Clulow, and Bain Attwood, eds. 2018. *Protection and Empire: A Global History*. Cambridge: Cambridge University Press.

Benton, Lauren, and Lisa Ford. 2016. *Rage for Order: The British Empire and the Origins of International Law 1800–1850*. Cambridge, MA: Harvard University Press.

Ben-Yehoyada, Naor. 2016. "'Follow Me, and I Will Make You Fishers of Men': The Moral and Political Scales of Migration in the Central Mediterranean." *Journal of the Royal Anthropological Institute* 22, no. 1: 183–202.

———. 2017. *The Mediterranean Incarnate: Region Formation between Sicily and Tunisia since World War II*. Chicago: University of Chicago Press.

Besteman, Catherine. 1996. "Representing Violence and 'Othering' Somalia." *Cultural Anthropology* 11, no. 1: 120–33.

———. 1999. *Unraveling Somalia: Race, Class and the Legacy of Slavery*. Philadelphia: University of Pennsylvania Press.

———. 2017. "Experimenting in Somalia: The New Security Empire." *Anthropological Theory* 17, no. 3: 404–20.

Bishara, Fahad Ahmad. 2017. *A Sea of Debt: Law and Economic Life in the Western Indian Ocean, 1780–1950*. Cambridge: Cambridge University Press.

Blaha, David. 2011. "Pushing Marginalization: British Colonial Policy, Somali Identity, and the Gosha 'Other' in Jubaland Province, 1895–1920." Master's thesis, Virginia Tech.

Blanchot, Maurice. 1995. *Writing of the Disaster*. Translated by Ann Smock. Lincoln: University of Nebraska Press.

Blok, Anton. 1974. *The Mafia of a Sicilian Village, 1860–1960: A Study of Violent Peasant Entrepreneurs*. Oxford: Blackwell Publishing.

Blum, Hester. 2003. "Pirated Tars, Piratical Texts: Barbary Captivity and American Sea Narratives." *Early American Studies* 1, no. 2: 133–58.

———. 2010. "The Prospect of Oceanic Studies." *PMLA* 125, no. 3: 670–77.

Bodin, Jean, and Julian H. Franklin. 1992. *On Sovereignty: Four Chapters from the Six Books of the Commonwealth*. Cambridge: Cambridge University Press

Bolt, Maxim. 2016. "Mediated Paternalism and Violent Incorporation: Enforcing Farm Hierarchies on the Zimbabwean–South African Border." *Journal of Southern African Studies* 42: 911–27.

Bourdieu, Pierre. 1977. *Outline of a Theory of Practice*. Cambridge, IL: University of Cambridge Press.

———. 1992. *An Invitation to Reflexive Sociology*. Chicago: University of Chicago Press.

Borradori, Giovanna. 2003. *Philosophy in a Time of Terror: Dialogues with Jurgen Habermas and Jacques Derrida*. Chicago: University of Chicago Press.

Bose, Sugata. 2009. *A Hundred Horizons: The Indian Ocean in the Age of Global Empire*. Cambridge, MA: Harvard University Press.

Boyer, Dominic. 2005. "The Corporeality of Expertise." *Ethnos* 70, no. 2: 243–66.

Braudel, Fernand. 1992. *Civilization and Capitalism, 15th–18th Century*, vol. 3: *The Perspective of the World*. Berkeley: University of California Press.

Brennan, James. 2008. "Lowering the Sultan's Flag: Sovereignty and Decolonization in Coastal Kenya." *Comparative Studies in Society and History* 50, no. 4: 831–61.

Brenner, Neil. 1999. "Beyond State-Centrism? Space, Territoriality, and Geographical Scale in Globalization Studies." *Theory and Society* 28, no. 1: 39–78.

Bueger, Christian. 2013. "Practice, Pirates and Coast Guards: The Grand Narrative of Somali Piracy." *Third World Quarterly* 34, no. 10: 1811–27.

Bueger, Christian, and Jan Stockenbrugger. 2013. "Security Communities, Alliances, and Macrosecuritization: The Practices of Counter-Piracy Governance." In *Maritime Piracy and Construction of Global Governance*, edited by Michael J. Struett, Jon D. Carlson, and Mark T. Nance, 99–124. London: Routledge.

Burchell, Graham, Colin Gordon, and Peter Miller, eds. 1991. *The Foucault Effect: Studies in Governmentality*. Chicago: University of Chicago Press.

Burton, Richard. 1856. *First Footsteps in East Africa*. London: Tylston and Edwards.

Bush, George W. 2002. "Address to a Joint Session of Congress and the American People." *Harvard Journal of Law & Public Policy* 25, no. 2: xviii.

Cabdi, Sucaad Ibrahim. 2005. "The Impact of the War on the Family." In *Rebuilding Somaliland: Issues and Possibilities*, edited by WSP International Somali Program, 269–325. Asmara: Red Sea Press.

Callon, Michel. 1998. *The Laws of the Markets*. Oxford: Blackwell Publishers.

———. 2012. "For an Anthropology of Atmospheric Markets: The Exemplary Case of Financial Markets. Theorizing the Contemporary." *Cultural Anthropology*, May 15, 2012. https://culanth.org/fieldsights/334-for-an-anthropology-of-atmospheric-markets-the-exemplary-case-of-financial-markets.

Candea, Matei. 2012. "Derrida en Corse? Hospitality as Scale-Free Abstraction." *Journal of the Royal Anthropological Institute* 18: S34–48.

Candea, Matei J., Jo Cook, Catherine Trundle, and Tom Yarrow, eds. 2015. *Detachment: Essays on the Limits of Relational Thinking*. Manchester: Manchester University Press.

Carrier, Neil. 2005. "The Need for Speed: Contrasting Timeframes in the Social Life of Kenyan *Miraa*." *Africa* 75, no. 4: 539–58.

———. 2007. *Kenyan Khat: The Social Life of a Stimulant*. Leiden: Brill.

———. 2017. *Little Mogadishu: Eastleigh, Nairobi's Global Somali Hub*. London: Hurst Publishers.

Cassanelli, Lee V. 1982. *The Shaping of Somali Society: Reconstructing the History of a Pastoral People, 1600–1900*. Philadelphia: University of Pennsylvania Press.

———. 1986. "Qat Changes in Production and Consumption of a Quasi-Legal Commodity." In *The Social Life of Things: Commodities in Cultural Perspective*, edited by Arjun Appaduarai, 236–57. Philadelphia: University of Pennsylvania Press.

Ceccarelli, Giovanni. 2001. "Risky Business: Theological and Canonical Thought on Insurance from the Thirteenth to the Seventeenth Century." *Journal of Medieval and Early Modern Studies* 31, no. 3: 607–58.

———. 2007. The Price for Risk-Taking: Marine Insurance and Probability Calculus in the Late Middle Ages. *Electronic Journ@l for History of Probability and Statistics* 3, no. 1. www.jehps.net/Juin2007/Ceccarelli_Risk.pdf.

Chamayou, Grégoire. 2012. *Manhunts: A Philosophical History.* Princeton, NJ: Princeton University Press.

Chaudhuri, K. N. 1983. *Trade and Civilisation in the Indian Ocean: An Economic History from the Rise of Islam to 1750.* Cambridge: Cambridge University Press.

Cicero, Marcus Tullius. 1833. *De Officiis Libri Tres: Accedunt in Usum Juventutis Notae Quaedam Anglice Scriptae.* Philadelphia: Hogan & Thompson.

Clark, Geoffrey. 1999. *Betting on Lives: The Culture of Life Insurance in England, 1695–1775.* Manchester: Manchester University Press.

Clarke, Kamari Maxine. 2009. *Fictions of Justice: The International Criminal Court and the Challenges of Legal Pluralism in Sub-Saharan Africa.* Cambridge: Cambridge University Press.

Clulow, Adam. 2012. "The Pirate and the Warlord." *Journal of Early Modern History* 16, no. 2: 523–42.

Coggins, Bridget L. 2016. "Failing and the Seven Seas? Somali Piracy in Global Perspective." *Journal of Global Security Studies* 1, no. 4: 251–69.

Cohen, Abner. 1969. *Custom and Politics in Urban Africa: A Study of Hausa Migrants in Yoruba Towns.* Berkeley: University of California Press.

Coleman, E. Gabriella. 2013. *Coding Freedom: The Ethics and Aesthetics of Hacking.* Princeton, NJ: Princeton University Press.

Comaroff, Jean, and John L. Comaroff. 1990. "Goodly Beasts, Beastly Goods: Cattle and Commodities in a South African Context." *American Ethnologist* 17, no. 2: 195–216.

———, eds. 2006. *Law and Disorder in the Postcolony.* Chicago: University of Chicago Press.

———. 2012. *Theory from the South: Or, How Euro-America Is Evolving toward Africa.* Boulder, CO: Paradigm Publishers.

———. 2016. *The Truth about Crime: Sovereignty, Knowledge, Social Order.* Chicago: University of Chicago Press.

Comaroff, John, and Simon Roberts. 1981. *Rules and Processes: The Cultural Logic of Dispute in an African Context.* Chicago: University of Chicago Press.

Coombe, Rosemary J. 1998. *The Cultural Life of Intellectual Properties: Authorship, Appropriation, and the Law.* Durham, NC: Duke University Press.

Cooper, Frederick, and Ann Laura Stoler. 1997. *Tensions of Empire: Colonial Cultures in a Bourgeois World.* Berkeley: University of California Press.

Cowen, Deborah. 2014. *The Deadly Life of Logistics.* Minneapolis: University of Minnesota Press.

Cruttenden, C. J. 1846. "Report on the Mijertheyn Tribe of Somalies, Inhabiting the District Forming the North-East Point of Africa." In *Transactions of the*

Bombay Geographical Society, vol. 7: *From May 1844 to December 1846.* Bombay: The Times Press.

Curtin, Philip D. 1984. *Cross-Cultural Trade in World History.* Cambridge: Cambridge University Press.

Daniels, Christopher. 2012. *Somali Piracy and Terrorism in the Horn of Africa.* Lanham, MD: Scarecrow Press.

Das, Veena, and Deborah Poole. 2004. *Anthropology in the Margins of the State.* Santa Fe, NM: School of American Research Press.

Dawdy, Shannon L., and Joe Bonni. 2012. "Towards a General Theory of Piracy." *Anthropological Quarterly* 85, no. 3: 673–99.

Daxecker, Ursula, and Brandon C Prins. 2017. "Financing Rebellion: Using Piracy to Explain and Predict Conflict Intensity in Africa and Southeast Asia. *Journal of Peace Research* 54, no. 2: 215–30.

De Genova, Nicholas. 2005. *Working the Boundaries: Race, Space, and "Illegality" in Mexican Chicago.* Durham, NC: Duke University Press.

de Goede, Marieke. 2003. "Hawala Discourses and the War on Terrorist Finance." *Environment and Planning D: Society and Space* 21, no. 5: 513–32.

———. 2004. "Repoliticizing Financial Risk." *Economy and Society* 33, no. 2: 197–217.

Dent, Alexander S. 2012. "Piracy, Circulatory Legitimacy, and Neoliberal Subjectivity in Brazil." *Cultural Anthropology* 27, no. 1: 28–49.

Derrida, Jacques. 2005. "The Principle of Hospitality: An Interview with Dominique Dhombres." Translated by A. Thompson. *Parallax* 11, no. 1: 6–9.

Desai, Gaurav. 2013. *Commerce with the Universe: Africa, India, and the Afrasian Imagination.* New York: Columbia University Press.

De Sardan, Olivier J. P. 1999. "A Moral Economy of Corruption in Africa?" *Journal of Modern African Studies* 37, no. 1: 25–52.

Dickinson, Edwin D. 1924. "Is the Crime of Piracy Obsolete?" *Harvard Law Review* 38, no. 3: 334–60.

Dickinson, Laura A. 2011. *Outsourcing War and Peace: Preserving Public Values in a World of Privatized Foreign Affairs.* New Haven, CT: Yale University Press.

Donahue, Charles. 1986. "Animalia Ferae Naturae: Rome, Bologna, Leyden, Oxford and Queen's County, N.Y." In *Studies in Roman Law in Memory of A. Arthur Schiller,* edited by Roger S. Bagnall and William V. Harris, 39–63. Leiden: Brill.

Dresch, Paul. 2012. "Aspects of Non-State Law: Early Yemen and Perpetual Peace." In *Legalism: Anthropology and History,* edited by Paul Dresch and Hannah Skoda, 145–72. Oxford: Oxford University Press.

Dua, Jatin. 2010. "A Modern-Day Pirate's Port of Call." *Middle East Report* no. 256: 20–23.

———. 2013. "A Sea of Trade and a Sea of Fish: Piracy and Protection in the Western Indian Ocean." *Journal of Eastern African Studies* 7, no. 2: 353–70.

———. 2015. "After piracy? Mapping the means and ends of maritime predation in the Western Indian Ocean" *Journal of Eastern African Studies* 9, no.3: 505–521.

———. 2019. "Hijacked: Piracy and Economies of Protection in the Western Indian Ocean." *Comparative Studies in Society and History* 61, no.3: 479–507.

———. 2016. "Dhow Encounters." *Transition* 119: 49–59.

———. 2017a. "A Sea of Profit: Making Property in the Western Indian Ocean." In *Legalism: Property and Ownership*, edited by Georgy Kantor, Tom Lambert, Hannah Skoda, 175–202. New York: Oxford University Press.

———. 2017b. "A Sino-Kenyan Story of Shipwreck and Salvation." In *Inhabiting the Corridor*, edited by Tau Tavengwa and Léonie Newhouse, 45–47. Göttingen, Germany: Max-Planck Institute for the Study of Religious and Ethnic Diversity in association with Cityscapes: Rethinking Urban Things.

———. 2018. "Privateers and Public Ends: Piracy as Global Moral Panic in the Atlantic and Indian Ocean." In *Panic, Transnational Cultural Studies, and the Affective Contours of Power*, edited by Micol Seigel, 27–45. New York: Routledge.

———. 2019. "Piracy and Maritime Security in Africa." *Oxford Encyclopedia of African Politics*, 1–23. New York: Oxford University Press.

Dunigan, Molly. 2013. A Lesson from Iraq War: How to Outsource War to Private Contractors." *Christian Science Monitor,* March 19, 2013. www.csmonitor.com /Commentary/Opinion/2013/0319/A-lesson-from-Iraq-war-How-to-outsource-war-to-private-contractors.

Dunn, Ross E. 1989. *The Adventures of Ibn Battuta: A Muslim Traveler of the 14th Century*. Berkeley: University of California Press.

Durril, Wayne. 1986. "Atrocious Misery: The African Origins of Famine in Northern Somalia, 1839–1884." *American Historical Review* 91, no. 2: 287–306.

Ebert, Christopher. 2011. "Early Modern Atlantic Trade and the Development of Maritime Insurance to 1630." *Past & Present* 213, no. 1: 87–114.

Economist, The (US, no author cited). 2018. "How Kidnapping Insurance Keeps a Lid on Ransom Inflation." *The Economist,* May 26, 2018, 64.

Edwards, David B. 1996. *Heroes of the Age: Moral Fault Lines on the Afghan Frontier*. Berkeley: University of California Press.

Elsea, Jennifer K. 2011. "Private Security Contractors in Iraq and Afghanistan: Legal Issues." *Current Politics and Economics of Northern and Western Asia* 20, no. 2: 359–407.

Ellickson, Robert C. 2009. *Order without Law: How Neighbors Settle Disputes*. Cambridge, MA: Harvard University Press.

Elyachar, Julia. 2010. "Phatic Labor, Infrastructure, and the Question of Empowerment in Cairo." *American Ethnologist* 37, no. 3: 452–64.

Ericson, Richard V., Aaron Doyle, and Dean Barry, eds. 2003. *Insurance as Governance*. Toronto: University of Toronto Press.

Evans-Pritchard, E. E. 1969. *The Nuer: A Description of the Modes of Livelihood and Political Institutions of a Nilotic People*. New York: Oxford University Press.

Ewald, François. 1991. "Insurance and Risk." In *The Foucault Effect: Studies in Governmentality*, edited by Graham Burchell, Colin Gordon, and Peter Miller, 197–210. Chicago: University of Chicago Press.

FAO (Food and Agricultural Organization of the United Nations). 2005. Profile: The Somali Republic. www.fao.org/fi/oldsite/FCP/en/SOM/profile.htm.

Favier, Jean. 1998. *Gold & Spices: The Rise of Commerce in the Middle Ages*. New York: Holmes and Meier.

Feldman, Gregory. 2011. *The Migration Apparatus: Security, Labor, and Policymaking in the European Union*. Stanford, CA: Stanford University Press.

Ferguson, James. 1985. "The Bovine Mystique: Power, Property and Livestock in Rural Lesotho." *MAN* 20, no. 4: 647–74.

———. 1999. *Expectations of Modernity: Myths and Meanings of Urban Life on the Zambian Copperbelt*. Berkeley: University of California Press.

———. 2005. "Seeing like an Oil Company: Space, Security, and Global Capital in Neoliberal Africa." *American Anthropologist* 107, no. 3: 377–82.

Finley, M. I. 1970. "Aristotle and Economic Analysis." *Past & Present* 47, no. 1: 3–25.

Forest, James J. F. 2012. "Global Trends in Kidnapping by Terrorist Groups." *Global Change, Peace & Security* 24, no. 3: 311–30.

Foucault, Michel. 2004. *Security Terror and Population: Lectures at the College de France, 1977–1978*. New York: Palgrave Macmillan.

Gabrielsen, Vincent. 2001. "Economic Activity, Maritime Trade and Piracy in the Hellenistic Aegean." *Revue des Études Anciennes* 103, nos. 1–2: 219–40.

Galemba, Rebecca B. 2018. *Contraband Corridor: Making a Living at the Mexico-Guatemala Border*. Stanford, CA: Stanford University Press.

Gambetta, Diego. 1996. *The Sicilian Mafia: The Business of Private Protection*. Cambridge, MA: Harvard University Press.

Games, Alison. 2006. "Beyond the Atlantic: English Globetrotters and Transoceanic Connections." *William and Mary Quarterly* 63, no. 4: 675–92.

Gandrup, Tobias. 2016. *Enter and Exit: Everyday State Practices at Somaliland's Hargeisa Egal International Airport*. DIIS Working Paper.

Gebissa, Ezekiel. 2004. *Leaf of Allah: Khat and Agricultural Transformation in Harerge, Ethiopia 1875–1991*. Oxford: James Currey.

Geertz, Clifford. 1963. *Peddlers and Princes*. Chicago: University of Chicago Press.

———. 1978. "The Bazaar Economy: Information and Search in Peasant Marketing." *American Economic Review* 68, no. 2: 28–32.

Gettleman, Jeffrey. 2017. "Somali Pirates Attack, Raising Fears that a Menace Is Back." *New York Times,* April 4, 2017.

Gieryn, Thomas F. 1983. "Boundary-Work and the Demarcation of Science from Non-Science: Strains and Interests in Professional Ideologies of Scientists." *American Sociological Review* 48, no. 6: 781–95.

Gigerenzer, Gerd, ed. 1989. *The Empire of Chance: How Probability Changed Science and Everyday Life*. Cambridge: Cambridge University Press.

Gilbert, Erik. 2004. *Dhows and the Colonial Economy of Zanzibar, 1860–1970*. Athens: Ohio University Press.

Gilmer, Brittany. 2017. "Hedonists and Husbands: Piracy Narratives, Gender Demands, and Local Political Economic Realities in Somalia." *Third World Quarterly 38*, no. 6: 1366–80.

Glück, Zoltán. 2015. "Piracy and the Production of Security Space." *Environment and Planning D: Society and Space* 33, no. 4: 642–59.

Gluckman, Max. 1963. *Order and Rebellion in Tribal Africa* (collected essays). London: Cohen and West.

Golomski, Casey. 2015. "Compassion Technology: Life Insurance and the Remaking of Kinship in Swaziland's Age of HIV." *American Ethnologist* 42, no. 1: 81–96.

Gordillo, Gastón. 2014. *Rubble: The Afterlife of Destruction.* Durham, NC: Duke University Press.

Gordon, Scott H. 1954. "The Economic Theory of a Common-Property Resource: The Fishery." *Journal of Political Economy* 62, no. 2: 124–42.

Gosse, Philip. 1932. *The History of Piracy.* New York: Burt Franklin.

Goswami, Manu. 2004. *Producing India.* New Delhi: Orient Blackswan.

Graeber, David. 2011. *Debt: The First 5,000 Years.* Brooklyn, NY: Melville House.

Grant, Bruce. 2009. *The Captive and the Gift: Cultural Histories of Sovereignty in Russia and the Caucasus.* Ithaca, NY: Cornell University Press.

Gregory, Chris. 2015. *Gifts and Commodities.* Chicago: HAU Books.

Greene, Jody. 2008. "Hostis Humani Generis." *Critical Inquiry* 34, no. 4: 683–705.

Grotius, Hugo. (1609) 2004. *The Free Sea.* Edited by David Armitage. Indianapolis: Liberty Fund.

———. (1625) 2005. *The Rights of War and Peace,* book 3. Edited by Richard Tuck. Indianapolis: Liberty Fund.

Grovogui, Siba N'Zatioula. 1996. *Sovereigns, Quasi Sovereigns, and Africans: Race and Self-Determination in International Law.* Minneapolis: University of Minnesota Press.

Gupta, Pamila. 2012. "Monsoon Fever." *Social Dynamics* 38, no. 3: 516–27.

Gusterson, Hugh. 2016. *Drone Remote Control Warfare.* Cambridge, MA: MIT Press.

Guyer, Jane. 2004. *Marginal Gains: Monetary Transactions in Atlantic Africa.* Chicago: University of Chicago Press.

Hagmann, Tobias, and Markus V. Hoehne. 2008. "Failures of the State Failure Debate: Evidence from the Somali Territories." *Journal of International Development* 21, no. 1: 42–57.

Hallaq, Wael. 2009. *An Introduction to Islamic Law.* Cambridge: Cambridge University Press.

Hansen, Stig Jarle. 2009. *Piracy in the Greater Gulf of Aden.* London: Norwegian Institute for Urban and Regional Research.

Hansen, Thomas Blom, and Finn Stepputat. 2006. "Sovereignty Revisited." *Annual Review of Anthropology* 35, no. 1: 295–315.

Hardin, Garrett. 1968. "The Tragedy of the Commons." *Science* 162, no. 3859: 1243–48.

Hardt, Michael. 2005. "Immaterial Labor and Artistic Production." *A Journal of Economics, Culture and Society* 17, no. 2: 175–77.

Hardt, Michael, and Antonio Negri. 2005. *Multitude: War and Democracy in the Age of Empire.* New York: Penguin Books.

Hari, Johann. 2009. "You Are Being Lied To about Pirates." *Independent,* January 4, 2009. www.independent.co.uk/voices/commentators/johann-hari/johann-hari-you-are-being-lied-to-about-pirates-1225817.html.

Harvey, David. 2005. *Spaces of Neoliberalization: Towards a Theory of Uneven Geographical Development.* Munich, Germany: Franz Steiner Verlag.

Heller-Roazen, Daniel. 2009. *The Enemy of All: Piracy and the Law of Nations.* Cambridge, MA: Zone Books.

Helmreich, Stefan. 2009. *Alien Ocean: Anthropological Voyages in Microbial Seas.* Berkeley: University of California Press.

Herskovits, Melville J. 1926. "The Cattle Complex in East Africa." *American Anthropologist* 28, no. 1: 230–72.

Herzfeld, Michael. 1985. *The Poetics of Manhood: Contest and Identity in a Cretan Mountain Village.* Princeton, NJ: Princeton University Press.

Heyman, Josiah. 1999. *States and Illegal Practices.* Oxford: Berg.

Hindu, The. 2010. "Somali Pirates Hijack Indian Dhows." March 30, 2010. www.thehindu.com/news/national/Somali-pirates-hijack-Indian-dhows/article16634530.ece.

Hirschman, Albert. 1977. *The Passions and the Interests: Political Arguments for Capitalism before Its Triumph.* Princeton, NJ: Princeton University Press.

Ho, Engseng. 2004. "Empire through Diasporic Eyes: A View from the Other Boat." *Comparative Studies in Society and History* 46, no. 2: 210–46.

———. 2006. *The Graves of Tarim: Genealogy and Mobility across the Indian Ocean.* Berkeley: University of California Press.

Hobbes, Thomas. 2006. *Leviathan, Or the Matter, Forme and Power of a Commonwealth Ecclesiasticall and Civil.* New Haven, CT: Yale University Press.

Hobsbawm, Eric J. 1959. *Primitive Rebels: Studies in Archaic Forms of Social Movements in the 19th and 20th Centuries.* Manchester: Manchester University Press.

Hoehne, Markus. 2016. "The Rupture of Territoriality and the Diminishing Relevance of Cross-Cutting Ties in Somalia after 1990." *Development and Change* 47, no. 6: 1379–1411.

Hofmeyr, Isabel. 2010. "Universalizing the Indian Ocean." *PMLA* 125, no. 3: 721–29.

Hopper, Matthew S. 2015. *Slaves of One Master: Globalization and Slavery in Arabia in the Age of Empire.* New Haven, CT: Yale University Press.

Huber, Valeska. 2013. *Channelling Mobilities: Migration and Globalisation in the Suez Canal Region and Beyond, 1869–1914.* Cambridge: Cambridge University Press.

Hutchins, Todd E. 2011. "Structuring a Sustainable Letters of Marque Regime: How Commissioning Privateers Can Defeat the Somali Pirates." *California Law Review* 99, no. 3: 819–84.

Hutchinson, Sharon. 1992. "The Cattle of Money and the Cattle of Girls among the Nuer, 1930–83." *American Ethnologist* 19, no. 2: 294–316.

Ibrahim, Mohamed. 2010. "Somalia and Global Terrorism: A Growing Connection?" *Journal of Contemporary African Studies* 28, no. 3: 283–95.

ICG (International Crisis Group). 2009. "Somalia: The Trouble with Puntland." Crisis Group Africa Briefing 64, August 12, 2009. www.crisisgroup.org/africa/horn-africa/somalia/somalia-trouble-puntland.

ILO (International Labour Organization). 2004. *The Global Seafarer: Living and Working Conditions in a Globalized Industry.*

IMB (International Maritime Bureau, International Chamber of Commerce). 2012. *Piracy and Armed Robbery against Ships: Report for the Period 1 January— 31 December 2012.* www.icc-ccs.org/reports/2017-Annual-IMB-Piracy-Report.pdf.

———. 2008. *Piracy and Armed Robbery against Ships: Report for the Period 1 January—31 December 2008.* www.rk-marine-kiel.de/files/piraterie/imb/imb_piracy_report_2008.pdf.

IMO-MKC (International Maritime Organization—Maritime Knowledge Centre). 2008. *International Shipping and World Trade: Facts and Figures May 2008.*

Jamali, Hafeez. 2013. *The Anxiety of Development: Megaprojects and the Politics of Place in Gwadar, Pakistan.* Crossroads Asia Working Series, no. 6. Bonn: Center for Development Research.

Johns, Adrian. 2009. *Piracy: The Intellectual Property Wars from Gutenberg to Gates.* Chicago: University of Chicago Press.

Johnston, W. Ross. 1973. *Sovereignty and Protection: A Study of British Jurisdictional Imperialism in the Late Nineteenth Century.* Duke University Commonwealth Studies Center Series, no. 41. Durham, NC: Duke University Press.

Kant, Immanuel. (1795) 2003. *Essay: Perpetual Peace: A Philosophical Sketch.* London: Hackett Publications.

Kaplan, Robert D. 2010. *Monsoon: The Indian Ocean and the Future of American Power.* New York: Random House.

Kapteijns, Lidwien. 1995. "Gender Relations and the Transformation of the Northern Somali Pastoral Tradition." *International Journal of African Historical Studies* 28, no. 2: 241–59.

———. 2008. "The Disintegration of Somalia: A Historiographical Essay." *Bildhaan: An International Journal of Somali Studies* 1, no. 1: 6–17.

Kar, Sohini. 2013. "Recovering Debts: Microfinance Loan Officers and the Work of 'Proxy-Creditors' in India." *American Ethnologist* 40, no. 3: 480–93.

———. 2017. "Relative Indemnity: Risk, Insurance, and Kinship in Indian Microfinance." *Journal of the Royal Anthropological Institute* 23, no. 2: 302–19.

Keane, Webb. 2008. "Market, Materiality and Moral Metalanguage." *Anthropological Theory* 8, no. 1: 27–42.

Kemp, Christopher. 2012. *Floating Gold: A Natural (and Unnatural) History of Ambergris.* Chicago: University of Chicago Press.

Khāfī Khān, Muḥammad Hāshim. 1869. *Muntakhab-ul-Lubab.* Edited by Mawlavi kabir al-Din Ahmad. Calcutta: Asiatic Society of Bengal.

Khaldun, Ibn. 1957. *The Muqaddimah: An Introduction to History.* Translated by Franz Rosenthal. Princeton, NJ: Princeton University.

Khalilieh, Hassan. 1998. *Islamic Maritime Law: An Introduction.* Leiden: Brill.

Kinsey, Christopher P., Stig J. Hansen, and George Franklin. 2009. "The Impact of Private Security Companies on Somalia's Governance Networks." *Cambridge Review of International Affairs* 22, no. 1: 147–61.

Knight, Frank H. 1921. *Risk, Uncertainty, and Profit.* Boston: Houghton Mifflin.

Knights, David, and Theo Vurdubakis. 1993. "Calculations of Risk: Towards an Understanding of Insurance as a Moral and Political Practice." *Accounting, Organizations, and Society* 18, nos. 7–8: 729–64.

Koselleck, Reinhart. 2004. *Futures Past: On the Semantics of Historical Time.* New York: Columbia University Press.

Kraska, James, and Brian Wilson. 2008. "Fighting Pirates: The Pen and the Sword." *World Policy Journal* 25, no. 4: 41–52.

Kuper, Adam. 1982. *Wives for Cattle: Bridewealth and Marriage in Southern Africa.* London: Routledge & Kegan Paul.

Kusow, Abdi M., and Stephanie R. Bjork, eds. 2007. *From Mogadishu to Dixon: The Somali Diaspora in a Global Context.* Trenton, NJ: Red Sea Press.

Laitin, David, and Said Samatar. 1984. "Somalia and the World Economy." *Review of African Political Economy* 11, no. 30: 58–72.

————. 1987. *Somalia: Nation in Search of a State.* Boulder, CO: Westview Press.

Lambert, Tom, George Kantor, and Hannah Skoda. 2017. *Legalism: Property and Ownership.* Oxford: Oxford University Press.

Lane, Anthony. 2013. "Dangerous Waters: 'Captain Phillips' and 'Parkland.'" *The New Yorker,* October 14, 2013. www.newyorker.com/magazine/2013/10/14/dangerous-waters.

Lane, Frederick C. 1979. *Profits from Power: Readings in Protection Rent and Violence-Controlling Enterprises.* Albany, NY: SUNY Press.

Lapidoth, Ruth. 1982. *The Red Sea and the Gulf of Aden,* vol. 5. Leiden: Martinus Nijhoff Publishers.

Larkin, Brian. 2008. *Signal and Noise: Media, Infrastructure, and Urban Culture in Nigeria.* Durham, NC: Duke University Press

Larkin, Peter A. 1977. "An Epitaph for the Concept of Maximum Sustained Yield." *Transactions of the American Fisheries Society* 106, no. 1: 1–11.

Layton, Simon. 2013. "The 'Moghul's Admiral': Angrian 'Piracy' and the Rise of British Bombay. *Journal of Early Modern History* 17, no. 1: 75–93.

Lee, Christopher J. 2013. "The Indian Ocean during the Cold War: Thinking through a Critical Geography History Compass." *History Compass* 11, no. 7: 524–30.

Leeson, Peter T. 2012. *The Invisible Hook: The Hidden Economics of Pirates.* Princeton, NJ: Princeton University Press.

Lehr, Peter. 2006. *Violence at Sea: Piracy in an Age of Global Terrorism.* New York: Routledge.

Lepselter, Susan. 2012. "The Resonance of Captivity: Aliens and Conquest." *HAU: Journal of Ethnographic Theory* 2, no. 2: 84–104.

Levinson, Marc. 2016. *The Box: How the Shipping Container Made the World Smaller and the World Economy Bigger.* Princeton, NJ: Princeton University Press.

Lewis, Ioan M. 1994. *Blood and Bone: The Call of Kinship in Somali Society*. Lawrenceville, NJ: Red Sea Press.

———. 1999. *A Pastoral Democracy: A Study of Pastoralism & Politics among the Northern Somali of the Horn of Africa*. Oxford: James Currey Publishers.

Little, Peter. 2003. *Somalia: Economy without State*. Bloomington: Indiana University Press.

Lobo-Guerrero, Luis. 2007. "Biopolitics of Specialized Risk: An Analysis of Kidnap and Ransom Insurance." *Security Dialogue*, 38, no. 3: 315–34.

———. 2012. *Insuring War: Sovereignty, Security, and Risk*. London: Routledge.

Luxemburg, Rosa. (1913) 2003. *The Accumulation of Capital*. London: Routledge.

Macguire, Eoghan. 2016. *Resurrection of Somali Pirate Attacks Feared after Tanker Shootout*. NBC News online, November 20, 2016. www.nbcnews.com/news/world/resurrection-somali-pirate-attacks-feared-after-tanker-shootout-n685731.

Machado, Pedro. 2014. *Ocean of Trade: South Asian Merchants, Africa and the Indian Ocean, c. 1750–1850*. Cambridge: Cambridge University Press.

Machiavelli, Niccolò. 1961 *The Prince*. Translated by George Bull. Baltimore: Penguin Books.

Mahan, Alfred. T. (1890) 1975. *The Influence of Sea Power upon History, 1660–1783*. Boston: Little, Brown.

Malgaonkar, Manohar. 1981. *The Sea Hawk: Life and Battles of Kanhoji Angrey*. New Delhi: Orient Books.

Malinowski, Bronislaw. 1926. *Crime and Custom in Savage Society*. London: Routledge & Kegan.

Mannov, Adrienne. 2015. *Economies of Security: An Ethnography of Merchant Seafarers, Global Itineraries, and Maritime Piracy*. PhD diss., Faculty of Social Sciences, University of Copenhagen.

Marchal, Roland. 1996. *The Post Civil War Somali Business Class*. European Commission, Somalia Unit.

Margariti, Roxani E. 2008. "Mercantile Networks, Port Cities, and 'Pirate' States: Conflict and Competition in the Indian Ocean World of Trade before the Sixteenth Century." *Journal of the Economic and Social History of the Orient* 51, no. 4: 543–77.

Markovits, Claude, Jacques Pouchepadass, and Sanjay Subrahmanyam. 2006. *Society and Circulation: Mobile People and Itinerant Cultures in South Asia, 1750–1950*. New York: Anthem.

Marston, Thomas E. 1961. *Britain's Imperial Role in the Red Sea Area, 1800–1878*. Hamden, CT: Shoe String Press.

Marx, Karl. 1867. *Capital: Volume 1: A Critique of Political Economy*. London: Penguin Classics.

———. (1893) 1993a. *Capital Volume 2: A Critique of Political Economy* London: Penguin Classics.

———. (1939) 1993b. *Grundrisse: Foundations of the Critique of Political Economy*. Translated by Martin Nicolaus. New York: Penguin Books, in association with New Left Review.

Mathew, Johan. 2016. *Margins of the Market: Trafficking and Capitalism across the Arabian Sea*. Berkeley, CA: University of California Press.

Maurer, Bill. 1997. *Recharting the Caribbean: Land, Law, and Citizenship in the British Virgin Islands*. Ann Arbor: University of Michigan Press.

———. 2002. "Anthropological and Accounting Knowledge in Islamic Banking and Finance: Rethinking Critical Accounts." *Journal of the Royal Anthropological Institute* 8, no. 4: 645–67.

———. 2005. *Mutual Life, Limited: Islamic Banking, Alternative Currencies, Lateral Reason*. Princeton, NJ: Princeton University Press.

———. 2006. "The Anthropology of Money." *Annual Review of Anthropology* 35, no. 1: 15–36.

———. 2007a. "Due Diligence and 'Reasonable Man,' Offshore." *Cultural Anthropology* 20, no. 4: 474–505.

———. 2007b. "Incalculable Payments: Money, Scale and the South African Offshore Grey Money Amnesty." *African Studies Review* 50, no. 2: 125–38.

———. 2012. Payment: Forms and Functions of Value Transfer in Contemporary Society. *Cambridge Anthropology* 30, no. 2: 15–35.

Mauri, Arnaldo. 1971. "Banking Development in Somalia." In *Banking Systems in Africa*, edited by G. Dell'Amore. Milan: Cariplo, Finafrica. https://ssrn.com/abstract=958442.

Mauss, Marcel. (1954) 2002. *The Gift: The Form and Reason of Exchange in Archaic Societies*. Translated by W. D. Halls. London: Routledge.

Mawani, Renisa. 2018. *Across Oceans of Law: The Komagata Maru and Jurisdiction in the Time of Empire*. Durham, NC: Duke University Press.

Mbembe, Achille. 1992. "Banality of Power and the Aesthetics of Vulgarity in the Postcolony." Translated by Janet Roitman. *Public Culture* 4, no. 2: 1–30.

———. 2008. *On the Postcolony*. Johannesburg: Wits University Press.

Mburu, Nene. 2005. *Bandits on the Border: The Last Frontier in the Search for Somali Unity*. Trenton, NJ: Red Sea Press.

McCay, Bonnie J., and James M. Acheson, eds. 1987. *The Question of the Commons: The Culture and Ecology of Communal Resources*. Tucson: University of Arizona Press.

McDow, Thomas F. 2018. *Buying Time: Debt and Mobility in the Western Indian Ocean*. Athens: Ohio University Press.

McEvoy, Arthur F. 1990. *The Fisherman's Problem: Ecology and Law in the California Fisheries, 1850–1980*. Cambridge: Cambridge University Press.

Melville, Herman. 2001. *Moby Dick*. New York: Penguin Books.

Menkhaus, Kenneth. 2007. "Governance without Government in Somalia: Spoilers, State Building, and the Politics of Coping." *International Security* 31, no. 3: 74–106.

Merry, Sally Engle. 2000. *Colonizing Hawai'i: The Cultural Power of Law*. Princeton, NJ: Princeton University Press.

———. 2006. *Human Rights and Gender Violence: Translating International Law into Local Justice*. Chicago, IL: University of Chicago Press.

Mezzadra, Sandro, and Brett Neilson. 2013. *Border as Method, or, the Multiplication of Labor*. Durham, NC: Duke University Press.

Miller, Michael D. 1994. *Marine War Risks*, 3rd ed. London: Lloyd's of London Press; Richmond: Informa Law from Routledge.

Mintz, Sidney. 1957. "The Role of the Middleman in the Internal Distribution System of a Caribbean Peasant Economy." *Human Organization* 15, no. 2: 18–23.

Miran, Jonathan. 2009. *Red Sea Citizens: Cosmopolitan Society and Cultural Change in Massawa*. Bloomington: Indiana University Press.

Mitchell, Timothy. 1991. "Limits of the State: Beyond Statist Approaches and Their Critics." *American Political Science Review* 85, no. 1: 77–96.

———. 2011. *Carbon Democracy: Political Power in the Age of Oil*. London: Verso.

Miyazaki, Hiro. 2007. "Between Arbitrage and Speculation: An Economy of Belief and Doubt." *Economy and Society* 36, no. 3: 396–415.

———. 2013. *Arbitraging Japan: Dreams of Capitalism at the End of Finance*. Berkeley: University of California Press.

Moeran, Brian. 2010. "The Book Fair as a Tournament of Values." *Journal of the Royal Anthropological Institute* 16, no. 1: 138–54.

Moore, Amelia. 2012. "The Aquatic Invaders: Marine Management Figuring Fishermen, Fisheries, and Lionfish in the Bahamas." *Cultural Anthropology* 27, no. 4: 667–88.

Mubarak, Jamil A. 1997. "The 'Hidden Hand': Behind the Resilience of the Stateless Economy of Somalia." *World Development* 25, no. 12: 2027–41.

Mullen, Carl T. 1991. *The Lucona Affair*. Paper presented at the Oceans 91 Conference Proceedings, Honolulu, October 1–3, 1991.

Munn, Nancy. 1992. *The Fame of Gawa: A Symbolic Study of Value Transformation in a Massim Society*. Durham, NC: Duke University Press.

Murphy, Anne. 2009. *The Origins of the English Financial Markets: Investment and Speculation before the South Sea Bubble*. Cambridge: Cambridge University Press.

Murphy, Martin N. 2009. *Small Boats, Weak States, Dirty Money: Piracy and Maritime Terrorism in the Modern World*. Oxford: Oxford University Press.

———. 2011. *Somalia, the New Barbary? Piracy and Islam in the Horn of Africa*. New York: Columbia University Press.

Officer of the Watch. 2012. "Nato Dhow Project." December 6, 2012. https://officerofthewatch.com/tag/pirate-skiff/.

Onley, James A. 2004. "The Politics of Protection in the Gulf: The Arab Rulers and the British Resident in the Nineteenth Century." *New Arabian Studies* 6: 30–92.

———. 2007. *The Arabian Frontier of the British Raj: Merchants, Rulers, and the British in the Nineteenth-Century Gulf*. Oxford: Oxford University Press.

Osanloo, Arzoo. 2012. "When Blood Has Spilled: Gender, Honor, and Compensation in Iranian Criminal Sentencing." *POLAR: Political and Legal Anthropology Review* 35, no. 2: 308–26.

Ostrom, Elinor. 2010. "Beyond Markets and States: Polycentric Governance of Complex Economic Systems." *American Economic Review* 100, no. 3: 641–72.

Pálsson, Gísli. 2004. "Enskilment at Sea." *MAN* 29, no. 4: 901–27.

Panikkar, Kavalam Madhava. 1959. *Asia and Western Dominance: A Survey of the Vasco da Gama Epoch of Asian History, 1498–1945.* London: G. Allen & Unwin.

Parkin, David, and Stephen C. Headley, eds. 2000. *Islamic Prayer across the Indian Ocean: Inside and Outside the Mosque.* Richmond, Surrey: Curzon Press.

Parry, Jonathan. 1986. "The Gift, the Indian Gift and the 'Indian Gift.'" *MAN* 21, no. 3: 453–73.

Pearson, Michael. 2003. *The Indian Ocean.* London: Routledge.

Percy, Sarah. 2007. *Mercenaries: The History of a Norm in International Relations.* Oxford: Oxford University Press.

———. 2009. *The Pirates of Somalia: Coastguards of Anarchy.* Cambridge: Cambridge University Press.

Peters, Rudolph. 2005. *Crime and Punishment in Islamic Law: Theory and Practice from the Sixteenth to the Twenty-First Century.* Cambridge: Cambridge University Press.

Pietsch, Tamson. 2016. "Bodies at Sea: Traveling to Australia in the Age of Sea." *Journal of Global History* 1, no. 2: 209–28.

Piot, Charles. 2010. *Nostalgia for the Future: West Africa after the Cold War.* Chicago: University of Chicago Press.

Pirie, Fernanda, and Judith Scheele. 2014. *Legalism: Community and Justice.* Oxford: Oxford University Press.

Pitt-Rivers, Julian. 1977. *The Fate of Shechem or, the Politics of Sex: Essays in the Anthropology of the Mediterranean.* Cambridge: Cambridge University Press.

Polanyi, Karl, Conrad M. Arensberg, and Harry W. Pearson. 1957. *Trade and Market in the Early Empires: Economies in History and Theory.* Glencoe, IL: Free Press.

Poovey, Mary. 1998. *A History of the Modern Fact: Problems of Knowledge in the Sciences of Wealth and Society.* Chicago: University of Chicago Press.

Portenger, Henderick. 1819. *Narrative of the Sufferings and Adventures of Henderick Portenger: A Private Soldier of the Late Swiss Regiment De Mueron, Who Was Wrecked on the Shores of Abyssinia in the Red Sea.* British Library Archive.

Povinelli, Elizabeth. 2011. *Economies of Abandonment: Social Belonging and Endurance in Late Liberalism.* Durham, NC: Duke University Press.

Prange, Sebastian R. 2011. "A Trade of No Dishonor: Piracy, Commerce, and Community in the Western Indian Ocean, Twelfth to Sixteenth Century." *American Historical Review* 116, no. 5: 1269–93.

———. 2018. *Monsoon Islam: Trade and Faith on the Medieval Malabar* Coast. Cambridge Oceanic Histories. Cambridge: Cambridge University Press.

Prestholdt, Jeremy. 2013. "Fighting Phantoms: The United States and Counterterrorism in Eastern Africa." In *From Moral Manic to Permanent War: Lessons and Legacies of the War on Terror,* edited by Gershon Shafir, Everard Meade, and William J. Aceves, 139–68. London: Routledge.

Rabb, Intisar A. 2015. *Doubt in Islamic Law: A History of Legal Maxims, Interpretation, and Islamic Criminal Law.* Cambridge: Cambridge University Press.

Raeymaekers, Timothy. 2010. "Protection for Sale? War and the Transformation of Regulation on the Congo-Ugandan Border." *Development and Change* 41, no. 4: 563–87.

Raffles, Hugh. 2010. *Insectopedia*. New York: Random House.

Ranganathan, Surabhi. 2015. *Strategically Created Treaty Conflicts and the Politics of International* Law. Cambridge: Cambridge University Press.

Redfield, Peter. 2012. "The Unbearable Lightness of Ex-pats: Double Binds of Humanitarian Mobility." *Cultural Anthropology* 27, no. 2: 358–82.

Rediker, Marcus. 2004. *Villains of All Nations: Atlantic Pirates in the Golden Age*. Boston: Beacon Press.

Rediker, Marcus, and Peter Linebaugh. 2013. *The Many-Headed Hydra: Sailors, Slaves, Commoners, and the Hidden History of the Revolutionary Atlantic*. Boston: Beacon Press.

Reese, Scott Steven. 2008. *Renewers of the Age: Holy Men and Social Discourse in Colonial Benaadir*. Leiden: Brill.

Riles, Annelise. 2000. *The Network Inside Out*. Ann Arbor: University of Michigan Press.

———. 2006. "Anthropology, Human Rights, and Legal Knowledge: Culture in the Iron Cage." *American Anthropologist* 108, no. 1: 52–65.

———. 2011. *Collateral Knowledge: Legal Reasoning in the Global Financial Markets*. Chicago: University of Chicago Press.

Risso, Patricia. 2001. "Cross-Cultural Perceptions of Piracy: Maritime Violence in the Western Indian Ocean and Persian Gulf Region during a Long Eighteenth Century." *Journal of World History* 12, no. 2: 293–319.

Ritchie, Robert. 1989. *Captain Kidd and the War against the Pirates*. Cambridge, MA: Harvard University Press.

Roach, J. Ashley. 2010 "Countering Piracy off Somalia: International Law and International Institutions." *American Journal of International Law* 104, no. 3: 397–416.

Robinson, Cedric. 1983. *Black Marxism: The Making of the Black Radical Tradition*. London: Zed Books.

Roitman, Janet L. 2005. *Fiscal Disobedience: An Anthropology of Economic Regulation in Central Africa*. Princeton, NJ: Princeton University Press.

———. 2006. "Ethics of Illegality in the Chad Basin." In *Law and Disorder in the Postcolony*, edited by Jean Comaroff and John L. Comaroff, 247–72. Chicago: University of Chicago Press.

———. 2014. *Anti-Crisis*. Durham, NC: Duke University Press.

Roll, Eric. 1954. *The History of Economic Thought*, 5th ed. London: Faber & Faber.

Rose, Carol M. 1985. "Possession as the Origin of Property." *University of Chicago Law Review* 52, no. 1: 73–88.

———. 1994. *Property and Persuasion: Essays on the History, Theory, and Rhetoric of Ownership*. Boulder, CO: Westview Press.

Rothman, E. Natalie. 2012. *Brokering Empire: Trans-Imperial Subjects between Venice and Istanbul*. Ithaca, NY: Cornell University Press.

Rowlandson, Mary. 1856 (1997). *A Narrative of the Captivity, Sufferings, and Removes, of Mrs. Mary Rowlandson, Who Was Taken Prisoner by the Indians; with Several Others . . . Written by Her Own Hand*. Boston: reprinted and sold by Thomas and John Fleet, at the Bible and Heart, Cornhill, The Mass. Sabbath School Society.

Rubin, Alfred P. 2006. *The Law of Piracy*. Honolulu: University Press of the Pacific.

Sahlins, Marshall D. 1974. *Stone Age Economics*. Piscataway, NJ: Transaction Publishers.

Samatar, Abdi Ismail. 1989. *The State and Rural Transformation in Northern Somalia, 1884–1986*. Madison: University of Wisconsin Press.

Samatar, Abdi Ismail, Mark Lindberg, and Basil Mahayni. 2010. "The Dialectics of Piracy in Somalia: The Rich versus the Poor." *Third World Quarterly* 31, no. 8: 1377–94.

Samatar, Ahmed I. 2003. Review of I. M. Lewis, *A Modern History of the Somali: Nation and State in the Horn of Africa*. H-Africa, H-Net Reviews, December, 2003. www.h-net.org/reviews/showrev.php?id=8552.

Sanchez, Andrew, James G. Carrier, Christopher Gregory, James Laidlaw, Marilyn Strathern, Yunxiang Yan, and Jonathan Parry. 2017. "'The Indian Gift': A Critical Debate." *History and Anthropology* 28, no. 5: 553–83.

Sandars, Thomas Collett, ed./trans. 1917. *The Institutes of Justinian*. Clark, NJ: The Lawbook Exchange.

Sarkar, Bhaskar. 2016. "Media Piracy and the Terrorist Boogeyman: Speculative Potentiations. *Positions* 24, no. 2: 343–68.

Scharf, Michael, Michael A. Newton, and Milena Sterio. 2015. *Prosecuting Maritime Piracy: Domestic Solutions to International Crimes*. New York: Cambridge University Press.

Scheele, Judith. 2012. *Smugglers and Saints of the Sahara: Regional Connectivity in the Twentieth Century*. New York: Cambridge University Press.

———. 2015. "The Values of 'Anarchy': Moral Autonomy among Tubu-Speakers in Northern Chad." *Journal of the Royal Anthropological Institute* 21, no. 1: 32–48.

Schmitt, Carl. 2006. *The Concept of the Political*. Chicago: University of Chicago Press.

———. 2008. *Land Und Meer: Eine Weltgeschichtliche Betrachtung*. Stuttgart, Germany: Klett Cotta.

Schwartz, Moshe. 2010. *Department of Defense Contractors in Iraq and Afghanistan: Background and Analysis*. Washington, DC: Congressional Research Service.

Scott, James C. 1998. *Seeing like a State: How Certain Schemes to Improve the Human Condition Have Failed*. New Haven, CT: Yale University Press.

Sekula, Allan, and Centrum voor Hedendaagse Kunst. 1995. *Fish Story*. Dusseldorf: Witte de With Center for Contemporary Art in collaboration with Richter Verlag.

Serres, Michel. 1980. *The Parasite*. Baltimore: Johns Hopkins University Press.

Shah, Alpa. 2006. "Markets of Protection: The 'Terrorist' Maoist Movement and the State in Jharkhand, India." *Critique of Anthropology* 26, no. 3: 297–314.

Sharpe, Christina E. 2016. *In the Wake: On Blackness and Being.* Durham, NC: Duke University Press.

Sheriff, Abdul. 2010. *Dhow Cultures of the Indian Ocean: Cosmopolitanism, Commerce, and Islam.* London: Hurst & Co.

Shields, Rob. 1991. *Places on the Margin: Alternative Geographies of Modernity.* London: Routledge.

Shipton, Parker. 2010. *Credit between Cultures: Farmers, Financiers, and Misunderstanding in Africa.* New Haven, CT: Yale University Press.

Shryock, Andrew. 2004. "The New Jordanian Hospitality: House, Host, and Guest in the Culture of Public Display." *Comparative Studies in Society and History* 46, no. 1: 35–62.

————. 2012. "Breaking Hospitality Apart: Bad Hosts, Bad Guests, and the Problem of Sovereignty." *Journal of the Royal Anthropological Institute* 18: S20–33.

Simons, Anna. 1995. *Networks of Dissolution: Somalia Undone.* Boulder, CO: Westview Press.

Simpson, Edward. 2006. "Apprenticeship in Western India." *Journal of the Royal Anthropological Institute* 12, no. 1: 151–71.

Singer, Peter W. 2003. *Corporate Warriors: The Rise of the Privatized Military Industry.* Ithaca, NY: Cornell University Press.

Singh, Curran, and Arjun Singh Bedi. 2012. "War on Piracy: The Conflation of Somali Piracy with Terrorism in Discourse, Tactic and Law." *Security Dialogue* 47, no. 5: 440–58.

Standing, Guy. 2011. *The Precariat: The New Dangerous Class.* London: Bloomsbury.

Starkey, David J., E. S. van Eyck van Heslinga, and Jaap de Moor. 1997. *Pirates and Privateers: New Perspectives on the War on Trade in the Eighteenth and Nineteenth Centuries.* Liverpool: Liverpool University Press.

Steensgaard, Niels. 1974. *The Asian Trade Revolution of the Seventeenth Century: The East India Companies and the Decline of the Caravan Trade.* Chicago: University of Chicago Press.

Steinberg, Philip E. 2013. "Of Other Seas: Metaphors and Materialities in Maritime Regions." *Atlantic Studies* 10, no. 2: 156–69.

Stern, Philip J. 2006. "British Asia and British Atlantic: Comparisons and Connections." *William and Mary Quarterly* 63, no. 4: 693–712.

————. 2008. "'A Politie of Civill & Military Power': Political Thought and the Late Seventeenth-Century Foundations of the East India Company-State." *Journal of British Studies* 47, no. 2: 253–83.

————. 2011. *The Company-State: Corporate Sovereignty and the Early Modern Foundations of the British Empire in India.* Oxford: Oxford University Press.

Stevenson, Jonathan. 2010. "Jihad and Piracy in Somalia." *Survival* 52, no. 1: 27–38.

Strathern, Marilyn. 2005. *Kinship, Law and the Unexpected: Relatives Are Always a Surprise.* New York: Cambridge University Press.

Strong, Pauline Turner. 1999. *Captive Selves, Captivating Others: The Politics and Poetics of Colonial American Captivity Narratives.* Boulder, CO: Westview Press.

Struett, Michael J, Jon D. Carlson, and Mark T. Nance. 2013. *Maritime Piracy and the Construction of Global Governance.* London: Routledge.

Subramanian, Ajantha. 2009. *Shorelines: Space and Rights in South India.* Stanford, CA: Stanford University Press.

Subramanian, Lakshmi. 2016. *The Sovereign and the Pirate.* Delhi, India: Oxford University Press.

Sullivan, George Lydiard. 1873. *Dhow Chasing in Zanzibar Waters and on the Eastern Coast of Africa: Narrative of Five Years' Experiences in the Suppression of the Slave Trade.* London: S. Low, Marston, Low & Searle.

Taussig-Rubbo, Mateo. 2011. Pirate Trials, the International Criminal Court, and Mob Justice: Reflections on Postcolonial Sovereignty in Kenya. *Humanity: An International Journal of Human Rights, Humanitarianism, and Development* 1: 51–74.

Thomas, Kedron. 2016. *Regulating Style: Intellectual Property Law and the Business of Fashion in Guatemala.* Oakland: University of California Press.

Thomas, Kedron, and Rebecca Galemba. 2013. "Illegal Anthropology: An Introduction." *PoLAR* 36, no. 2: 211–14.

Tilly, Charles. 1985. "War Making and State Making as Organized Crime." In *Violence: A Reader,* edited by Catherine Besteman, 35–60. New York: NYU Press.

———. 1990 *Coercion, Capital, and European States, A.D. 990–1990.* Cambridge, MA: Basil Blackwell.

Trennery, Charles Farley. 1926. *The Origin and Early History of Insurance, Including the Contract of Bottomry.* London: P. S. King & Son, Ltd.

Trivellato, Francesca. 2012. *Familiarity of Strangers: The Sephardic Diaspora, Livorno, and Cross-Cultural Trade in the Early Modern Period.* New Haven, CT: Yale University Press.

Tsing, Anna Lowenhaupt. 2009. "Supply Chains and the Human Condition." *Rethinking Marxism* 21, no. 2: 148–76.

———. 2013. "Sorting Out Commodities: How Capitalist Value Is Made through Gifts." *HAU: Journal of Ethnographic Theory* 3, no. 1, 21–43.

———. 2015. *The Mushroom at the End of the World: On the Possibility of Life in Capitalist Ruins.* Princeton, NJ: Princeton University Press.

Turner, Victor. 1967. *The Forest of Symbols: Aspects of the Ndembu Ritual.* Ithaca, NY: Cornell University Press.

UK Department for Transport. 2011. "Change in UK Policy on Employing Armed Guards to Protect against Somali Piracy." December 11, 2011. http://webarchive .nationalarchives.gov.uk/20120607094600/http://www.dft.gov.uk/news/press-releases/dft-press-20111206a.

UN (United Nations). 1982. *United Nations Convention on the Law of the Sea.* http:// www.un.org/depts/los/convention_agreements/texts/unclos/unclos_e.pdf.

UNCTAD (United Nations Conference on Trade and Development). 2018. *Review of Maritime Transport.* https://unctad.org/en/PublicationsLibrary/rmt2018_ en.pdf.

UNODC-WB (United Nations Office on Drugs and Crime/World Bank). 2013. *Pirate Trails: Tracking the Illicit Financial Flows from Pirate Activities of the*

Horn of Africa. Washington, DC: A World Bank Study. http://documents .worldbank.org/curated/en/408451468010486316/Pirate-trails-tracking-the-illicit-financial-flows-from-pirate-activities-off-the-Horn-of-Africa#.

UNSC-SEMG (United Nations Security Council/Somalia and Eritrea Monitoring Group). 2012. *Report of the Monitoring Group on Somalia and Eritrea Pursuant to Security Council Resolution 2002* (S/2012/544). https://www.undocs .org/S/2012/544.

USEIA (United States Energy Information Administration). 2017. *World Oil Transit Chokepoints.* https://www.eia.gov/beta/international/analysis_includes/special_ topics/World_Oil_Transit_Chokepoints/wotc.pdf.

Valentine, David. 2016. "Atmosphere: Context, Detachment, and the View from above Earth." *American Ethnologist* 43, no. 3: 511–24.

Van Gennep, Arnold. 1960. *The Rites of Passage.* Translated by Monica B. Vizedom and Gabrielle L. Caffee. London: Routledge & Kegan Paul.

van Schendel, Willem, and Itty Abraham. 2005. *Illicit Flows and Criminal Things: States, Borders, and the Other Side of Globalization.* Bloomington: Indiana University Press.

Verdery, Katherine. 2003. *The Vanishing Hectare: Property and Value in Postsocialist Transylvania.* Ithaca, NY: Cornell University Press.

Vergès, Françoise. 2003. "Writing on Water: Peripheries, Flows, Capital, and Struggles in the Indian Ocean." *Positions* 11, no. 1: 241–57.

Vink, Markus. 2007. "Indian Ocean Studies and the 'New Thalassology.'" *Journal of Global History* 2, no. 1: 41–62.

Virno, Paolo. 1996. "The Ambivalence of Disenchantment." In *Radical Thought in Italy: A Potential Politics,* edited by Paolo Virno and Michael Hardt, 13–33. Minneapolis: University of Minnesota Press.

Volkov, Vadim. 2002. *Violent Entrepreneurs: The Use of Force in the Making of Russian Capitalism.* Ithaca, NY: Cornell University Press.

Warsame, Amina. 2004. *Queens without Crowns: Somaliland Women's Changing Roles and Peace Building.* Printed by the Somaliland Women's Research and Action Group.

Weber, Max. 1958. "The Three Types of Legitimate Rule." Translated by Hans Gerth. *Berkeley Publications in Society and Institutions* 4, no. 1: 1–11.

———. (1968) 1978. *Economy and Society: An Outline of Interpretative Sociology,* vol. 1. Berkeley: University of California Press.

Wedeen, Lisa. 2008. *Peripheral Visions: Publics, Power, and Performance in Yemen.* Chicago: University of Chicago Press.

Weeks, Kathi. 2011. *The Problem with Work: Feminism, Marxism, Antiwork Politics, and Postwork Imaginaries.* Durham, NC: Duke University Press.

Weitzberg, Keren. 2017. *We Do Not Have Borders: Greater Somalia and the Predicaments of Belonging in Kenya.* Athens: Ohio University Press.

Weldemichael, Awet T. 2012. "Maritime Corporate Terrorism and Its Consequences in the Western Indian Ocean: Illegal Fishing, Waste Dumping and Piracy in Twenty-First-Century Somalia." *Journal of the Indian Ocean Region* 8, no. 2: 110–26.

Weskett, John. 1781. *A Complete Digest of the Theory, Laws, and Practice of Insurance. Compiled from the Best Authorities in Different Languages, Which Are Quoted and Referred to Throughout the Work.* London: Richardson & Urquhart.

Wick, Alexis. 2016. *The Red Sea: In Search of Lost Space.* Berkeley: University of California Press.

Williams, Eric. 1944. *Capitalism and Slavery.* Chapel Hill: University of North Carolina Press.

World Bank. 2013. *The Pirates of Somalia: Ending the Threat, Rebuilding a Nation.* http://documents.worldbank.org/curated/en/182671468307148284/The-pirates-of-Somalia-ending-the-threat-rebuilding-a-nation.

Wright, Charles, and C. Ernest Fayle. 1928. *A History of Lloyd's: From the Founding of Lloyd's Coffee House to the Present Day.* London: Macmillan and Company.

Zelizer, Viviana A. Rotman. (1979) 2017. *Morals and Markets: The Development of Life Insurance in the United States.* New York: Columbia University Press.

INDEX

Note: Page numbers in *italics* denote illustrations.

Burton, Richard, 188n24
Bush, George W., 141

camels: dhows likened to, 37–38, 39; and obligation to share, 37–38; and pastoral "camel complex," 38–39; popularity of (2011), 171
Canada: Africa Oil, 179–80; Somcan (Somali-Canadian company), 57, 58, 190n19
Candea, Matei, 162–63
capital: diya groups as source of, 73–75; for Red Sea vs. Indian Ocean–based piracy, 66–67
capitalism: and ambergris, 40; capitalist divination, 125; circulation time and, 85, 86–87, 193n14; enclave capitalism, 102, 194n10; finance capitalism as dependent on insurance as form of capital accumulation, 194n13; incorporation of northern Somalia into, 40; racial capitalism, 139; rise in violence alongside, 40
Captain Phillips (film), 157–58, 159, 169
captivity: as central to dynamics of hospitality, 150–51; dhow as mothership as space of, 150–51, 161–63, 166–67; prisons and slavery as, 150; and tensions of empire, 171–73
capture: as attempt to break the credit/debt relationship, 43–44; bride capture, 150; as mode of sociality, 150; moral economy of, 43–44; at sea, as creating property, 40–44, 46. *See also* capture and redistribution economies; capture by pirates
capture and redistribution economies: ambergris communities as, 40–41; artisanal fishing as, 41–42; diasporic seafaring communities and, 11, 186n12; pastoral logic of, 39, 43, 46, 150; reciprocity and return and, 43–44; scalar transformations of, 59
capture by pirates: of container ships compared to dhows, 159–60; dhow as mothership as technology of, 151; as disaster without history or context, 159; divination/logistical support for finding ships to hijack, 123–25, 127, 195–96nn3–6;

freeboard (height above the water) as factor in, 124–25; narratives of, ix–x, 1–3, 90–91, 97–98, 101–2, 105, 120, 156–59; narratives of, by pirates, 133–34; as no guarantee of profit, 122; recovery of crewmembers from, 158; *Surviving Piracy off the Coast of Somalia* pamphlet, 79, 82; as threshold event, 159; violence and, 157–58, 159, 160. *See also* dhows as motherships; ransom negotiations
carbon democracy, 154–55
Carrier, Neil, 78
cartaz system, 20, 21
cattle complex, 38
Ceccarelli, Giovanni, 108
cell phones: pirate search through contact lists of, 135, 136; reception, 121, 122, 132
Central America, kidnappings in, 127
Central Somalia Piracy Network, 180
chance: and capture as creating property, 41; seeking profit from, insurance and sanctions against, 107, 108, 109, 194n12
Charles II, 93
chemical tankers, 2, 3, 158–59
China: and counter-piracy, 100; One Belt One Road Initiative, 8
Cicero, 12, 186–87n13
circulation milieu, 103–4
circulation time, and capitalism, 85, 86–87, 193n14
clanism: criminalization of, 51; MOD (Marrehaan, Ogadeen, and Dulbahante clans), 51; patronage system under Barre, 51; and population upheavals following collapse of Somali state, 55; and private economy under Scientific Socialism, 51; Puntland formation and, 55; Somali society believed to be organized according to, 71, 192n7. *See also* diya groups; kinship
class: and capture of dhow motherships, 161, 163; geographies of toxicity and, 33
coastguards: armed confrontations with local protection groups, 56; private security companies as, 54, 55–56, 57–58, 143, 190n19

Cold War: end of, and return of maritime piracy, 15; erasure of irregular wars of, in declaration of "new and different" War on Terror, 141–42; oscillation of newly independent countries' alignment, 48; oscillation of Somalia's alignment between Soviet Union and United States, 30, 31, 48, 50, 52

colonialism: clan as transformed during, 192n7; and dhows, attempts to regulate, 153, 154; and diya groups, attempts to regulate, 72, 73; erasure of violence of, in declaration of "new and different" War on Terror, 141–42; natural law vision of the commons as allowing expropriation, 35–36; patronage for English pirates in the U.S., 94–95; and pirates as anticolonial heroes, 187n16; and rise in violence alongside capitalism, 40; and rituals of Mombasa High Court, 17–18. *See also* decolonization

Combined Task Force 150, 97–98

common law: and first possession/rule-of-capture, 42–43; and rituals of Mombasa High Court, 17–18

commons: communitarian management of, 45–46, 190n12; and dispossession, 33, 35–36; as emerging through capture and redistribution, 33–34; failures of governance and geographies of toxicity in, 33; overexploitation of (tragedy of the commons), 44–45, 46, 189n10, 190nn11–12; at sea, vs. property on land as elemental bias of Western natural law, 35–36. *See also* pastoral commons, the sea as

Comoros Islands, 93

Computer (Abdulkhadar), 124, 125, 195–96n3

container ships, 5; and Berbera trade, 30; *Captain Phillips* film narrative of hijacking of, 157–58, 159, 169; development of containerization, 155, 198n5; dhows as connecting locales excluded by itineraries of, 151, 155–56, 198n7; Suez-max size, 166; TEU (twenty-foot equivalent unit), 197n10

cornicello (devil's horn) amulet, 126–27

costs of piracy: overview, 122; fuel costs for increased speed through the Gulf of Aden, 122; graph illustrating costs to industry and government, *123*; insurance, 118; internalization of, 21; naval policing, 95–96, 122; private guards, 182; and private guards, racial hierarchy of, 182; ransom as small portion of overall costs, 122; to ship and cargo owners, 3. *See also* supplies for piracy

costs of privatization of the U.S. military, 142

counter-piracy, *97*; and the anthropological critique, anticipation of, 194n7; armed convoys, prior to European imperialism, 20; authorization of naval presence, 16–17, 99; authorization of naval presence curtailed, 144; "catch and release" of pirates back to Somalia, 96; and construction of piracy into a global problem, 94–95, 96–97; definition of, 91; and distinguishing between fishing vessels and pirate boats, 19, 102, 104, 105; as driving pirates out of the Red Sea and into the Indian Ocean, 66–67, 99–100, 151, 152; exclusion of Somali actors from policy making, 96–97, 195n16; fiction of Somali maritime sovereignty gradually disbanded, 98; force and contract as intimately tied together in, 92, 120; imprisonment of pirates, 180; Indian Navy and, 150; insurance as protecting, 109, 110, 118, 119; Internationally Recommended Transit Corridor (IRTC) in the Gulf of Aden, 99–100, 103–5; legal architecture for, 17–19, 98–99; as locally solvable funding issue, 96; management from afar, 101–2, 104, 194n7; management of piracy incidents within an optimal range as goal of, 103–4, 194n11; Mombasa as port of call for navies, 124; narrative of patrol vessel experience, 102–5; new global war on piracy, 98, 193–94n5, 197n11; private security guards approved by governments (2011), 143–44; private security guards opposed by governments and insurance companies, 143; prosecutions at Mombasa High Court (Kenya), 17–19, 24; as protecting global trade, 19; as scaling up of processual dispute resolution, 120, 195n16; scope of operation, 100–101; studies of, as perpetuating the distinction between force and contract, 91–92; technology and, 104; United Nations Resolution 1816, 15–17, 99; videos of bursts of action in, 104–5; and violence, 105; visual surveillance, 104, 183–84. *See also* costs of piracy; private security companies

crewmembers: embedded maritime nations and, 138; of European and American sailing ships, 153; hired through recruiting agencies vs. shipping companies, 138–39; racial hierarchy of labor among, 138–39, 154; racial hierarchy of labor and value of ransom, 139, 147; recovery from capture at MtS in Mombasa, 158. *See also* capture by pirates; families of hostages; ransom negotiation

Cruttenden, C. J., 30

Cuba, health clinics in Somalia, 30

Curtin, Philip, 65

Dawdy, Shannon, 187n17

decolonization: and decline of dhow trade, 154–55; and oscillation of newly independent countries' alignment between the Soviet Union and the United States, 30, 31, 48, 50, 52

de Hoop Scheffer, Jaap, 119

detachment, 129–32, 170, 196–97n8

developmentalism, 49

Dhow Project (NATO/EU), 152, 167, 170

dhows: and Berbera trade, 30; and Bosaso trade, 37, 148; colonial empires and attempts to regulate trade of, 153, 154; container ship itineraries, servicing locales excluded from, 151, 155–56, 198n7; and cosmopolitan ethos of Indian Ocean commerce, 153; decolonization and the rise of oil and decline of, 154–55; definition of, 152–53, 185n1; and gendered economy, 156–57; India and Pakistan as homeports of, 148, 156;

Indian government attempts to regulate, 160; likened to a camel, 37–38; as motorized vessel (MSV), 37, 155; nineteenth-century recasting of, as piratical, 153, 198n3; as primary target of Somali piracy prior to the *Nori*, 15; and short-wave radios, 157; sized for Somalia's shipping needs, 166; "Somali route," importance of, 166; and transshipment, 156, 198n7; upsurge of piracy and increase of trade via, 37. *See also* dhows as motherships

dhows as motherships, *168*; breakdown and, 168–70; as camouflage and cover, 152; captivity and, 150–51, 161–63, 166–67; capture of, 156–57, 159, 160–62; as capture technology, 151; collusion as issue and, 167, 170; and counter-piracy as driving pirates from the Red Sea to the Indian Ocean, 151, 152; definition of mothership, 151–52; departures and, 167, 170; dependence of pirates on captain and crew of, 162–63; detachment and, 170; and Dhow Project of NATO/EU, 152, 167, 170; and familiarity of pirates, 166; food and, 165, 168; gift offerings to boarding pirates, 159, 160; hospitality and, 163–67; initial hijacking (2010), 152; and new diaspora, 151; pirates as taking without giving, 160, 163; and protection, 152, 165–66, 168, 170; as stability in the monsoonal open waters, 152, 165; violence in, 160, 161, 163, 168–70; weapons laid down, 161, 163, 168, 169

diaspora, Somali: diya groups and connectivity of, 74; higher contributions (*qaaran*) to diya group expected from, 70–71; new construction built by, 30; in Pakistan, 149; piracy in the Indian Ocean as, 151; returning to become intermediaries in piracy, 121

diasporic seafaring communities and piracy/raiding as form of commercial transaction, 11, 186n12

Dickinson, Edwin, 14

Dietmar, Dirty, 106

digital piracy, 187–88n19

disaster, without history or context, 159

dispossession: the commons and, 33, 35–36; failed governance and, 33

divination: capitalist/technologies of imagination, 125; economic use of random events as, 108, 109; Gosha, 124, 196nn4,6; by intermediaries finding ships for pirates to hijack, 123–25, 127, 195–96nn3–6; payment and, 125, 196nn5–6. *See also* magic

diya groups: *aqila* (male relatives) as responsible for financial compensation, 68; boundaries of civil/criminal and crimes against the individual/state as blurred in, 68; and capital, credit, and collateral, 73–75, 93, 192n8; and connectivity among the diaspora, 74; definition of, 68; as distributing obligations to broader social universe, 68; flexibility in, 69, 71; as functioning like insurance, 69, 70, 71; government attempts to regulate, 72–73; inequalities and, 71; Islamic law and, 68; kinship as collateral in, 74, 87, 88, 192n8; as *mag* payment groups (Somali), 69; matrilineal, as alternate source of support, 69, 83; as patrilineal, 69; and piracy, credit for, 74–76; and public shaming, 72; *qaaran* (obligatory payment) to, and enforcement of, 70–71; and remittances from abroad, 74; as restitution, payment as mode of, 68; and trust of business owners for pirates, 61, 68, 75, 86, 87, 89; and violence, management of, 71–72

Djibouti, 102–3, 143, 194nn9–10

djinns, 165

driving in Somalia, and accidents, 69–70, 72

Dubai, and dhow trade, 156

Dubai Ports World, 102

Dutch East India Company (VOC): and Dutch empire building, 187n14; as "internalizing" the costs of protection, 21; taking of the *Santa Catarina,* 35–36

economic globalization, 63–64

Eel Haamed, Somalia, 52

Elizabeth I, 93

Elyachar, Julia, 63–64

empire. *See* colonialism; decolonization; European empire

enclave capitalism, 102, 194n10

England. *See* British empire; Great Britain

Enterprise. See MV Enterprise

entertainment: Bollywood DVDs, 81, 163, 165; *Lion King* soundtrack, 103

Ethiopia: Barre regime conflicts with, 54; khat cultivation in, 60, 78

European empire: and attempts to regulate dhow trade, 153, 154; captivity and tensions of, 171–73; instability of meaning of protection and justification of conquest, 21; monsoon pattern discovery as enabling, 65–66; privateering and creation of, 12, 94, 187n14. *See also* British empire; colonialism

European law: fugitive property, 189n7. *See also* insurance

Europeans, and racialized hierarchies: private security, 182; shipping labor, 139

European Union: Dhow Project, 152, 167, 170; and Kenya as prosecution site for piracy, 17, 18

European Union counter-piracy mission (EU-NAVFOR-ATALANTA), 100–105, 194nn7,9–11

European Union Naval Force, *Surviving Piracy off the Coast of Somalia,* 79

Evans-Pritchard, E. E., 38

Ewald, François, 114

Executive Outcomes, 141

expropriation, 33, 35–36

Eyl, Somalia, 52, 57

families of hostages: asked to pay part of ransom, 120, 170; entanglement with pirates by negotiators for pirates, 135; facilitators hired to work with, 136; isolated from pirates by negotiators for shipowners, 129–30

Fancy, 93

Fateh Muhammad, 92

Feldman, Gregory, 194n11

Ferguson, James, 102, 190n16, 194n10

Filonardi company, 50

financialization, 63–64

Findlater jet, 39

fishing and fishermen: artisanal fishing, 41–42, 54; becoming pirates, 32, 57–59; factory ships, 151; fish factory development projects, 31–32, 46–47; and GDP, 52; illegal fishing, Somali piracy as revolt against, 13, 33, 181, 182, 189n3; industrialized fishing, Barre regime and establishment of, 31, 52; local protection groups formed among, 53–54, 56; pastoralists resettled into, 52, 53, 57–58

fishing licensing: appropriation and redistribution and, 54; armed confrontations between competing coastguards, 56; environmental damage caused by, 54; as form of capture, 51; informal licensing systems, 53, 55–56, 147; jurisdiction as property created by, 53; local protection groups and, 53–54, 56; maximum sustainable yield (MSY) treaty and establishment of, 52–53, 190n17; pastoralists creating redistributive networks of, 53; piracy as extension of, 34, 54, 55, 56, 57–59, 143; private security company coastguards and official licensing regime, 54, 55–56, 57–58, 143, 190n19; as socialist vs. neoliberal enterprise, 190n16

fishing vessels, *38*; fiber skiffs, 30–32; mechanized, Scientific Socialism and, 52; as primary target of Somali piracy prior to the *Nori*, 15

flags of convenience and open registries, 113

Florence, and insurance industry, 108

Food and Agricultural Organization of the United Nations (FAO 2005), 52

Foucault, Michel, 103–4, 194n11

France: and *abaan* protection, 22; and counter-piracy, 102; Djibouti independence from, 102; English privateering targeting trade of, 93; and global war on terror, 1; privateering and creation of empire of, 12, 94

freeboard (height above the water) as factor in capture, 124–25

fugitive property, 42–44, 189n7

Gabrielsen, Vincent, 186n12

Ganj-i-Sawai, 92–93, 94–95

Gayer, Sir John, 93

Geertz, Clifford, "The Bazaar Economy," 196n7

gender, geographies of toxicity and, 33

gendered economy: and camel milk, 76; and the dhow trade, 156–57; and the khat trade, 77, 137; and piracy as spectacle, 82; and ransom negotiations, 136–37; women as prominent in trade, 76–77, 137; and women's cooperatives, 76

Genoa, insurance industry in, 108

geographies of toxicity, 33

Germany: and counter-piracy, 98; and global war on terror, 1

Gieryn, Thomas, 192n11

gift/commodity binary, 196n5; khat as defying distinction of, 87, 193n15

gift-exchange, and reciprocity, 196n5

gifts: offered to pirates boarding dhows, 159, 160; from the sea, ambergris as, 40, 175

Gilbert, Erik, 153

global trade: protection of, as role of the navies, 19; statistics on numbers of ships and seafarers utilized in, 5

Global War on Terror: Combined Task Force 150 (multinational counter-terrorism force), 97; declaration of, 141; and historical amnesia, 141; naval patrols, 1, 97; new global war on piracy as alongside, 98, 193–94n5; and privatization of the military, 141–42

Gluckman, Max, 195n16

Gordillo, Gastón, 189n2

Gordon, H. Scott, 45

Gosha, 124, 196nn4,6

Goswami, Manu, 49

governance failures, as explanation of renewed global dispossession, 33. *See also* Somali state failure

Grant, Bruce, 171

Great Britain: and *abaan* protection, 22; Admiralty Courts, 95; approval of private security guards onboard ships, 143–44; Assurance Act (1601), 109–10; Board of Trade, 95; Bubble Act (1720), 109; Chamber of Assurances (1576), 109; Court of Assurances, 109; ex-military men and private security companies, 55; and Kenya as prosecution site for

118, 119; as decentralized practice, 109; diya groups functioning like, 69, 70, 71; "economic interest" as sorting out legitimate and illegitimate forms of profiteering via, 109–10, 131; English law regulating, 109–10; finance capitalism as dependent on, as form of capital accumulation, 194n13; and flags of convenience, 113; frauds, 105–6, 107; future possibilities and, 109; and governance over shipping, 111–13; Greek bottomry practice, 107–8, 178–79; hull and machinery (H&M) policies, 115; Indian Ocean practices of, 107; as industry, development of, 110; intra-European trade not usually insured, 108; Joint War Committee (JWC), 115, 117, 118; kidnap-and-ransom (K&R) packages, 118–19, 127; life insurance, 109; mania for, 109; as originating with oceanic commerce, 107; piracy exclusion clause, 114; probability and, 118; "rich trades" as focus of, 108; risk as both peril and profit, 106–7; and risk pooling/risk management, 107, 110, 111, 113, 114, 117–18; and seeking profit from chance, sanctions against, 107, 108, 109, 194n12; separate policies for ship and cargo, 111–12; transformed into system of protection and profit, 108, 109, 110, 114–15; underinsured vessels, 120; and usury, sanctions against, 107, 108; and violence, 112; war-risk cover, 115–16, *116*, 117–19, 182, 195n15. *See also* insurance companies; kidnap-and-ransom (K&R) insurance packages

insurance companies: alerted to hijacking, 91; as not distinguishing between territorial and international waters, 99; as opposed to private security companies for protection, 143; as rendering marine war risks governable, 193n1. *See also* insurance company recommendations for protection; insurance underwriters; Lloyd's of London

insurance company recommendations for protection: carrying replica guns, 91; discounts for use of deterrents, 114,

125–26; hiring of private guards, 114, 182; list of best practices, 91; security companies licensed by insurance companies, 119, 182; shipping companies cutting corners on, 91, 182. *See also* vessel hardening

insurance underwriters: contracts, 113–15; on the costs of ransom negotiations, 3; development of, 108; manuals for, 108; methodology of research and, 24

intellectual property rights, 187–88n19

intermediaries: as central to a variety of projects and processes, 122, 195n1; divination/logistical support for pirates finding ships to capture, 123–25, 127, 195–96nn3–6; institutionalization of, 127; and openings for profit and monetary gain, 125, 127, 196nn5–6; private security companies seeking legitimization as, 144–46; transformation and replacement of, 122. *See also* private security companies (PSCs); ransom negotiators for pirates; ransom negotiators for shipowners

International Crisis Group (ICC), 55

International Labour Organization (ILO), 138

international law: codification of piracy and, 14; and instability of meanings of protection, 21; institutionalization of, 14

Internationally Recommended Transit Corridor (IRTC), 99–100, 103–5

International Maritime Bureau (IMB), 15, 188n20

International Maritime Organization (IMO), 112, 125, 128

international nature of shipping, 112–13

International Underwriting Association (London), 115

intimacy, and methodology of research, 25

Iran: and counter-piracy, 100; and dhow trade, 156, 171

Iraq, and dhow trade, 156

Iraq invasion (2003): private security companies denied immunity from prosecution by Iraq, 142; and privatization of the military, 141, 142, 144

Iraq war (1990–91), 156

IRTC. *See* Internationally Recommended Transit Corridor

Islam: ecumenical, and ancient trade routes, 8; *sadaka/sadaqa* (voluntary charity), 70; *sako/zakat* (compulsory alms), 70; in sanctuary of the dhow as mothership, 165–66; and women as traders, 77

Islamic banks, and *mudarabah* contracts, 191

Islamic law: diya groups and, 68; *hudud* (restriction), 68; and licit and illicit takings, 44; and piracy distinctions between just and unjust takings, 187n18; *qisas* (retaliation), 68; Scientific Socialism and, 49

Isman Mahmoud, 11

Israelis, and racialized systems of compensation in private security, 182

Italy: and *abaan* protection, 22; expatriate population in Malindi, 66; and fishing cooperatives, 52; fishing licenses granted to, 53; and Puntland shipwreck economy, 10, 11; and rescaling of economy under Scientific Socialism, 50; security companies from, 126–27; and Somaliland, 78; and violent entrepreneurs, 187n14

Japan, fishing licenses granted to, 53

Jeddah, Saudi Arabia, 143

jiwar practice, 164

Johanna (pirate port), 95

Joint War Committee (JWC), war-risk areas determined by, 115, 117, 118

jurisdiction: *abaan* protection as claim to, without sovereignty, 22–23; and Kenyan prosecution of pirates, 17, 18–19, 24; over ransom negotiations, 130, 134; as property, fishing licensing and creation of, 53

Justinian, 43

K&R. *See* kidnap-and-ransom (K&R) insurance packages

Kant, Emmanuel, 71

Kenya: Barre regime conflicts with, 54; colonial past of, 17–18; and dhow trade, 156; and history of contentious relations between Somalia and Kenya, 195n2; khat cultivation in, 60, 78; Merchant Shipping Act (2009), 18; as prosecution site for piracy, 17–19, 24; Somali refugees and residents in, 55, 124, 195n2. *See also* Mombasa, Kenya

khat (*Catha edulis*): as addiction, 83; circulation time and, 86–87, 193n14; cultivation in highlands, 60, 78, 84–85; daily truck deliveries of, 60–61, 85; as deception, 84; definition of, 185n2; distinction between gift and commodity as defied by, 87, 193n15; effects of, 77–78, 81, 137; and the gendered economy, 77, 137; khat tycoon, as aspirational status, 85; as literary foil for piracy, 80, 82, 83, 192n11; as losing potency within 48 hours, and need for speed, 60–61, 78, 84–85; the *mafresh* (khat chew) and spaces of sociality, 79, 80–82, 192n12; and piracy, khat as linked with, 78–80, 82, 83, 84, 88; pirates as ensnared by, 87–88; prices of, 78; and ships, khat as compared to, 137–38; and spectacle, 82; in supplies sent to hijacked ships, 2, 79–80, 85, 86, 88

Kidd, Captain William, 12, 95

kidnap-and-ransom (K&R) insurance packages: development of, 118, 119; disclosure of carrying as grounds for cancellation of insurance, 127; gender, race, and occupational kinship in, 137; and institutionalization of intermediaries, 127; racial hierarchy of labor and payout values of, 139; secrecy and, 127–28. *See also* ransom negotiators for shipowners

kidnap-and-ransom economy. *See* hijack-and-ransom economy

kidnapping ransoms, 127

kinship: *abaan* protection as oriented within, 22; as collateral, in diya groups, 74, 87, 88, 192n8; flexibility and, 69; pastoralism and, 39; stateless societies as organized by, 71, 192n7. *See also* clanism; diya groups

Mbembe, Achille, 163, 190n16
Mburu, Nene, 195n2
media piracy, 187–88n19
Mediterranean: protection payments in medieval and premodern trade, 20. *See also* insurance
Melville, Herman, *Moby Dick,* 174, 175
mercenaries: antimercenary bias in Europe and North America, 142; private security companies distinguished from, 141; rehabilitation of, and privatization of the military, 142. *See also* private security companies
Merchant Shipping Act (Kenya, 2009), 18
methodology: overview, 23–26; and khat, 60, 61; multilingual requirements, 26; plurality of actors and, 26; positionality of researcher, 25, 26, 61, 76, 167; protection and security of researcher, 25–26; pseudonyms and anonymity, x
migrant smuggling (*tahrib*), 181
Miller, Michael, 115
Mission to Seafarers (MtS) clubs, 158
Mitchell, Timothy, 119–20, 154
Miyazaki, Hiro, 194n9
mobility: and capture as creating property, 44; labor of, 86; between navies, slaving, privateers, and pirates, 93, 94; railways and, 154; steamships and, 154
Moby Dick (Melville), 174, 175
Mogadishu, Somalia, 6, 9, 48, 74, 78, 164
Mombasa, Kenya: as first port of call for vessels released from captivity, 124; and history of contentious relations between Somalia and Kenya, 195n2; Mission to Seafarers (MtS) club in, 158; as "modern day pirate's port of call," 124; as prosecution site for piracy, 17–19, 24; Somali investments in real estate market of, 82, 124; Somali neighborhoods in, 124; Vasco de Gama's hostile reception in, 66; weapons not allowed on merchant ships in, 143
Mongolia, as flag state, 113
monsoons: and ambergris, 40; centrality of, in Indian Ocean society, 65, 192n5; currents of, 39–40; discovery of, and European incursion into the Indian

Ocean, 65–66, 192n6; local humor about, 64; map of currents of, 65; piracy as transitioning into activity of, 66–67; and seasonal rhythm of life, 64–65, 67; steamships and railways as freeing trade from rhythms of, 154
Montreux Document, 144–45, 197n15
motherships, whaling, 151. *See also* dhows as motherships
motorized sailing vessel (MSV), 37, 155
MSY. *See* maximum sustainable yield (MSY)
mudarabah (profit and risk-sharing contract), 62, 107, 191n2
mudarib. See mudarabah
mujir (protector/host) and *mustajir* (protected/guest), 164
Muntakhab al-Lubab (Maulavi Kabir al-Din Ahmad), 92–93
musharakah (risk-sharing) partnerships, 107
MV Danica White, 58–59, 97–98, 188n21
MV Enterprise, 90–91, 120
MV Golden Nori, 1–4, 15, 67, 98, 177, 188n21
MV Seabourn Spirit, 188n21
MV Sirius Star, 59, 67, 98, 180

nationalism, and turn from the ocean, 155
nation-state: antimercenary bias and virtue of, 142; rise of, and instability of meanings of protection, 21; Scientific Socialism and building of, 49–50. *See also* Somali state failure; sovereignty
NATO: counter-piracy mission of, 91, 100; Dhow Project, 152, 167, 170; as insurance business, 119
natural law: bias of property/land and commons/sea in, 35–36; and privateering, 12, 94
navies: British, 93; British Indian, 37, 148; Indian, 150; Maratha, 187n16; mobility between slaving, privateers, pirates and, 93, 94. *See also* counter-piracy; United States Navy
Navigation Acts, 95
negotiation. *See* ransom negotiation

neoliberalism: ethnography of counter-piracy as seeking to shift the contours of debate about, 119–20; insurance as key to, 111; and licensing, 190n16; and privatization of the military, 142, 144

Netherlands: privateering and creation of empire of, 12, 94, 187n14; and violence in the Indian Ocean, 20. *See also* Dutch East India Company (VOC)

NGOs, women's cooperatives established through, 76

9/11 attacks, 117–18. *See also* Global War on Terror; terrorism

Nori. See MV Golden Nori

Northwood, England, EU counter-piracy mission, 100–102, 194n7

Norway: and fishing, 53, 54; Somali refugees in, 55

Nuer cattle complex, 38

obligations: anchoring of pirates in world of, 63–64, 84, 86, 88–89; camel ownership and obligation to share, 37–38; and capture as creating property, 44; and governance without government, 87; insurance as reorienting relationships of, to the individual, 111; shipwreck economy of the Majeerteen as creating, 11. *See also* diya groups

Oceansecure, 141, 143

oikos (household): definition of, 188n25; and labor of mobility, 86; and piracy, 163, 191n4

oil: and decline of dhow trade, 154–55; discovery of offshore oil, and decline of piracy, 179–80, 181; Somalis working in the Middle East in oil boom, 73–74; statistics on amount moved per day, 5–6

Oman, and dhow trade, 156

open registries and flags of convenience, 113

Operation Enduring Freedom—Horn of Africa, 1

Ostrom, Elinor, 190n12

Pakistan: and dhow trade, 148, 156; Somali diaspora in, 149

Pálsson, Gisli, 41

Panikkar, Kavalam Madhava, 192n6

Parry, Jonathan, 196n5

participants: Abdallah, 149; Abdi, 51; Abdul, ix–x; Abdullahi, 138; Absaame, 80–82; Adan, 133–34; Admiral Ahmed, 29, 32; Aisha, 61, 62, 76–77, 79, 84–87, 88, 89; Ali, 41–42, 44; Arale, 180–81; Asad, 13–14; Ayan, 172; Badi, 121, 132–33, 134–35, 136, 137; Badoon, 66–67; Bob, 136, 139, 147; Bole, 81; Cawil, 165, 171; Colonel Pierre, 100, 101–2, 194n7; Dalmar, 37–38, 39; Faisal, 71–72, 73–74; Farah, 57, 146–47; Greg, 113–14; Gurey, 2, 3; Hafiz, 90–91; Haji Ali, 161–63; Hanif, 83–84; Hashi, 57; Hassan, 83; Hirsi, 75, 84; Hodan, 137; Jack, 141, 142, 143, 144, 146; Jafaan, 149–50, 164–65; James, 128–32, 134, 147; Jeff, 145–46; Johan, 158–59; Joole, 46–47; Karl, 104; Mohamed, 53, 56; Musa, 29, 30–32, 36, 46; Nadeem, 169–70; Neil, 117–18; Nicholas, 183–84; Philip, 111, 113; Rahimullah, 160–63, 166; Rajesh, 135–36, 137, 139, 147; Ramu, 169; Rashid, 148–49; Ron, 145; Said, 61, 76; Salim, 124–25, 127; Samir, 2, 182; Shafiq, 156–57, 159–60, 170, 171; Sheikh Usman, 40–41, 61–63, 76, 87–88, 89, 174–75, 176–77; Shirmayo, 175–77; Simon, 117, 118, 119; Suraj, 90–91, 120; Timo, 70–71

pastoral commons, the sea as: and capture and redistribution economies, 39, 43, 46; definition of, 34, 39; interdependence as created by, 46; and the *maraja* (the edge), 39, 189n5; and material/metaphorical transformation of fish into goats and camels, 46; mobility and, 44; obligation and reciprocity as necessary to, 44; and politics of recognition, 44

pastoralism: camel complex, 38–39; cattle complex, 38; drought of 1974 and resettlement of nomads into fishing, 52, 53, 57–58; and kinship/clan formation, 39; private property retained for, during Scientific Socialism, 50, 51; and raiding economies of capture and redistribution, 39, 43, 46, 150 payment, 125, 196nn5–6

Penning, Mike, 143–44

perfume industry, 40, 41

Periplus Maris Erythraei, 6, 8, 20

Phillippines: as maritime labor supplier, 138, 139; and private security, 182

Pietsch, Tamson, 154

piracy and pirates: overview, 14; as "bad" pirates pitted against the "good" counter-piracy coalition, 4–5; as business enterprise, 13–14, 187n17; as criminal, 4, 12, 14; defensive piracy, 189n3; early twentieth-century assumption that piracy was obsolete, 14; as enemy of all mankind/threat to imperial order, 4, 11–12, 186–87n13; golden age of, ending in trials and executions, 12, 94, 95; and intellectual property rights, 187–88n19; Islamic law and distinctions of just and unjust takings, 187n18; and legality, as loaded and polemical terms, 33, 189n3; legitimate protection claimed by, 13, 187n16; "life has no value for them," 161; as natural form of acquisition, 163, 191n4; privateers being defined by authorities as, 94; privateers going rogue as, 12, 93; and protection, systems of, 4–5, 21–22, 122, 177–78; redistributive shipwreck economy labeled as, 11, 13; resource piracy, 189n3; as romanticized figures of popular culture, 4; steamship technology as sounding death knell of, 14; as system of transfer and redistribution, 11, 12, 186n12; upsurge of, despite modern international navies and technologies, 4; Western natural law transforming into lawful form of taking, 35–36. *See also* piracy off the coast of Somalia; privateers

piracy off the coast of Somalia: as addiction, 83; and deception, 83–84; and dhow trade, increases in, 37; end of era of, 147, 179–83; ethics of piracy/code of conduct, 62, 191n2; everyday worlds, piracy as part of, 24–25; fishing licensing regime and emergence of, 34, 54, 55, 56, 57–59, 143; and Gulf of Aden declared

an insurance war-risk area, 115–16, *116,* 117–19; khat as ensnaring pirates, 87–88; khat as likened to, 78–80, 82, 83, 84, 88; khat as literary foil for, 80, 82, 83, 192n11; loss and ruin and, 83–84; map of high-risk area, *116;* map of range of attacks, *16;* and *mudarabah* (profit and risk-sharing contract), 62, 191n2; the *Nori* hijacking as scaling up ransom payments, 15; oil wealth as alternative to, 179–80, 181; pirates as heroic figure, 81–82, 192n12; pirates as normal people, 61–62, 96, 191n1; pirates as poor people, 161, 163; "pirate style," 69–70, 83; private security companies as inadvertently instrumental in training first generation of, 56, 57, 143; return of, 183; and spectacle, 82–83; statistics on numbers of, 3, 15, 67, 179; transition from the Red Sea to the Indian Ocean, 66–67, 99–100, 151, 152; upsurge of, despite modern international navies and technologies, 4; and wealth accumulation, 76, 82–83, 195n2. *See also* capture by pirates; costs of piracy; counter-piracy; dhows as motherships; diya groups; hijack-and-ransom economy; khat; obligations; pirate action groups; ransom negotiation; supplies for piracy

pirate action groups, 67, 75; and diya groups, 74–75, 83; narrative of failed attempts to join, 149–50, 165; narrative of interview with pirate boss, 80–82

"pirate style," 69–70, 83

Pisa, and insurance industry, 108

PMCs. *See* private military companies

PMSCs. *See* private maritime security companies

poetry: *abaan* protectors in, 22; exalting the raider in, 82, 192n12; and khat traditions, 78

Pompei, 180

Poovey, Mary, 107

Portugal: *cartaz* system of, 20, 21; decline in the Indian Ocean, 20–21; monopolization of shipping viewed as act of aggression, 35; and privateering financed by rival empires, 12, 94; seizure of the

Santa Catarina by VOC, 35–36; Vasco de Gama epoch, 20, 66, 192n6
positive law, and privateering, 12, 94
Prange, Sebastian R., 20
primitive accumulation, 33
Prince, Erik, 142–43
Prince, The (Machiavelli), 142
prison: as captivity, 150; pirates sentenced to, 180
privateers: authorities redefining as pirates, 94; empires built through, 12, 94, 187n14; going rogue, 12, 93; royal license for, as only distinction from piracy, 94; as waging public wars by private means, 12, 94; and war on pirates, 12
private maritime security companies (PMSCs), 141, 142
private military companies (PMCs), 141, 142–43
private security companies (PSCs): as coastguards for official fishing licenses, 54, 55–56, 57–58, 143, 190n19; cost of, as prohibitive, 182; and end of the ransom economy of Somali piracy, 147, 179; governments and insurance companies opposed to private counter-piracy via, 143; governments approving private counter-piracy via (2011), 143–44; high-tech vessel hardening measures sold by, 125–27; hired by shipping companies, 119, 142–44; as inadvertently instrumental in training the first generation of Somali pirates, 56, 57, 143; insurance companies licensing, 119, 182; legitimization of, as intermediaries, 144–46; licensed by insurance companies, 119; mercenaries distinguished from, 141; and privatization of the U.S. military, 141–42, 144; profiteering as question for, 145; racialized systems of compensation in, 182; regulation of (Montreux Document), 144–45, 197n15; Somali retired pirate attempts to start, 146–47; and surplus population of armed, trained men due to privatization of the military, 144; trigger-happy security guards, 145; and weapons restrictions of ports, 143, 146

private security consultants: technologies of imagination produced by, 125. *See also* ransom negotiators for shipowners
privatization: ambiguities of, 119; as Hardin's solution to tragedy of the commons, 45; of the U.S. military, 141–42, 144
professional security class. *See* security companies
Proksch, Udo, 106
property: capture at sea as creating, 40–44, 46; jurisdiction as, fish licensing and, 53; on land, vs. the commons at sea, 35–36; physical possession and use as defining, 35; socialist regimes of, 50–51, 190n15
property law: first possession, 43; fugitive property, 42–44, 189n7; qualified property, 43, 44
protection: *abaan* (Arabic: *aman*) as land-based form of, 22–23, 81, 82, 146, 188n24; anthropology of, 23, 178–79; British treaty with Puntland against shipwreck economy (1838), 11; collateral as, 192n8; dhows as motherships and, 152, 165–66, 168, 170; diya groups as providing, 75–76; instability of meanings of, 21; *jiwar* practice as mixture of coercion and, 164; and methodology of research, 25–26; as modality of governance, 190n19; and safety, 23; as source of resource extraction, 190n19. *See also* diya groups; fishing licensing
protection systems for long-distance trade: overview, 4, 19, 23; counter-piracy as, 119–20; insurance transformed into, 108, 109, 110, 114–15; internalization of costs, 21; in the Mediterranean, medieval and premodern, 20; multiple scales of, 19; and piracy/counter-piracy as alternative system of connectivity and possibility within, 4–5, 21–22, 122, 177–78; and plurality of regulatory figures, 23; taxes for, prior to European imperialism, 20; trust and law as bridged by, 188n22; and violence after European incursion, 19–20; and violence before the arrival of European imperialism, 20. *See also* insurance underwriters; risk pooling and protection

PSCs. *See* private security companies

Puntland: British treaty with, to protect ships and nationals (1838), 11; conflict with Somaliland, 31, 136; and divination/logistical support for finding ships for pirates to capture, 124–25, 195–96n3; establishment of, 55; and fishing licensing, 55–56; Maritime Police Force (PMPF), 179, 181, 182; and methodology of research, 25–26; Ministry of Maritime Transport, Ports, and Counter-Piracy, 36–37, 95–96; and offshore oil exploration, 179–80; rumors of excessive wealth in, 82–83; and transition of piracy from the Red Sea to the Indian Ocean, 66; weak but functional governance of, as necessary to piracy, 9, 186n10. *See also* Bosaso, Puntland

Qawasim piracy, 187n15
qualified property, 43, 44
Qur'an, 68, 189n5

rabb al-mal. See mudarabah
Rabb, Intisar, 68
race: geographies of toxicity and, 33; hierarchy of labor, 138–39, 154; hierarchy of labor and value of ransom, 139, 147; hierarchy of private security compensation, 182; racial capitalism, 139
railways, 154
RAND Corporation, 142
Range Resources, 179–80
ransom negotiations, *140*; overview, 122–23; costs incurred by pirates during (*see* supplies for piracy); costs incurred by ship and cargo owners during, 3; families of hostages asked to pay portion of ransom, 120; gendered and racialized ideologies and assumptions shaping quality and quantity of ransoms, 122–23, 137–39, 147; narratives of, 120, 121, 128–31, 135–36; release of hijacked vessels, Mombasa as first port of call for, 124; as secretive enterprise, 127–28, 133; timeframes for, 122, 134–35; as "tournaments of value," 131, 197n9; violence and threat as shaping quality and quantity

of ransoms, 122–23; worry, anxiety, and fear of hostages, 134, 135, 136. *See also* capture by pirates; ransom negotiators for pirates; ransom negotiators for shipowners; ransom payments; supplies for piracy

ransom negotiators for pirates: assessment of potential value of crew and ship, 137–39; beginning process of negotiation immediately after capture, 133–34; day of radio silence, 134; as distancing themselves from pirates, 132–33; and entanglement within kinship relationships, 134–35; family and clan obligations not a consideration for hiring of, 136; and humanity of the hostages/shipowners (as "family man"), 135; incompetent negotiator, 136; narratives of, 134–35; new negotiator replacing incompetent one, 136, 137; proof of correct company/owner, 134; women as negotiators, 136–37; and worry, creation of, 134

ransom negotiators for shipowners: baseline professionalism and setting the affective tone, 130, 131; and bazaar economies, 129, 196n7; and detachment from emotion, 129–32; and fair price, 129, 131; as homogenous world, 128; and humanity of the hijacker (as profit-maximizing rational actor), 131–32, 135; immediate involvement of, 128–29; and incompetent negotiator for pirates, 136; isolation of pirates from shipowners and families, 129–30; local knowledge and language as secondary to, 131, 132; narratives of, 128–31, 136; offers and counteroffers, 129, 130–31, 132, 196n7; payoff matrix/game theory, 130; proof of life, 130, 134; secrecy and, 128; view of, by pirate negotiators, 135

ransom payments: annual amount paid globally, 127; delivery of payment (often by airdrop), 3, 122, 139; failed attempts at gaining, 183; as legally ambiguous due to laws on support for terrorism, 127; as small portion of total costs of piracy, 122

Ras Asir (Cape Guardafui), Somalia: lighthouse for, 10, 61, 174; shipwreck economy of, 10–11, 13

reciprocity: and capture as creating property, 44; and gift-exchange, 196n5; taking without giving, 160, 163

Redfield, Peter, 196–97n8

Rediker, Marcus, 193n3

refugee communities, Somali, 55

regulatory arbitrage, 156

riba (usury), 107

Rift Valley Fever, 37

risk: as both peril and profit, 106–7; "risk society," 111. *See also* risk pooling and protection

risk pooling and protection: insurance and, 107, 110, 111, 113, 114, 117–18; methodology of research and, 24; *mudarabah* and, 191n2

Roitman, Janet, 193n16

Romania, 50–51

Rome, ancient: division of the universe into things within human patrimony and things outside human patrimony, 34–36; and fugitive property, 43, 189n7; pirates and piracy in, 11–12

Rose, Carol M., 189n10

rubble, 30, 32, 189n2

Rubin, Alfred, 186–87n13

Rubin, Alfred P., 186n12

ruination, 33

ruins, rubble vs., 189n2

Russia: and counter-piracy, 100; and violent entrepreneurs, 187n14. *See also* Soviet Union

safety, protection and, 23

Sahlins, Marshall, 43–44

sailing vessels: European and American, 153–54; transition to steam from, 153–54. *See also* dhows

Saint Marie (pirate port), 95

Samatar, Abdi Ismail, 189n3

Samatar, Ahmed, 192n7

Samatar, Said, 47–48

Sandline, 141

Santa Catarina, 35

Saudi Arabia: Al Habibi (private security company), 58; livestock trade ban, 37; Somalis working in, 73–74

Schmitt, Carl, 35

Scientific Socialism (*hanti-wadaagga 'ilmu ku disan*) (1969–75): overview, 34; and banking, 73; clanism as reified and criminalized under, 51; criticism of, as un-Islamic, 49; and dissolution of the Somali state, 48; and diya groups, attempts to regulate, 72–73; establishment of, 48; fish factories and fish eating, 46–47, 52; fishing cooperatives built for resettled nomads, 52; nationalization/appropriation of property and, 50–51, 73; nation-building and, 49–50; rescaling of the economy and remaking of property during, 48–51, 190n15; Social Security Act (1970), 72–73. *See also* Barre, Muhammad Siyad, government of; fishing licensing; Somali state failure

sea: as commons, vs. land as property, 35–36; nationalism and turn from, 155; turn to, in the humanities, 8, 185n6. *See also* pastoral commons, the sea as; territorial waters

"sea-blindness," 6, 185n3

security companies. *See* private security companies

security consultants. *See* private security consultants; ransom negotiators for shipowners

Sekula, Allan, 185n3

September 11, 2001 terrorist attacks, 117–18. *See also* Global War on Terror; terrorism

Serres, Michel, 163

Shafi'I school of jurisprudence, 8

Sharjah, United Arab Emirates, 156

Sheriff, Abdul, 153

ship guards: prior to European imperialism (*asakir al-marakib*), 20. *See also* counter-piracy; private security companies

shipowners: entangled with pirates by pirate negotiator, 134–35; isolated from pirates by shipowner negotiators, 129–30. *See also* ransom negotiators for shipowners shipping pools, leased vessels and, 3

Ship Safe, 113, 116–19

shipwreck economy of the Majeerteen, 10–11, 13

Shirmarke, ʿAbd ar-Rashid ʿAli, 47

Shryock, Andrew, 162–63, 166

Sirius Star. See MV Sirius Star

skill, and capture as creating property, 41

slavery. *See* transnational slave trade

"social banditry," 62, 191n3

sociality, khat and spaces of, 79, 80–82, 192n12

socialization of piracy, methodology of research and, 25

soft law organizations, 195n15

SOMAFISH, 30–32

Somalia: coastline length of, 6; coast of, as geographically inhospitable, 6, 29; Cold War oscillation between Soviet Union and United States, 30, 31, 48, 50, 52; and Ethiopia, history of conflicts with, 54; fish-eating as uncommon in, 32, 46–47; histories of ports and trade, 6, 8–9, 10–11, 185nn5–6; and Kenya, history of contentious relations with, 195n2; map of, 7; occupation of, and belief it would end piracy, 103; wind patterns and oceanic currents and, 6. *See also* dhows; diaspora, Somali; diya groups; Puntland; Somaliland; Somali Republic

Somali Civil War, 30, 31, 76–77

Somali Commercial Bank, 73

Somali jet, 67

Somaliland: conflict with Puntland, 31, 136; and diya groups, government attempts to regulate, 72; and khat, 78; and methodology of research, 25; and Somali Civil War, 30, 31. *See also* Berbera, Somaliland

Somali Republic: assassination of first president of, 47; military coup (1969), 47–48; nationalization of institutions and industries, 50–51; Supreme Revolutionary Council (SRC), 47–48. *See also* Barre, Muhammad Siyad, government of; Scientific Socialism

Somali Savings & Credit Bank, 73

Somali state failure: clan as object of analysis as naturalizing, 192n7; conflicts with Ethiopia and Kenya and, 54; and construction of governance without government, 87; continuance of life despite, 9; and disbanding of Somali maritime sovereignty, 98; and diya groups as source of capital, collateral, and connection, 74; and exclusion of Somali actors from counter-piracy policy making, 96–97; fishing licensing and, 54; governance without government and, 186n8; insurgent groups and, 54–55; piracy as blamed on, 9, 186n9; piracy as requiring governance despite, 9, 186n10; refugee communities created by population upheavals following, 55

Somcan company, 57, 58, 190n19

South Africa, and private security companies, 55, 182

South America, kidnappings in, 127

Southeast Asia, piracy in, 15, 181

South Sea bubble, 194n12

sovereignty: *abaan* as jurisdiction without claim to, 22–23; ambiguities of, 119; of BEIC, 95; fiction of interstate conflict as central to the project of, 141; of Iraq, and denial of immunity to PSCs, 142; open-registry system and marketable identity, 113; order without state law, as question, 71; Somali maritime, as gradually disbanded, 98

Soviet Union: fishing licenses granted to, 53. *See also* Cold War; Russia

Spain, and privateering financed by rival empires, 12, 94

Sri Lanka, and private security, 182

stateless societies, order within, 71

status: *abaan* protection and, 22–23, 81, 82, 146–47; act of capture as creating, 150; to be feared as form of, 176; khat tycoon, 85; pirate bosses and, 81–82, 192n12

steamships: and British identity, 154; coaling stations required by, 37, 148, 154; and consolidation of global control of the oceans, 14; expansion of the Indian Ocean region and, 154; as freeing trade from monsoon rhythms, 154; as sounding death knell of maritime piracy, 14; transition from sailing to, 153–54

Steensgaard, Niels, 21

Stern, Philip, 95

Straits of Malacca, 15

sudfa (seeking profit from chance), 107

Suez Canal: and increased size of container ships, 166; number of vessels per year transiting, 5; opening of, as transforming the world of sail, 153–54; opening of, incorporation of Somalia into global capitalism, 40

Sufis, and khat use, 78

supplies for piracy: as boon to local business, 67, 68; and debts of pirates, 2, 68, 79–80, 83, 86, 139; diya groups as guaranteeing payment for, 68, 86; diya groups as providing capital for, 74–75; and food shortages on land, 62; khat as part of, 2, 79–80, 85, 86, 88

Surat, India, 92, 93

Sweden, privateering and creation of empire of, 94

Taar family, 58, 190n19

Taar, Xiif Ali, 58

technologies: and coastguard initiatives for fishing licensing, 55, 58; and counter-piracy, 104; of imagination/capitalist divination, 125; upsurge of piracy despite profusion of, 4; vessel hardening, 125–26. *See also* steamships

territorial waters: additional UN Resolutions dissolving distinction between international waters and, 99; Barre government and extension of Somalia's, 52; international law as inapplicable in, 98–99; solidification of role of the state in governing, 14; UN Resolution 1816 removing safe haven of, 15–17, 99

terrorism: khat as linked to, 78–79, 82; and legal ambiguity of ransom payments, 127; and secrecy about carrying K&R insurance, 127; and war-risk cover, 117–18. *See also* Global War on Terror

TEU (twenty-foot equivalent unit), 197n10

Thailand, 56, 100

thresholds, 159

Tilly, Charles, 21

tournaments of value, 131, 197n9

toxicity, geographies of, 33

toxic waste containers, tsunami depositing, 175–76

transnational slave trade: and captivity, 150; Lloyd's of London as major profiteer in system of, 111; and mobility between navy, slaving, privateer, and pirate, 93, 94

transregional economy: diya groups and, 73–74; khat and, 78; Scientific Socialism and rescaling of, 50

transregional geography, 8; overview, 9–10; dhows and trade network in, 156; monsoons and connectivity in, 64–65

transshipment, 156, 198n7

Trump, Donald, 83

trust: diya groups and trust of business owners for pirates, 61, 68, 75, 86, 87, 89; and long-distance trade, 188n22

Tsing, Anna, 193n15

tsunami (2004), 175–76

United Arab Emirates: British protectorate treaties with, 187n15; and livestock trade ban, 37; Somalis working in, 73–74; Somcan company registered in, 190n19

United Nations: Convention on the Law of the Sea (UNCLOS) (UN 1982), 47, 52–53, 98–99; Food and Agricultural Organization, 52; monitoring group on Somalia and Eritrea, 182; Resolution 1816 on piracy (2008), 15–17, 99; resolutions on counter-piracy (2008), 99; on tsunami of 2004 and exposure to radioactive substances, 176; UNCTAD revised insurance clause, 115

United States: approval of private security guards on ships, 144; and collapse of the Somali state, 74; colonial patronage for English pirates, 94–95; and global control of the oceans, 14; and Kenya as prosecution site for piracy, 17; and racialized hierarchy of shipping labor, 139; and racialized systems of compensation in private security, 182; and role

United States *(continued)*
models for quick money of piracy, 83.
See also Cold War
United States military, privatization of,
141–42, 144
United States Navy: deaths of crew members, 15; and EU counter-piracy task-force, 100; fiction of Somali maritime sovereignty gradually disbanded, 98; local humor about monsoons and, 64; and *MV Danica White* hijacking, 97–98; and the *Nori* hijacking, 1, 2, 98; shooting pirates, 177; upsurge of piracy despite hegemony of, 4
U.S. Department of Defense: Logistics Civil Augmentation Program, 142; and private contractors in Iraq and Afghanistan, 142
USS Carter Hall, 97–98
USS Cole, 193–94n5
USS Porter, 1

vahaans. See dhows
Valentine, David, 196–97n8
van Gennep, Arnold, 159
Vasco da Gama, 20, 66, 192n6
Verdery, Katherine, 50–51
vessel hardening: barbed wire, 91, 119, 125, 133; discounts on insurance for taking measures of, 114, 125–26; high-tech nonlethal measures, and sales conventions for, 125–27; loudspeakers, 119; sound guns, 119, 125; sticky foam, 126; water cannons, 91, 126, 133, *133. See also* insurance company recommendations for protection
vessels: anchoring of, 63; assessment of value of, 137–39; bulk carriers, 37, 136, 137, 139, 154–55, 189n4; fiber fishing skiffs, 30–32; flags of convenience and open registries, 113; khat compared to, 137–38; methodology of research and, 26; navy destroyers, 103; registration of, and embedded maritime nations, 138; ships as source of order in the ocean, 103; TEU cargo capacity of, 197n10. *See also* container ships; dhows; steamships; vessel hardening

violence: and *abaan* protectors, 23; of capture by pirates, 157–58, 159, 160; of counter-piracy, 105; insurance and, 112; privateering and demarcation of acceptable and unacceptable violence, 94; and researcher, 176–77; and rise of capitalism, 40; view of European incursion as introducing, 19–20, 192n6; view of existence of prior to European incursion, 20, 192n6
violent entrepreneurs, 12, 187n14. *See also* privateers
VOC. *See* Dutch East India Company
Volkov, Vadim, 187n14

war, as natural mode of acquisition, 191n4
War on Terror. *See* Global War on Terror
war-risk cover, insurance and, 115–16, *116,* 117–19, 182, 195n15
Wedeen, Lisa, 192n12
Weitzberg, Keren, 195n2
West Africa, piracy in, 15, 181
western Indian Ocean: counter-piracy as driving pirates out of the Red Sea and into, 66–67, 99–100, 151, 152; histories of ports and trade in, 6, 8–9, 10–11, 185nn5–6; megaport-development projects in, 8–9; statistics on numbers of vessels and seafarers in, 5–6. *See also* dhows as motherships
Western legal thought, land/sea distinction, 35–36
whales, bans on hunting, 41
whaling motherships, 151. *See also* dhows as motherships
Williams, Eric, 111
Wilson, J. T., 154
women: deceiving/robbing pirates, 83–84; as negotiators for pirates, 136–37. *See also* gendered economy
World Bank report (2013), 15
World Food Program (WFP), 37

Yemen, 37, 78, 192n12. *See also* Aden, Yemen
YouTube, counter-piracy videos on, 104–5
Yussuf, Abdullahi, 58, 190n19

Founded in 1893,
UNIVERSITY OF CALIFORNIA PRESS
publishes bold, progressive books and journals
on topics in the arts, humanities, social sciences,
and natural sciences—with a focus on social
justice issues—that inspire thought and action
among readers worldwide.

The UC PRESS FOUNDATION
raises funds to uphold the press's vital role
as an independent, nonprofit publisher, and
receives philanthropic support from a wide
range of individuals and institutions—and from
committed readers like you. To learn more, visit
ucpress.edu/supportus.